Peggy Gilbert & Her All-Girl Band

Ex Libris. Peggy drew this for the portfolio to accompany her application to art school, 1923.

Peggy Gilbert & Her All-Girl Band

Jeannie Gayle Pool

The Scarecrow Press, Inc.
Lanham, Maryland • Toronto • Plymouth, UK
2008

SCARECROW PRESS, INC.

Published in the United States of America
by Scarecrow Press, Inc.
A wholly owned subsidiary of
The Rowman & Littlefield Publishing Group, Inc.
4501 Forbes Boulevard, Suite 200, Lanham, Maryland 20706
www.scarecrowpress.com

Estover Road
Plymouth PL6 7PY
United Kingdom

British Library Cataloguing in Publication Information Available

Library of Congress Cataloging-in-Publication Data

Pool, Jeannie G.
Peggy Gilbert & her all-girl band / Jeannie Gayle Pool.
p. cm.
Includes bibliographical references (p. 235), filmography (p. 187), and index.
ISBN-13: 978-0-8108-6102-2 (pbk. : alk. paper)
ISBN-10: 0-8108-6102-X (pbk. : alk. paper)
1. Gilbert, Peggy. 2. Women jazz musicians—Biography. 3. Big bands—United States—History—20th century. I. Title. II. Title: Peggy Gilbert & her all-girl band.
ML419.G53P44 2008
781.65092—dc22
[B] 2007041449

∞™ The paper used in this publication meets the minimum requirements of American National Standard for Information Sciences—Permanence of Paper for Printed Library Materials, ANSI/NISO Z39.48-1992.

Designed by Beverly Simmons.
Manufactured in the United States of America.

Contents

Foreword

Lily Tomlin celebrating Peggy Gilbert's one hundredth birthday.

Peggy Gilbert will always be an inspiration to us. Peggy first delighted us twenty years ago when we saw her on the Johnny Carson show. She appeared with her all-woman band, playing her tenor sax, and we were blown away. We became immediate fans, and then were lucky enough to become devoted friends.

Peggy was born in 1905, and by her early twenties was a brilliant musician and bandleader. Peggy's extensive early performing career is vividly documented in this biography; she obviously loved making music and living in the moment. In spite of her unique talent and style, however, Peggy also struggled against the prejudices of a sexist era when men refused even to play in the same band with women. She was a pioneer in those early days by advancing the rights and opportunities for women musicians everywhere. Eighty years later, at the age of 102, she was still an activist for all women in the music business.

Often interviewed for books and articles on women in jazz, Peggy humbly focused on the women with whom she had played, rather than on her own impressive accomplishments. Peggy felt that, because she had survived so many women in the business, it was her obligation to keep their memories alive. For many decades, she carried the torch for several generations of women instrumentalists. Her biography is not only her story but also the story of women of the last century struggling to be independent and to express themselves.

Peggy herself innocently summed up her personality at her one hundredth birthday: in 2005, at the Musicians Union auditorium of Local 47 (an auditorium which Peggy helped build), we attended the party honoring her birthday. We asked Peggy where her horn was. "Oh, I sold it," she said. When we protested, she explained, "It was just too good a horn not to be played." Although the world lost Peggy in 2007, we love knowing that somewhere out there, Peggy's horn is still making music.

Peggy was witty, cool, progressive, and hip—as only a jazz musician can be. Her music enriched the world and her friendship enriched our lives. We were touched and moved by this biography and know that you will be, too.

—Lily Tomlin and Jane Wagner
September 2007

Introduction and Acknowledgments

Peggy Gilbert is the most remarkable person I know. Not just because she has reached 102 years of age. Not because she has had an extraordinary career as an entertainer. Nor because she is a staunch advocate of women musicians, even before the day she arrived in Hollywood in 1928. Not because she was a pioneer radio broadcaster, beginning in 1924 in Sioux City, Iowa. Nor because she serves as a one-woman network to help women musicians get jobs and have successful lives in music.

Peggy Gilbert is remarkable because she teaches all of us how to live, how to love, how to care for one another, how to reach our most cherished goals through perseverance and diligence, and how to become better human beings by keeping focused on what matters most—our relationships. She also teaches us how to have careers in the music business. Rather than tearing down the barriers that prevented her generation of women musicians from being full professionals, Peggy figured out how to circumvent them. Through her efforts, she laid the groundwork for a later generation of women musicians who would overcome those obstacles, during a reinvigorated feminist movement of the late 1960s and '70s. Had Peggy been a man, without a doubt she would have been one of the great American bandleaders of the Swing Era.

I met Peggy in 1983. As host of a radio program at KPFK radio in Los Angeles, nearly every time I did a program on women in music, someone would call the station and tell me I should contact Peggy Gilbert. When we finally did meet, I was pleased to discover that she had already written in her column for the musicians' union publication, *The Overture*, about my work to establish the International Congress on Women in Music.

While I was researching all-women's orchestras in California, with a grant from the California Council for the Humanities, Peggy became one of my informants; she introduced me to dozens of women musicians who played in all-girl bands in the Swing Era. In 1986, Peggy and I organized the Pioneer Women Musicians of Los Angeles Luncheon, a reunion honoring 106 women, held at the historic Ambassador Hotel. The event was presented by the International Institute for the Study of Women in Music, which I co-directed with Beverly Grigsby.[1]

Later that year, with the assistance of Pacific Bell Telephone, I produced a documentary about the all-women's orchestras in California. A recording of Peggy Gilbert and The Dixie Belles, which I produced for Cambria Records, was released as an LP album, also in 1986.[2]

Whenever Peggy was interviewed for radio and oral history during the 1980s, her focus was on promoting The Dixie Belles, her senior citizen women's band, then performing regularly in the Los Angeles area. She gave me some photographs from her early career, but did not share many details about her life, except that she had toured with Fanchon and Marco's vaudeville extravaganzas, had taken her band to Hawaii, had appeared in a few films as a "sideliner," and did a USO tour to Alaska with comedic actress Thelma White.

To celebrate Peggy Gilbert's ninetieth birthday in 1995, I wrote an article for the *International League of Women in Music Journal*,[3] then another for her ninety-fifth birthday in 2000, and yet another for her one hundredth birthday in 2005. Although Peggy always hoped to write a book "on the subject of girl musicians in the big band days,"[4] she never did it. But when women jazz musicians have died, Peggy is often the one to write their obituaries for *The Overture.*

In anticipation of her one hundredth birthday, I contacted Peggy's friend Serena Kay Williams, then Secretary/Treasurer of Local 47 of the American Federation of Musicians (AFM), and asked the union to host a party. With Serena, percussionist Judy Chilnick, and saxophonist and bandleader Ann Patterson, we organized a party on Monday, January 17, 2005, in the auditorium of Local 47 on Vine Street in Hollywood. It was attended by more than 120 people. As part of the celebration, I produced a presentation about Peggy's life and career, including about eighty photographs. Many of Peggy's friends expressed surprise at the photos, saying that, although they had known her for years, they had no idea how extensive her career had been. One party-goer was the actress Lily Tomlin, a longtime friend of Peggy's. She decided to help me make a documentary film using these photos, and agreed to serve as narrator. A friend of Lily's, who had videotaped the party, offered footage for use in the documentary. With funding from the Silva Watson Moonwalk Fund, and additional funding from the Schutrum-Piteo Foundation, we began production in summer 2005.[5]

While working on the documentary, I began gently to encourage Peggy to share with me more documents about her life and career. Although I knew—from testimonies of dozens of people—that she had always functioned as a one-woman network for women musicians in Los Angeles, I was impressed with how many women musicians she had hired over the years. With the deadline for the film project looming, Peggy offered more and more materials on her life and career, including videotapes of performances, TV appearances, news reports, and videotapes of films in which she had appeared. Her personal archive contains dozens of photographs of other all-girl bands, as well as photos of individual women musicians, most of whom she can identify. Peggy Gilbert is the "keeper" of the story of the all-girl bands.

Peggy's column in *The Overture*, "Tuning in on Femme Musicians," offered reports on female musicians, their activities, and their whereabouts, monthly from 1979 to 1984. However, she never wrote her own story. When researchers would appear at her door to inquire about the all-girl bands, Peggy generously talked to them, yet she was humble about her own accomplishments. Several writers who interviewed her hardly mention her in their books and articles; they did not understand her life's purpose and work.[6]

As you read *Peggy Gilbert & Her All-Girl Band*, you will discover that Peggy was a central figure for professional women musicians working in Los Angeles between 1928 and 1998, a staunch advocate, and a behind-the-scenes activist, creating more opportunities for them to practice their art. You will also understand how Peggy, and her partner, Kay Boley, have helped musicians—particularly elderly musicians—cope with illness, old age, and loneliness. Their service to the Los Angeles community of musicians is remarkable, even while Peggy and Kay themselves have dealt with their own frailties.

Many thanks to Peggy Gilbert and Kay Boley for sharing their stories and lives with me. Thanks to my editor, Beverly Simmons, whose encouragement and support made it possible for me to complete this book; she also helped with the archival work on Peggy's personal papers and memorabilia, designed this book, and edited the photographs. Thanks to Jenice Rosen, assistant producer for the documentary film. Thanks to Lance Bowling for providing insight and additional materials, both for this book and for the documentary film. Thanks to Serena Kay Williams and archivists Chris Ogrodowski and Gordon Carmadelle of AFM Local 47. Thanks to Lily Tomlin, Jane Wagner, and Vivian Schneider for making this research possible. Thanks to Linda Crane and Don J. Savarese of the Schutrum-Piteo Foundation for their support of the documentary.

Additional thanks to JoAnn Baldinger, Audrey Barnett, Harry Brown and the family of Sally Brown, Doug Caldwell, Judy Chilnick, Karen Donley, Ross Duffin, David Simmons-Duffin, Selena Simmons-Duffin, Janice Frey, Larry Gelbart, Deon Nielsen Price, Stephen M. Fry, Larry Gelbart, Ted Hegvik, Nellie Lutcher, Leonard Maltin, Georgia Shilling, Fern Spaulding Jaros, Jerrie Thill, the family of Kay Boley, the family of Peggy Gilbert, Ben Millar, E. J. Oshins, Ann Patterson, Cecilia Rasmussen, the family of Natalie Robin, Ken Rosen, Jane Sager, Ruth Ashton Taylor, Eldridge Walker, Denise Wells, June Derry Weston, and Glenn and Karen Winter.

Thanks also to the California Council for the Humanities, the state affiliate of the National Endowment for the Humanities, and California State University, Northridge.

All of this support enabled me to write this book while Peggy is still here to help me do it. What a privilege, indeed, to present this remarkable story.

—Jeannie Pool
January 2007

Illustrations

Sidebars

Chronology

January 17, 1905	Margaret Fern Knechtges Gilbert is born in Sioux City, Iowa, to John Darwin and Edith Gilbert Knechtges.
Summer 1912	Peggy begins piano lessons with local teacher; studies violin with father.
Summer 1913	Peggy tours with Highland Dance Troupe with Sir Harry Lauder, in Nebraska, Iowa, and South Dakota.
January 1923	Peggy graduates from Sioux City High School; briefly attends Morning Side College.
Summer 1923	Peggy starts band of girls and guys at Lake Okoboji, on Iowa Great Lakes.
1925	Peggy starts her first all-girl band, The Melody Girls, to perform at the Martin Hotel, Sioux City.
1927	The Melody Girls are heard live on nightly radio broadcasts over KSCJ.
November 1927	Father, John Knechtges, dies.
May 1928	Peggy, mother, and grandmother move to Los Angeles.
July 1928	Sister-in-law, Zanona Gunn Knechtges, dies, and Peggy, mother, and brother bring brother's son and daughter to Los Angeles.

Summer 1928	Peggy takes over all-girl band at El Mirador Hotel in Palm Springs.
October 1928–May 1929	Peggy tours with saxophonist Rudy Wiedoeft in Fanchon and Marco show, "Saxophobia Idea."
October 1929–May 1930	Peggy tours with Fanchon and Marco show, "Jazz Temple Idea."
September 1930–Spring 1931	Peggy tours with Fanchon and Marco show, "Busy Bee Idea."
1931	Peggy organizes all-girl band to appear in MGM movie, *Politics*.
1932	Peggy organizes all-girl band to appear in MGM movies, *The Wet Parade* and *That's My Boy*.
Spring 1932	Peggy tours California with her all-girl band; also plays Las Vegas Meadows Casino and parties for Marion Davies.
August 1932	Peggy organizes all-girl band to tour with entertainer Vivian Duncan.
December 1932	Peggy visits Sioux City and joins Boots and Her Buddies Band to go on tour.
Spring 1933	Peggy leaves Boots and Her Buddies and returns to Los Angeles; she performs with all-girl band (not her own) at the Paramount Theater in downtown Los Angeles.
May 1933	Other members leave Boots and drive from Texas to Los Angeles to join Peggy's all-girl big band in Hollywood.
September 1933	Peggy's band plays in Bakersfield, California, and appears on experimental television station W6XAH.
October 1933	Peggy's band goes on tour to Hawaii with E. K. Fernandez's organization.
December 1934	Peggy's band returns to Los Angeles to play nightclubs and ballrooms.
February 1935	Peggy's band plays for Opening Ceremonies of Boulder [Hoover] Dam.

1935	Peggy's band plays at The Italian Village and Club New Yorker in Hollywood; broadcasts live over KFWB, KFOX, and KFXM Radio.
1937	Peggy organizes all-girl jazz band to appear in film, *Melody for Two* (Warner Bros.).
March–May 1937	Peggy's band goes to Greensburg, Pennsylvania, to play at Albert Penn Hotel; Peggy meets First Lady Eleanor Roosevelt.
1937–1938	Peggy's band plays at the Zenda Ballroom.
1938	Peggy organizes band "The Early Girls and Three Chirps" for KMPC Radio.
April 1938	Peggy's article appears in *Downbeat* magazine.
1938	Peggy contracts women musicians to perform in "Beer Garden Scene" of film, *The Great Waltz* (MGM); she appears with her band in the film, *Reckless Living* (Universal).
1939	Peggy's band appears at Blue Lantern Café, Hollywood Café, Gay White Way, and at benefits for the Fraternal Order of Police.
1940	Peggy organizes all-girl band to perform in film, *Lillian Russell* (Twentieth Century Fox); she also performs at the Bud Taylor Café.
April 19, 1940	Niece Darlene Maryland Knechtges dies from fall in Griffith Park, Los Angeles.
1941	Peggy works at Local 47 to get enlisted servicemen placed in military bands.
1942	Peggy forms band, The Jacks and Jills, with brother Orval on drums.
August 1942	Nephew John Darwin Knechtges, an apprentice seaman in the U.S. Navy, is declared "missing in action" in the Solomon Islands.
Fall 1942	Peggy leads band for Ona Munson's show on CBS. The Victory Belles entertain troops with live radio broadcast heard Saturday nights.

June 28, 1942	Peggy marries sound engineer, James G. Wright, just before he is shipped overseas for military duty.
1943	Grandmother Carrie Adell Hazzard Gilbert dies at age eighty-nine.
1944–45	Peggy goes on USO tour with Thelma White to East Coast, Canada, and Alaska.
1944	Peggy meets Kay Boley at the China Bowl Restaurant.
1945	Kay Boley comes to live with Peggy's family.
1946	Peggy's band is playing at the Figueroa Ballroom, when their contract is terminated with no notice, to be replaced by "boys" returning from war.
1947	Peggy appears as sideliner in film, *Sirens of Atlantis* (United Artists).
1949–1950	Peggy serves on Building Committee at Local 47, which builds union headquarters at 817 Vine Street; Peggy begins full-time clerical work for Local 47.
1951	Peggy plays with Ada Leonard's band on KTTV in Los Angeles.
1950s	Peggy continues to perform with her band, The Jacks and Jills, with her brother.
September 1953	Peggy leaves job at Local 47, to work briefly for barbeque manufacturing company, but soon returns to Local 47.
May 21, 1957	Peggy appears on Ralph Edwards's *This Is Your Life*, in episode honoring Thelma White.
1961	Peggy organizes all-girl band to play in *The Second Time Around* (Twentieth Century Fox).
1961	Peggy appears as extra in film, *How the West Was Won.*
July 29, 1967	Surprise Tribute to Peggy Gilbert, involving sixty women from the Big Band days.
March 15, 1968	Mother Edith Knechtges dies at age eighty-seven.
1970	At age sixty-five, Peggy retires from job at Local 47.

1974	Peggy starts senior citizen Dixieland jazz band, The Dixie Belles.
1975	Peggy appears as extra in film, *At Long Last Love* (Twentieth Century Fox).
1979	Peggy appears as extra in film, *The In-Laws* (Warner Bros.).
FEBRUARY 1979	Peggy begins to write column, "Tuning in on Femme Musicians," for the union's monthly publication, *The Overture.*
1980	Peggy appears as extra in film, *The Competition* (Columbia Pictures).
JANUARY 1, 1980	Peggy Gilbert and The Dixie Belles appear in The Rose Bowl Parade on the Confectionary Workers Union's float.
SEPTEMBER 19, 1981	Peggy Gilbert and The Dixie Belles appear on *The Tonight Show Starring Johnny Carson.*
SEPTEMBER 23, 1982	Peggy appears in episode of *Madame's Place.*
1985	Peggy Gilbert and The Dixie Belles record album for Cambria Master Recordings, Los Angeles.
MARCH 8, 1986	Luncheon to celebrate Pioneer Women Musicians of Los Angeles, at Ambassador Hotel Ballroom.
FEBRUARY 2, 1988	Brother Orval Lloyd Knechtges dies at age eighty-seven.
OCTOBER 22, 1988	Peggy appears as "Esther" in episode #42 of *The Golden Girls.*
JANUARY 17, 2005	Peggy's one hundredth birthday is celebrated with party at Local 47.
SEPTEMBER 2006	Documentary film, *Peggy Gilbert & Her All-Girl Band,* is completed.
OCTOBER 2006	*Peggy Gilbert and The Dixie Belles: Dixieland Jazz* is reissued by Cambria Master Recordings as compact disc.
FEBRUARY 12, 2007	Peggy Gilbert dies at age 102.

Margaret Fern Knechtges with her brother Orval Lloyd, c.1912.

CHAPTER 1
The Early Years

Margaret Fern Knechtges Gilbert[7] was born on January 17, 1905, in Sioux City, Iowa. Both her parents were professional musicians, paving the way for her also to go into the music business. Her father, John Darwin Knechtges (1870–1927), was a violinist who played in theater pit bands in Sioux City and the immediate area. In addition to playing for operas, dances, and string quartets, he later managed the Hawkeye Concert Orchestra.[8] Late in life, he injured a finger on his left hand, so he turned his attention to fancy wood finishing. Peggy's mother, Edith Ella Gilbert (1880–1968),[9] was a singer for the opera house, then called a "super singer" (a.k.a. "sup" or "extra"), singing in opera choruses for touring productions appearing in Sioux City.

John's parents emigrated from Germany. His father, Paul Knechtges (1827–1915), and mother, Magdelena (1843–1912),[10] were married in 1860 in St. Norbert's Catholic Church in Roxbury, Wisconsin. Although Paul was a bridge builder by trade, education was a high priority in the family. They had eight children: Clara Lu (1861–1953); Henry (1863–1935); Anthony (1865–1934); John; Paul (1872–?); Magdelena (1876–1903); Elizabeth (1882–1904); and Margaret (1884–?).[11] Peggy was named after her Aunt Margaret, who was a teacher. Her uncles Paul and John were professional musicians. Peggy recalls that, up until World War I, most in the Knechtges family spoke German to one another,[12] although they were all fluent in English.

Of her father, Peggy says:

> He was a soft-spoken man, had a quick and fascinating smile, blond curly hair, and blue eyes. His skin, after shaving, seemed so light and smooth, I

> loved to see the difference in color when he blushed, as often he did, especially when Mama said something that embarrassed him or complimented him in front of people. He was a retiring and fun-loving man, in spite of the fact that he was a show-off when it came to playing music. He also was an expert wood finisher, and always had a piece of furniture from some friend's house at our place, where he would work on it in his spare time—sanding and oiling for hours, until it looked more beautiful than you can imagine. He loved wood, and often said, "Remember this: you can improve on God's creating, but you cannot create something that is His work." I used to look at a small piece of wood and count the lines and feel with my fingers the ridges in it, and ask him about it. He always had a beautiful explanation to give, which only made my admiration greater.[13]

John Darwin and Edith Ella Gilbert Knechtges.

When Peggy was born, Theodore Roosevelt (1858–1919) was President, having succeeded William McKinley, who was assassinated in 1901. At age 42, Roosevelt was the youngest ever U.S. president, a Republican and a reformer. In office until 1909, he instituted regulations for control of large corporations, particularly railroads and the processed food industry, and improved the conditions for laborers. A central figure of the Progressive Movement, he tried to reign in the big monopolies and to look after the country's greater welfare.[14]

According to Peggy, "I was raised to respect all types of music and to love all kinds of music. I grew up hearing music every day in our house. I had a wonderful family and a wonderful background in the music business and I loved every minute of it."[15] Peggy recalls her first piano: "My dad bought me a piano even before I was born. As soon as I was old enough to walk, I walked up to the piano and put my teeth against the piano. It was mahogany and I put my signature right there, and he never took it off."[16]

Soon after starting piano lessons at age eight, Peggy accompanied her father for some of his stage shows. Her first professional engagement was playing at a dance with her father's band:

> My dad was the manager and first violinist with the Hawkeye Symphony[17] in Iowa and I learned that part. I had a piano teacher first and, every time I put in an extra note, she would say, "No! If the composer had meant that note to be in there, he would have put it there." I'd get my hand slapped, you know. I didn't like that. I liked to fill in the notes.[18]

Peggy recalls that, "When Dad said something, he meant it and we knew it. He made the family a large wooden rocking horse and was quite artistic and could sketch, draw, and paint."

Her brother, Orval Lloyd Knechtges, was born in 1900, four-and-a-half years before Peggy. Of her upbringing, Peggy wrote:

> My father played violin and could have been great and made a big name for himself, had he not fallen in love with my mother and married her. He still performed and gave of his talents to the people in the area where we lived. We had many, many good friends and a happy household, where music was the dominant factor in our everyday life. Dad had an orchestra and they would rehearse almost every week at our house. My brother and I thoroughly enjoyed the music, the good fellowship, and the coins that were sometimes left us when we finally went to sleep during rehearsals, curling up on two chairs pulled together in the dining room, or on a couch in the living room—not too far from the music, ever.

Having learned from her parents how to give a party for musicians, Peggy continued the family tradition.

> We lived in a household where there were no rules . . . except that we never interfered with grownups to the extent of joining in their parties, but we were never forbidden entrance, either. We did know that we could not attract attention to ourselves, except for maybe asking for a small sip of beer, which we were given from time to time—or enjoying the delightful "Dutch Lunches" that our mother always had on the table for all of our guests. This invariably consisted of various kinds of cheeses, bologna, cold roast beef, home-made potato salad, various types of pickles, and the usual olives. We always had home-made bread, which mother made [by] herself in our old-fashioned coal and wood stove in the kitchen. I can smell that delicious fragrance even to this day. We were not poor; we had most of the essentials of life, including, always, good plain food.[19]

The family's home was on the street that divided the city, Rebecca Street; the house was owned by her Grandmother Gilbert, who rented it to them. That side of town was mixed race—white, black, and Native American. The other side of town was where the wealthier white people lived. Peggy recalls going to elementary school for the first time to find students of all colors and backgrounds there. Her brother insisted they go home, because it was clear to him that they "didn't belong there." When they got home, they told their parents about the school, but were sent back again. They were told by their parents emphatically that prejudices would not be tolerated in their family. Peggy said, "We learned right from the beginning to treat everyone with respect and consideration, regardless of race or ethnicity."[20]

The ebb and flow of family home life was determined by her parents' extensive musical activities. Peggy's development as a musician began with solid classical training:

> My father, being a "legit" violinist, I was aware of that type of music all my life. My first instrument was piano. My father taught me to respect the keyboard. He said, "Whatever you do, whatever you take up as an instrument, learn piano first, because that's the foundation of all." . . . When he had his chamber music groups and various string group rehearsals at the house, I was about nine or ten years old, and I was sitting there playing *Cavalleria Rusticana* and *Bohemian Girl* and all these long drawn-out things, while the other kids were all playing. I was playing the keyboard, you know, never dreaming that I would wind up as a saxophone player.
>
> I've been very aware of all types of music all my life. The fact that I chose jazz was mostly because I enjoyed it. . . . It was a release to be inventive. I didn't have to just read what was there. I could do what I felt I wanted to do. . . . But I never lost track of the fact that I loved symphony music and I still do, to this day.[21]

Sioux City had instrumental music in the schools when Peggy was growing up, including large school orchestras, even in the elementary schools. Born into the music business, it was not surprising that Peggy began working professionally as a child. She toured with the immensely popular Scottish cultural ambassador Sir Harry Lauder (1870–1950):[22]

> Harry Lauder came to town and I happened to be in third grade at that time. I had a teacher named Miss McFadden. She was Scottish, of course. She took some of us from her class and taught us the "Highland Fling." Harry Lauder had heard about her and about us, and he came to town from Scotland with his own musicians, and came to us and said, "I heard about girls who dance the 'Highland Fling' who are about seven years old. I'd like to meet them."
>
> So they met at our house. Naturally, that was where everybody met. He [Harry Lauder] came over and talked to us and he had all the girls dance and show him what they did. He was amazed. We had never been to Scotland. We had little dresses, the outfits, and everything. And he took us on his

Peggy *(top row, right)*, at age seven, with Harry Lauder dance troupe.

whole tour that summer, to the Chambers of Commerce in Nebraska, South Dakota, Iowa, and North Dakota, and, well, we were busy all summer.

You know, no one went with me. My folks considered that to be my business. Someone was in charge. They didn't worry about me. At seven years old, I was out trouping! I had a ball. That was my first dancing. I never intended to ever be a dancer, but it ended up that I had to do some dancing to keep playing the horn. And that comes later.[23]

With Peggy's classroom teacher, Miss McFadden, as chaperone, the parents did not worry about their daughters going on a regional tour.

Grandma Gilbert

Peggy's maternal grandmother, Carrie Adell Hazzard Gilbert (1854–1943),[24] was a strong, determined, and formidable woman, who had a tremendous influence on Peggy. Carrie Hazzard had a difficult early life and had married three times. Her first marriage was to an older traveling salesman when she was still a teenager. Peggy recalls Grandma Gilbert:

> We were blessed. We had a grandmother who lived nearby—a widow. She was very independent and, much to my consternation at times, showed very plainly that she preferred boys to girls. But, in spite of my hurt feelings at times, when my brother . . . would get a new toy or be given a shiny new dollar to spend by my grandmother, and even though I would be standing right beside him looking longingly and hopefully into my grandmother's eyes, she would ignore me completely, or say, "Orval is a young man, and he has to have these things. You are just a little girl." That explanation was to satisfy me entirely because I did not receive any present or extra plaything—I was just a girl, period. I have often wondered if that particular phase in my life had anything to do with my own destiny. . . .Grandma, as we called her, was a regal looking woman, who carried herself straight and walked with the distinct step of knowing where she was going and getting there as soon as possible.[25]

Even at a young age, Peggy felt the sting of injustice based on gender preference. She learned in her family that she would have to work hard to get what she wanted and that she was expected to step aside meekly and give priority to the needs of her male relatives. The irony of this is apparent in the fact that, in the 1930s, after her father's death, Peggy became the main financial provider for her mother, grandmother, and her brother's children. Peggy earned money by playing the saxophone (considered a masculine instrument), by taking charge of her own band (when bandleader was considered a masculine role), and by developing substantial skills in financial management.[26]

> Grandma had been through much hardship, prone to those who had come by covered wagon from Wisconsin to the Middle West. Her life as a child in Wisconsin on a farm was another story indeed. . . . Grandma was of "hearty" stock and very proud to call herself a "Yankee," which she did on every possible occasion. She had brothers and sisters, some of whom were still living when we were small, [including] Uncle George, who was a jovial, beloved fellow and who always had time to stop and talk for no matter how long, even though the house may be burning down, or his wife was having a baby and he would be on his way to the doctor. Everyone loved Uncle George, including my brother and me. His wife, Aunt Jennie, was a very slight woman, [with] black, black hair and a strong face with wide set black eyes that made me feel, as a child, that she could see right through me and know every thought I was thinking. We spent many happy days with them at a little home they had on a small lake in Iowa, where I learned to fish. I had the greatest respect for [Grandma], since she represented a strength to me that even my own father did not project.

Peggy's life was greatly impacted by her brother Orval's actions, as well:

> My brother Orval was like my father in many ways—his fast, easy, and quick smile mostly. He had a way with people—and especially women. From the moment I became aware of the fact that I was "just a girl," I also saw the way women looked at him, with a different kind of smile than they had for me.
>
> Orval, who grew up in the same surroundings I did, somehow believed life was all perfectly great, and he never thought he should not have had this or that because we didn't have the money. He eventually did get almost everything he wanted—somehow [he] became aware of the fact that his charm worked. Even the teachers at school liked him. I was a few grades behind him, and when I came into class where he had been, they would always remember my brother Orval. They would have a smile and twinkle in their eyes when they spoke of him. His grades were not high; in fact, he just skimmed through one class [grade level] to another. He was a good ball player and ice skater. He had that certain something, indefinable, that brought people to him.
>
> In trying to compete with my brother, I attempted other ways to obtain the friendships and companionship and love of my classmates. I always had good grades, and Orval was the first to brag about it to everyone. This made me very happy. So I would try that much harder. He would sometimes let me play marbles in the backyard with his friends and himself. Invariably, I would win all the marbles, because I seriously practiced to be better than they were, and it paid off. They would laugh, and I would laugh, and eventually—perhaps at dinner that night—Orval would offer to pay me for my winnings, and I would sell all the marbles back to him. He then would return them to his friends the next day. Later, we would play the same game again. Sometimes I thought maybe they let me win—but, after thinking it over several years later, I'm sure they didn't—I just won, period.

> The early '20s in our town was like a spring flower just budding and coming into full bloom. All things were wonderful and unbelievable at the same time. My brother was beginning to wear clothes to look like a young dude. He wore candy-striped silk shirts, or wild colors, and tight collars. He wore what they called "pipe-stem pants," and I remember he had to put them on before he put on his shoes, because the bottom of the legs was so tight. He had broad shoulders, carried himself very erect and proud, and wore the very latest in fashions, including, at that time, bright bow ties. I used to look at him when he was dressed and ready to go out with the boys, and think how wonderful it would be to be able to dress like that. Many times, when the folks were out, and I found a few moments alone in the house, I would dress completely in his clothes, and stand before the mirror in admiration, thinking how wonderful it was to be a man.[27]

Peggy had a large extended family in the Sioux City area. In addition to her father's family of musicians, her mother's brother, Uncle Bert, worked in the stockyards and was an expert in Morse code.[28] His wife, Aunt Lett, had a restaurant near the "car barns," where the street cars were housed at night. At one time, Uncle Bert had a cigar store near the stockyards and Peggy's mother worked there. Uncle Bert was "a talker," often having big discussions with Aunt Lett's customers in the restaurant.[29]

Sioux City had a rich, diverse, and active cultural life during the early years of the twentieth century.

> The big theater, the auditorium, there was where all the operas came and my dad often played in the pit, and on the stage behind the performers. It was a good place to go to hear good music, especially, and musicals that were coming in at that time. We kept up on everything. At the same time, my mother was called to be in the background every once in awhile to be a singer. We used to laugh, "Mother, you are on stage tonight." She'd say, "I really wasn't on stage. I'm in the background."[30]

When Peggy was a child, Sioux City's largest performing venue was the Peavey Grand Opera House. Located at the corner of Fourth and Jones, its construction was paid for by several wealthy industrialists. The Chamber of Commerce, banks, and other businesses were housed in the front of the building. The theater had approximately 1,700 seats, including 500 inexpensive ones in the gallery. In 1919, the theater was closed and used as a warehouse and auto repair shop. A fire in 1931 forced the building's demolition.

Riverside Park was also a popular entertainment center in Sioux City. It had the first amusement park in the area, including a roller coaster, as well as country clubs, baseball fields, race tracks, and picnic grounds. People could swim, canoe, or row on the river; many took steamboat rides. Accessible by streetcar from downtown, the country clubs had live entertainment for dancing, and rooms for card playing and pool shooting. The Interstate Fair took place there from 1903 until 1926, under the leadership of F. L. Eaton. Farmers from the tristate area bought and sold livestock there, among extensive exhibitions and races.

For several decades, the Sioux City Brick & Tile Company was one of the largest employers in the area. Other major employers included the Sioux City Vinegar and Pickling Works, and repair shops for Chicago, Milwaukee, St. Paul, and Pacific railroads. Many people worked in the stockyards and the meat-packing industry.[31]

Prohibition began on January 16, 1920, with enactment of the 18th Amendment to the U.S. Constitution. Known as the Volstead Act, it prohibited the manufacture, sale, and possession of alcohol in the United States. This "noble experiment" failed miserably; by 1925, there were more than one hundred thousand speakeasies in New York City alone. The Mob operated nightclubs with floor shows and great bands. People drank alcohol in tea cups, in case the place was raided by police. Outside of big cities, people drank "bathtub gin," and Sioux City had its share. Normal law-abiding folks became criminals in the eyes of the law. Prohibition continued for thirteen years, ending on December 5, 1933, when the 21st Amendment repealed the 18th.

Within six months of the start of Prohibition, women won the right to vote, as a result of the efforts of the Suffrage movement.[32] Nevertheless, flappers were the rage during the Jazz Age of the 1920s. They wore short skirts and bobbed their hair, smoked cigarettes and drank alcohol. They went to speakeasies and nightclubs, partying and dancing all night.

It was in this era that Peggy Gilbert came of age. There was great optimism in America about its future. Peggy recalls the hardships suffered by many American families during World War I, as well as the big parade and celebration in Sioux City that was held at war's end. Horrified by the experiences of World War I, Americans were determined to enjoy themselves and pursue their dreams in the "Roarin' Twenties."

There were substantial changes in the music business during this time, as well. By World War I, most families with some degree of education owned a piano and played music at home—both solo piano music and popular songs. But with the advancement in technology for phonographs, recordings began to outsell sheet music. By the mid 1920s, the sale of a hit song recording surpassed the sale of its sheet music. Bandleader Paul Whiteman's famous 1920 recording of the Schonberger-Coburn-Rose song "Whispering"[33] purportedly sold two million copies.

Radio was making a big impact. The first commercial radio station, KDKA in Pittsburgh, was established in 1920. By 1930, there were more than six hundred commercial radio stations, coast-to-coast. Peggy's family kept up with the latest in popular music by listening to their Atwater Kent radio set at home.

Sioux City High School

Peggy attended Sioux City High School, which had been dedicated in May 1893, and was later known as Central High School. Costing more than $104,460 to build,[34] it was constructed of brownish-pink Lake Superior sandstone, also called Sioux Falls granite, and featured a central ventilating system, electric bells, and thermostatically controlled heating in the classrooms. Among its alumnae were twins Esther Pauline "Eppie" and Pauline Esther "Popo" Friedman, better known as advice columnists Ann Landers and Abigail Van Buren, who graduated in 1936. Peggy particularly remembers the high school's basement, known as the "dungeon," with its 960-seat auditorium as the site of many performances and other community events.

> The high school was called the "castle on the hill" and it was a great big building. Three stories high. It was all brick. . . . We had terrific teachers. I graduated from that school, mid-year in 1923 . . . and it gave me a good start. I thought that my life would be music. It had to have something to do with music. So that was the direction I was taking.
>
> Except I really wanted to go to Chicago Art Institute,[35] but my folks at the time were facing a lot of . . . financial problems, so I couldn't go there. So I went to Morningside College for about 6 months, but thought, "This is not is for me," so I got out and went into the music business. That's where I belong.[36]

In high school, Peggy took some secretarial courses, learning to type and take shorthand. She developed an excellent command of the English language and learned to write quickly and effectively. These skills served her throughout her career, particularly when, in mid-life, she had difficulty making a living as a musician.

In addition to weekly piano lessons, Peggy continued her education to the best of her ability. Her heart was never quite in it, because music was so strongly embedded in her life. At that time, she was listening to big dance bands and stage bands at the Orpheum Theater.[37] She was thrilled to hear the band break into a progression of wild and raucous brass sounds in fanfares before the curtain would open.[38]

Also during high school, Peggy worked as a movie usher at the Paramount Theater. She remembers the theater's pipe-organ, popular in the days before talking pictures. She worked her way up to the position of "head girl," seating people in the orchestra section, the highest priced tickets. One of the things she disliked about her job was having to direct black theatergoers to the balcony, where they were required to sit. "That just made me sick!"[39]

Peggy knew about vaudeville from a young age. A style of theater which flourished in North America from 1880 through the early 1930s, vaudeville included multiple acts, ranging from acrobats, singers, and dancers to strongmen, escape artists, freak acts, comedians, magic, animal acts, Shakespeare, virtuosic instrumentalists, celebrities, lectures by intellectuals, and bands. Beginning with a "dumb act," for example, acrobats, or jugglers—so that latecomers would not interrupt dialogue-intensive performances—the show usually had a "flash act," with its own lavish set, special effects, and chorus. The headliner appeared as the highlight or penultimate act of the show, which concluded with a "chaser," an act dull enough to "chase" the audience from the theater, thereby clearing the house for the next performance. The Orpheum Circuit[40] was the best known in the Western states, eventually acquired by the Keith-Albee Circuit, which dominated in the East.

By the 1890s, vaudeville shows played in large and small venues in nearly every reasonably sized city and town in North America. With standardized booking and sophisticated promotion, they enjoyed a large and loyal audience. Only public schools and churches rivaled vaudeville in the size of their community gatherings. When films began to be presented commercially, they were shown in vaudeville halls, incorporated into the overall show. In the larger theaters, these films were accompanied by orchestras, with nine to thirty-three musicians.

Eventually the film screening became the focus of the show, with the vaudeville stage acts only introducing and supplementing it. Vaudeville shows had a touring ensemble of headliners and special acts, but often hired local bands, emcees, and backup singers and musicians to supplement the touring group. Peggy's parents often performed in these shows; her father sometimes led the orchestra for a silent film. The form of vaudeville productions later became the basis of television variety shows; some performers from vaudeville had careers in early television.[41]

Peggy's brother, Orval, began playing professionally as a drummer with several area bands, and Peggy often went to hear him play. Some of the bands with which Orval played toured in the tristate region. He was making money and having fun. As her brother became more and more the "man about town," Peggy remembers that her father told him, "Son, if you quit school, and start to work—as long as you live here in this house with us—you will contribute the same as I do." Orval contributed to the household expenses and "the cup was never empty." Literally, there was a cup in the pantry and Orval helped to keep it filled with money to cover the family's expenses.[42]

AMERICAN VAUDEVILLE PERFORMERS AND MUSICIANS

Although some vaudeville performers were involved in film and radio performances, by the Great Depression, many found themselves out of work. With the advent of talking pictures and the "Mighty Wurlitzer" theater organ, orchestral musicians who accompanied silent film screenings found themselves unemployed practically overnight. Within months of the release of the first "talkie," *The Jazz Singer*, orchestras in movie theaters were disbanded. By 1930, some 22,000 theater jobs were lost by the musicians who had accompanied silent films and vaudeville shows. New technology in the recording industry only created a few hundred new jobs to replace them.

The American Federation of Musicians protested the loss of jobs due to "canned" music, but could neither prevent nor slow the transformation. Due to the difficulty of synchronizing music to picture, the union was able to negotiate high prices for musicians working in that business. In 1930, the AFM even created the Music Defense League to raise the public's awareness of the problem. By the summer of 1930, sound was installed in 83 percent of all theaters in the United States.

Many of these Midwestern musicians went to Hollywood in search of work. They became the backbone of the music business in Los Angeles, performing in Hollywood studio orchestras, stage shows, nightclubs, cafeterias, tearooms, and tourist attractions. Most of the nation suffered terribly with the Depression, but musicians in Los Angeles during the 1930s did well, including Peggy Gilbert.

Peggy remembers difficult times for her family in the 1920s:

> Now came the period of our lives when our father started getting ill and, after spending some time in the hospital, . . . became less and less able to keep up his job. Orval felt that he would have to stop traveling so much and find time to be home, where he could be of some help both financially and physically. In the meantime, I was continuing in school, working in theaters as an usherette, etc. Life was not altogether without problems, but we were a family who shared them together and so we got along. Papa worked off and on, but was not physically strong and had limited activities. We still had our musicales at home, and continued to enjoy friends as we had always done.

> In my last year of high school, I noticed that Orval was becoming very attentive to one girl. She was only sixteen years old, and a beautiful young lady, who lived at home with her family and other brothers and sisters. . . . When I questioned him about his new girlfriend, he would tend to brush it aside, but smile at me like he would say, "nothing to think about—or worry about—I like her a lot and she likes me, and we are not going to settle down yet." That, of course, turned out to be wrong.[43]

Orval married Zanona "Nona" Gunn in 1923 and they soon had three children.[44] Orval's young family required all of his resources. So, when Peggy was a senior in high school, she started to help support her parents.

Peggy was eighteen when she took up the saxophone, starting with the E-flat alto. She says, "The first time I tried one, I said, 'This is it!' I loved the feel of it—free and loose. And there weren't many girls playing horns in those days. As soon as I got the saxophone or clarinet in my hands, it was an entirely different thing with me. I felt an emotional charge."[45] The style of music she played was ragtime, the predecessor to jazz. She joined the Musicians Union in Sioux City. She says, "My father was a charter member of the Musicians Union in Sioux City. He helped organize it. He said if you are ever going to become a professional, be union, and be a professional with professionals and act like one. So I always tried to."[46] Women musicians were accepted into the Musicians' Union beginning in 1903, when it joined the American Federation of Labor, which prohibited discrimination against women workers.

Peggy credits her ability to play jazz to listening to national radio broadcasts of the Coon-Sanders Original Kansas City Nighthawks in the early 1920s. Drummer Carleton Coons and pianist Joe Sanders met in 1919 at the Jenkins Music Store in Kansas City, Missouri. In 1920, they formed the Coon-Sanders Novelty Orchestra and performed at the Pompeiian Room of the Baltimore Hotel and at the Newman Theater, as part of a vaudeville show. In 1921, they recorded four songs for Columbia Records. By 1922, they were broadcast regularly over WDAF, a station owned by the *Kansas City Star*. Their nightly broadcasts could be heard from Maine to Hawaii, 11:30 p.m. to 1 a.m. Changing their name to Nighthawks, they formed the first radio fan club, which grew within two years to 37,000 members. By 1926, they moved to the Blackhawk Restaurant in Chicago, at the corner of Wabash and Randolph, and were heard over WGN.[47]

In 1925, Peggy visited an aunt in Los Angeles and decided that she would return there someday to live. At the time, she had two aunts and uncles living in Southern California. During that same year, her parents bought a house on Isabella Street in Sioux City.

PEGGY GILBERT: THE SWITCH FROM PIANO TO C-MELODY SAX[48]

I had a natural talent for music. Piano was first, and I made my mark all through grammar school playing loud and precise marches on the old battered upright piano in the hallway for the students to march in every morning and march out every afternoon. This was my first experience of getting noticed through music and I discovered early in life that the mood of the musician sets the scene and if I played hard and fast, they marched the same way. If I felt like dragging it out, they walked stooped-shouldered and monotonously to their respective rooms, uninspired by what they heard. My playing could either get them off happily and quickly or on a downbeat drag. So much for that—already I felt superior in that I could control the actions of my fellow students and hence, music was the only profession in the world for me. Not the kind I played and practiced at home, but that great four-letter word JAZZ. I loved it from the time I became aware of a combination of notes and beats that make my blood tingle and my heart race.

Piano was not for me. Much to my regret, I found out through many lean years later, that pianists always worked, many times when there was no money for other musicians. But, no—I loved a saxophone. So be it. My first paycheck earned as an office girl in an insurance company went for a down payment on a "C" melody saxophone. I brought it home with me, not knowing much about it except that I knew I would play the H--- out of it or die in the process. My grandmother, who was never at a loss for words in expressing her personal feelings said, "What are you going to do with that thing?" My father, who was an excellent violinist and who taught me to do it right when studying the piano, yelling from the basement through the thick floor boards, almost bouncing me head first off the piano stool, "Stop! Do that over again. You hit the wrong note!" Whereupon I would grudgingly go over the passage until he stopped screaming from the cellar, where he made the best homemade brew in town. Getting back to the entrance of a horn in my life, my dad followed my grandmother's remark with, "You'll never see a saxophone in a symphony orchestra. It is a bastard instrument only for effect." I said, "I don't care. I don't want to play symphony music. I like it and when I learn to play it, you'll be surprised what I will do with it." Grandma retorted, "I won't be surprised and I could tell you what to do with it, but I'm a lady." Well, so that was my beginning. Discouraged? No, not in the least. In fact, so determined was I that I found the scale that night and by 12 midnight the neighbors were calling on the phone, making smart remarks like, "Stick to the piano!" "Who does she think she is? Rudy Wiedoeft?"[48]

CHAPTER II
The Melody Girls

In the 1920s, Margaret—as everyone called her then—was well aware of all-girl bands, having heard several of them in Sioux City. She would go to the theater to meet them and ask questions about being on the road: Who do you know? How does one become successful in this business? Other all-girl bands popular in the 1920s and '30s included Edna White's Trombone Quartet, Bobbie Grice's Fourteen Bricktops, Bobbie Howell's American Syncopators, The Dixie Sweethearts, The Darlings of Rhythm (with tenor saxophone player Margaret Backstrom and alto saxophone player Josephine Boyd), Eddie Durham's All-Star Girl Orchestra, The Parisian Redheads (from Paris, Indiana), and The Twelve Vampires. The best-known and most successful girl band of the '20s was Babe Egan and Her Hollywood Redheads.[49]

BABE EGAN AND HER HOLLYWOOD REDHEADS

Mary Florence Cecilia Egan, known as "Babe," died at Rockhaven Sanitarium in Verdugo City at 2:45 am Monday February 7, 1966. She suffered her third stroke a week ago. Dot Sauter took her record player and the records made in Hamburg [Germany] to entertain her but she'd had the stroke the day before and no one could see her. She couldn't see and her left side was affected. She died at the age of 68.

Miss Babe Egan was born in Seattle, Washington [May 1, 1897]. She played violin professionally when very young—played in the pits there. Her family moved to Hollywood where Miss Egan soon got a job at the studios playing mood music for the greats of the silent era. Jim Cruze[50] was her hero, and he gave her advice about getting her own orchestra. She organized the Babe Egan's Hollywood Redheads in about 1924. She rehearsed in theaters and got bookings as far as Honolulu that way. Played in Honolulu for three months, changing the show each week. In those days the megaphone was used so a singing trio was part of the band—everyone did everything, sing, dance, play and look pretty. We wore blazers and copied ourselves after Fred Waring and his Pennsylvanians. We played in Chatiner's Ravenna Theater for several months, playing the pit and on the stage. Then we took off on the Keith-Orpheum Circuit. Played the circuit for many years. Would stay in N.Y.C. for a year at a time, in those days playing the subway circuit so-called. Worked with Burns and Allen, Jimmy Durante, then known as Clayton Jackson and Durante. Phil Silvers [1911–1985] was a kid in an act called "In Any Apartment." He had a crush on the drummer. He was 14 and she was 16. Our clarinet player taught him clarinet which he plays to this day. Also drums.

We took off for Europe in 1929 and were gone one year, touring 14 countries. Babe Egan was a fine manager and was worshipped by the girls. Her word was law. She was a natural redhead and had an Irish temper but we understood her. We were billed as the best girl band in the world and were treated as great artists by Europeans. Not just scum musicians as in the U.S.A. We ate up the hand kissing and the publicity, although the plumbing was bad. The food was delightful except in England. Three months in England and the girls were starved to death and glad to open in Berlin. Berlin in 1929 was modern and beautiful. Some of the girls would swim and sightsee in the daytime and find a pool where the waves were turned on every ten minutes. Night clubs where a telephone would be at each table—Wow! Talk about affairs of the heart. The girls stayed pretty much to themselves as they were a little afraid of foreigners.

After a year in Europe, the girls became homesick and sick of looking at castles and museums so took the "Isle de France"[51] and came back to the States. Playing the Palace in N.Y. and subsequently three times a headline act. Worked with Ted Healy [1896–1937] and his Stooges. The same Stooges who are so popular with the kids today. Moe and Shemp and "what's his name." After touring the U.S. again and visiting our families, we took off for Europe again, with an enlarged band—16 pieces this time and had just as a successful tour—a year as well, until the usual homesickness overtook the girls. It was 1933 then, and Hitler was in power, especially in Czechoslovakia. One of the girls was Jewish and she visited her relatives in Vienna and barely escaped with her life and later got her relatives out in the nick of time. Miriam Stieglitz was her name. She still plays the sax and clarinet in N.Y.C. Dorothy Sauter still plays bass professionally. Having played with Jack Benny and an 'X–mas' T.V. show three years ago. All the other girls are married and are now grandmothers. The band joined up with Thelma White at this time. Thelma having joined the band in Europe and changed the act all around. No longer the collegiate type but a more daring costumed band. Needless to say it didn't go over and the band soon broke up, as the depression was on anyhow. Later Miss Egan and Thelma White

Babe Egan *(at the piano)* and Her Hollywood Redheads *(left to right)*: Geraldine Stanley, saxophone; Billie Farley, bass; Shirley Thomas, trumpet; Edith Griffith, piano; Dot Sauter, bass; Fern Spaulding, trombone; Estelle Dilthey, drums; and Juanita Klein, saxophone.

organized a new band and went to Australia where they were quite successful. Picking up most of their musicians over there.

Miss Egan later quit the music business and had a string of dancing schools where she was quite successful. She bought a house in the [San Fernando] Valley and settled down. Later, she retired and bought a huge trailer in about 1958. This she had hauled to Palm Springs where she planned to spend the winters and the beach in the summers. She suffered a stroke. Her second one as she had one on the Isle of Majorca while visiting rich friends there a few years previous. She lay, for no one knows how many days, until her dog attracted attention and saved her life. She was taken to the hospital and later to Rockhaven Sanitarium where she has been receiving the finest of care ever since. Her brain was affected but Babe never forgot the band or the names of places and people we worked with. She wrote everyone of the band and received answers from all who knew her. Yes, she was happy in Rockhaven. Good bye, Babe.[52]

Among the women who played in Babe Egan's band were: Dorothy "Dot" Sauter,[53] bass, tuba, cello; Estelle Dilthey [Hamburgh], drums, xylophone; Elva Dilthey [MacNair], saxophone; Billie Farley, guitar, banjo; Edith Griffith,[54] piano; Fern Spaulding, trombone; Geraldine "Jerrie" Stanley,[55] saxophone; Shirley Lee Thomas [Brush], trumpet; Juanita Klein, saxophone, clarinet. Babe played violin. The band appeared at the inaugural performance at the Omaha Orpheum on October 10, 1927, making quite an impression.

Entering the Music Business

From her friend, saxophonist Maynard Foster, who had a band in Sioux City, Peggy learned more about the business of having a band. They dated and, at one point, even considered marriage. However, when Maynard jokingly threatened to hit a dog in the middle of the road one night, she decided to break up their relationship.

The first band Peggy organized in Sioux City played at Lake Okoboji, one of the Iowa Great Lakes. Peggy played saxophone and clarinet; Marjorie "Midge" Kelley, piano; Dorothy Kelley, banjo and accordion; Orval Knechtges, drums; and Ruth Dubnoff, violin. A young man played trumpet and another young man played bass and tuba, but their names are not remembered. They played at The Inn, which was a large, popular ballroom.

Next was Peggy's first all-girl band, The Melody Girls, which included some of the musicians from the Lake Okoboji band:

> It was not easy being accepted as a woman musician. First of all, women musicians who played instruments like trumpets, trombones, drums, saxophones were not too well-known, because they were just starting out to be accepted at that time, and so it wasn't easy. However, I was very lucky, because I had a good group. I had some fine musicians and we were able to contact places and be accepted, and we went from there.[56]
>
> I organized the first all-girl band in Sioux City. I talk as if it was a big band, but it was a small band, five pieces, sometimes six. I played a lot around town. The Elks Club, all the clubs, Chamber of Commerce. I broke in my band that way. Then we started really working. I got a connection with the Martin Hotel. . . . We were there for two years and it was wonderful. I had a time finding girl musicians that could play.
>
> Pardon the expression "girl musicians." I know that *girl* musicians is not the way to describe a girl band nowadays. It is *women*. But we weren't "women," we were "girls" . . . the bands that were girls were girl bands . . . that's what we called ourselves. We had a good time. We enjoyed every minute of it.[57]

> We rehearsed at my house, just as my dad did, and he would give us little suggestions. I'd take an orchestration and cut it up. We didn't know what we were doing, but I did. Up here [pointing to her head], I knew what I wanted. We'd make arrangements from the orchestrations to fit the group. We were on radio every night on KSCJ. We used to get stacks of mail with requests from people who wanted us to play tunes and dedicate them.[58]
>
> That's the way we got started. A very small way. A very secure way. It wasn't anything special to me. We were just making a living. I didn't want to be a star or anything. . . . I just wanted to make a living. It happened to be that music was the best thing for me.[59]

Peggy credits her father with teaching her how to make her own arrangements from sheet music. This skill served her well throughout her career.[60]

A photograph of the band from around 1926–27 shows Charlotte Nordstrom, drums; her sister Viola Nordstrom,[61] violin; Marjorie Kelley, piano; her sister Dorothy Kelley, banjo; and Peggy [Margaret Knechtges], saxophone, clarinet, vocals, and leader. Peggy often referred to this as the "First Melody Girls Orchestra."

The Melody Girls, 1928.

When the Martin Hotel opened in 1912, it was Sioux City's largest, most modern and elegant hotel. Built by Sioux City businessmen James P. and Louis B. Martin, it was designed by Chicago architect Louis Sullivan. It was six stories high, with a classical theme, built on a two-story base at the corner of Fourth and Pierce streets. A seventh floor was added in 1918.[62]

Peggy's band at the Martin Hotel was broadcast nightly over KSCJ, the radio station of the *Sioux City Journal* at 1360 AM.[63] The station first went on the air on April 4, 1927.[64] Thus, Peggy began her work as a pioneer radio broadcaster. She recalls that they had only one large microphone hanging from the ceiling, which she had to pull down to announce the selections from the bandstand. A program from the Hotel Martin dated October 16, 1927, gives the names of the Melody Girls as: Margaret Knechtges, director, saxophone; Marjorie Kelley, banjo and piano; Ruth Dubnoff, violin; Charlotte Nordstrom, drums; Sarah Brown, trumpet.[65]

Trumpeter Sarah "Sally" Viola Brown[66] (1909–2000) was born in Dakota City, Nebraska,[67] and played in the Brown Family Orchestra as a child. At age three, her left arm got caught in the wringer of a washing machine and "was chewed up." Doctors wanted to amputate, but her father refused; although her arm healed, she remained badly scarred. As a high school senior, she beat twenty-five male contestants to win Nebraska State Championship in trumpet. According to Peggy, she played "a fabulous trumpet."[68]

SONG FORM

Song form dominated popular music and jazz up until the 1950s. Typically in song form, there are one or two verses followed by a thirty-two-bar chorus in four phrases and in set patterns: AABA, ABAB, ABCA, or AABC. Verses were increasingly left out and by the 1930s, songwriters often did not write a verse at all.

The music was basically triadic, diatonic, and tonal, but harmonies became more and more complex, including seventh and ninth chords, and triads with added sixths and seconds, and chromatically altered chords. In the 1930s and '40s, there were modulations to remote keys in the second or third section of a song. Syncopation or syncopated rhythms from dance music dominated popular songs in the 1920s, '30s, and '40s.

Jazz relied heavily on thirty-two-bar, four-phrase songs, with the first and last statement of the song played by the entire band. Between the first and last statement was a succession of improvised solos.

At the Martin Hotel, the band played two shows a day: luncheon and dinner in the main dining room. It is likely that they performed and were broadcast six nights a week during 1927 and early 1928. The list of tunes includes:

"Shanghai Honeymoon" (Shockley, Hausman, Melrose, 1926)

"I Can't Believe That You're in Love With Me" (Jimmy McHugh, Clarence Gaskill, 1926)

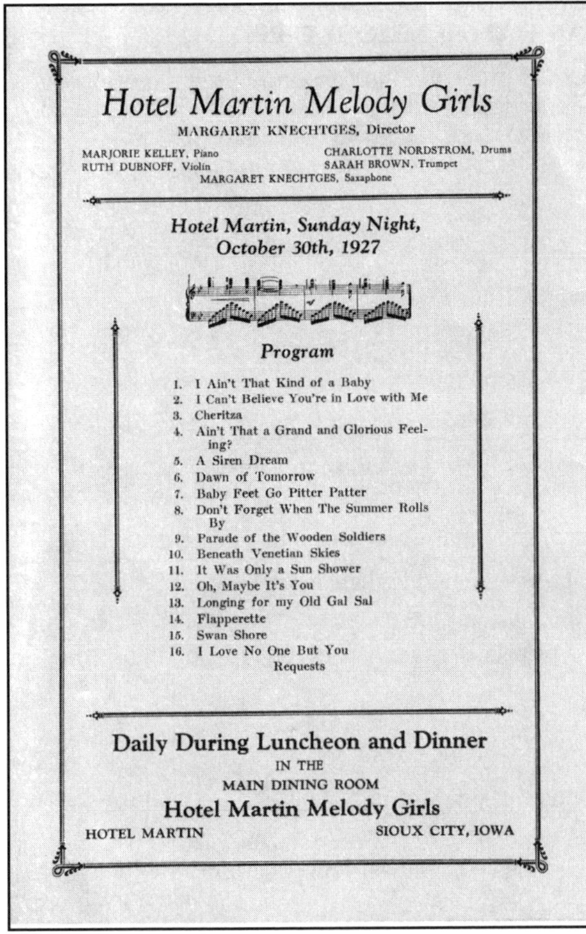

Hotel Martin Melody Girls

MARGARET KNECHTGES, Director

MARJORIE KELLEY, Piano — CHARLOTTE NORDSTROM, Drums
RUTH DUBNOFF, Violin — SARAH BROWN, Trumpet
MARGARET KNECHTGES, Saxaphone

Hotel Martin, Sunday Night, October 30th, 1927

Program

1. I Ain't That Kind of a Baby
2. I Can't Believe You're in Love with Me
3. Cheritza
4. Ain't That a Grand and Glorious Feeling?
5. A Siren Dream
6. Dawn of Tomorrow
7. Baby Feet Go Pitter Patter
8. Don't Forget When The Summer Rolls By
9. Parade of the Wooden Soldiers
10. Beneath Venetian Skies
11. It Was Only a Sun Shower
12. Oh, Maybe It's You
13. Longing for my Old Gal Sal
14. Flapperette
15. Swan Shore
16. I Love No One But You

Requests

Daily During Luncheon and Dinner
IN THE
MAIN DINING ROOM
Hotel Martin Melody Girls
HOTEL MARTIN — SIOUX CITY, IOWA

Original program for The Melody Girls at the Martin Hotel, Sioux City, Iowa, October 30, 1927.

"Cheerie-Beerie Be" (from *Sunny Italy*, by Mabel Wayne, 1927)

"Baby Your Mother (... like she Babied You)" (Joe Burke, 1927)

"Hallelujah!" (from *Hit The Deck,* by Vincent Youmans, Clifford Grey, Leo Robin, 1927)

"Indian Love Call" (from *Rose Marie*, by Rudolf Friml, 1924)

"Just Once Again" (Walter Donaldson, Paul Ash, 1927)

"Flapperette" (Jesse Greer, 1926)

"By The Waters of the Minnetonka" (Thurlow Lieurance, 1920)

[What'll we do...] "On A Dew Dew Dewy Day" (Howard Johnson, Charles Tobias, Al Sherman, 1927)

"March of the Dolls" [unknown composer]

"Sweetheart Memories" (Benny Davis, Joe Burke, 1927)

"Highways Are Happy Ways" (Larry Shay, 1927)

"Sometimes I'm Happy" (from *Hit the Deck,* by Youmans, Grey, Robin, 1927)

"Russian Lullaby" (Irving Berlin, 1927)

"Doll Dance" (Nacio Herb Brown, 1921)

MAIL FOR THE MELODY GIRLS

"Compliments on your nice programs. The Announcer [Peggy Knechtges] sure deserves special praise as she is fine. The rest of your Orchestra is fine. P.S. Is there some way you can keep C. from interfering with your programs. He sounds as though he has mush in his mouth."

—Sioux City, IA

"This is probably lengthy for a request but your music is extraordinary. The general blah and bland is missing—a credit to you. Hoping that you continue your entertaining over KSCJ."

"That sax juggler holds my envy." —Sioux City, IA

"Dear Melody Girls—Music Sounds Wonderful!" —Marcus, IA

"Hoping you girls will keep up your good stuff!" —Waterbury, NE

"I listen to your program each night and think it is nice."

—Your listener

"Melody Girls sure have good music and program!" —Ponca, NE

"You have got one of the best orchestras that I have heard over many big stations." —Le Mars, IA

"Hello Girls! Listened to your program last evening. Don't think your orchestra could be beat." —Carroll, NE

"I was listening last night and must say you girls surely possess "IT" which goes to make up a real dance orchestra." —Decatur, NE

"You girls are the best on the air in the line of music." —Emerson, NE

"Listen to the Melody Girls orchestra at every chance and think they are the best orchestra on the air. I enjoyed your singing on 'The Tin Can Parade,' Margaret." —Waterbury, NE

Monday nights featured "Special Requests." Among the songs requested by mail:

"What'll You Do"
"There Must Be Somebody Else"
"My Blue Ridge Mountain Home"
"Moonlit Waters"
"Together We Two"
"The Sweetheart of Sigmaki"
"My Blue Heaven"
"Hallelujah"
"Rio Rita"
"Under the Moon"
"Just Once Again"
"I Told Them All About You"
"Broken Hearted"

"Lopaloma"
"I Can't Get the One I Want"
"My Bungalow of Dreams"
"Side by Side"
"Doll Dance"
"So Tired"
"Among My Souvenirs"
"Baby Your Mother as She Babied You"
"You Only Want Me When You're Lonesome"
"The Tin Pan Parade"
"Highways Are Happy Ways"
"I Ain't Got Nobody"
"Thanks for the Buggy Ride"
"Here Comes Your Sugar"
"Red Lips Kiss My Blues Away"
"The Song Is Ended But the Melody Lingers On"

One listener, "Percy H. G.," wrote them a poem, dated March 20, 1928:

Melody Girls

In signing off, we'll say good night,
We wish that you could see
The pleasure that your letters bring
The Girls of Melody

We hope our programme met your taste;
Our aim is but to please,
If you but tell us what you want
We'll send it with the breeze.

From six till eight each Monday night
We're on Sioux City's air
And from the Journal's station send
Our songs to everywhere

KSCJ is signing off;
The precious moments flee,
As once again we say good night—
The Girls of Melody.

While Peggy's band was performing at the Martin Hotel, the all-girl band Gibson's Navigators appeared at the Orpheum Theater in Sioux City[69] around 1926–27. Because some of the band members were staying at the Martin Hotel, they heard Peggy's band in the dining room and the women became friendly.[70] Peggy was especially impressed with trombonist Fern Spaulding,[71] with whom she would later work professionally.[72]

An article entitled, "Sailor Maids Fill Theater with Melody: Beth Gibson's Band is Palace Hit," describes Gibson's Navigators in detail:

> Nine young women, possessing more than their share of good looks and filling the theater with pervasive melody, are a big reason for the high popularity of the present show at the Palace Theater. They are Beth Gibson's "Navigators." Smartest looking sailors you ever did see.
>
> The girls—none is more than 21—fill their act with the spirit of youth. After a melody or two they get prankish and clown a bit and sing and dance. They are clever in all of it and easily create the impression of being one of the best among the many bands that come to the Palace.
>
> Fern Spaulding is an exceedingly accomplished trombone player and a leader in the comedy moments. You will not overlook the lass at the drums, Marvell Tanner, whose skillful handling of her outfit and contribution to the fun making are highly agreeable. Miss Sandahl's manipulation of the piano keys stands out in the triumphs of the band, which is directed modestly and efficiently by Miss Gibson.
>
> The "Navigators" will be one of the attractions at the opening of the new Orpheum theater in Madison, Wis., next Thursday.
>
> The Palace's show is an enthusiastic affair, with a heap of clean fun in it. Everybody likes Joseph B. Stanley, especially his dancing. Stanley has wit and accomplishments in comedy touches. Small and Mays are wonderfully talented lads, tuneful in song, and with music in their heels. One of them is a master of the ukulele. McGrath and Deeds capitalize their unique partnership to good returns. George W. Moore, cheerful of presence and one of the best of jugglers, starts the show off in just the right way.[73]

Another article, "Beth Gibson's Navigators to Be at Majestic," names the band members as Beth Gibson, Nell Gibson [tuba];[74] Nellie Sandahl, piano; Christal [sic] Harvey;[75] Edris Christi [saxophone]; Nina Locke [violin?]; Marvell Tanner, drums; Fern Spaulding, trombone; and Mae McFarland [trumpet?]. Also on the bill were Ernest Hiatt, comedian; Harry Hayden, actor; Reis Pamella, Lela Bliss, and Richard Lane, actors; Cuby and Smith; Bud Coulter and Billy Rose "will display their ability as delineators of the Southern Negro"; Corinne Villa and Bill Strigo "will entertain with musical instruments of unique design, while Jenny and Nylin are speed demons on roller skates."[76]

Peggy was offered several jobs on the road while still in Sioux City, including a gig with the Jazz Pirates. A telegram from Vincent and Stewart offers: "Jazzy Pirates: Pay forty dollars per week and transportation. Play high class picture shows and vaudeville theaters. We furnish costumes. Steady work. Answer at once to Strand Theater, Newton, Iowa if you want engagement. Will want you both[77] to join August 8. One Weeks rehearsal." This was

Gibson's Navigators *(top row, left to right)*: Mae McFarland, trumpet(?); Marvell Tanner, drums; Edris Christi, saxophone; *(bottom row, left to right)*: Nellie Sandahl, piano; Nell Gibson, tuba; Crystal Harvey, guitar, banjo; Fern Spaulding, trombone; Nina Locke, violin(?); and Beth Gibson, leader.

addressed to Margaret Knechtges at The Inn, Okoboji, Iowa, but has no date (probably 1927). Another telegram from Stewart Cash, sent from Fairfield, Iowa, states, "Can use both in 2 weeks. Summer salary $40 per week. I'm coming that way. Answer this to Strand Theater, Boone, Iowa."

Move to Los Angeles in 1928

Peggy's father died in November 1927, at the age of fifty-six, after several years of ill health.[78] "As long as I live," Peggy recalls, "I will never forget his funeral. My mother had to decide whether she wanted to take the money or have a beautiful funeral and she decided to spend the money on his funeral." The parade down a major street in Sioux City was a moving demonstration of the high esteem in which her father had been held in the music community. It included a marching band of twenty-four musicians from the Sioux City Musicians' Union, then a small marching string group, and the casket, followed by the entire family.

Soon after John Knechtges's death, the family faced severe financial problems. They lost their house, because they could not make the mortgage payments.[79] Peggy decided it was time to start her career in the entertainment business, so she could help support her mother and grandmother. To facilitate this, they decided to move to Los Angeles. Peggy drove out in her 1926 Dodge sedan, with a custom rooftop luggage rack. After she left, the Melody Girls continued at the Martin Hotel under the leadership of Peggy's friend, trumpeter Sarah Brown.

Along with her, she took a letter of recommendation from the Eppley Hotels Company, Omaha, Nebraska:

> To Whom It May Concern,
>
> For the past several seasons Miss Margaret Knechtges and Her Melody Girls have played at Hotel Martin, Sioux City, Iowa, to our entire satisfaction. The personnel of Miss Knechtges' combination is above average, and we feel sure these girls would do justice to any work they undertake.[80]

Immediately upon their arrival in California,[81] they received a telegram from Orval urging them to come back to Sioux City. His wife had died suddenly, at the age of twenty-three, of what was then called "quick consumption."[82] He had a four-year-old daughter, a two-year-old son, and a three-month-old baby, who had been born with consumption. Peggy returned to Sioux City, bought a car, and brought the children and Orval back to Los Angeles to live with her, her mother, and her grandmother. The baby stayed with its maternal grandparents.[83]

Peggy offers this description of Los Angeles in 1928, when she first arrived:

> The entertainment business was probably the most exciting thing that Los Angeles and Hollywood had to offer. . . . The motion picture studios were all running full blast and they were all over town, in all ends and in all

> sections of the town. They were making pictures on the streets. . . . In Culver City, on Adams Streets where the big homes were, all over the Valley, all over the place, you could see them, because they didn't have the big studios, the facilities that they have now. . . .
>
> They had many theaters here. They had stage shows connected with the motion pictures. Everybody who wanted to work as a musician had all the opportunity in the world. They were playing the studios. They were playing in all of the theaters, in the pits; they had bands on the stages. Everything. All the cafeterias had tea dances going on downtown. All the cafeterias had string instruments and groups playing. There was no limit . . . if you really wanted to go, were ambitious, and had a desire to play in any direction, whether it was classical or jazz or whatever. Opportunity was here.[84]
>
> At that time, the competition among women was not very steep. Most of the women at that time were playing in symphonies.[85] They were the string players, the harpists, and particular instruments that have been associated with feminine women. At the time I came out here, in 1928, jazz was just beginning to come into its own and some of the female musicians who were excellent at jazz had just now begun to discover that they had a place and they could be found. But, frankly, you'd have to work with all-girl orchestras, because the men at that time were not into using women jazz musicians yet. But there was plenty of work for girls if they were good, in the jazz field, in all fields, for that matter. Women musicians at that time, especially on wind instruments, were not as prevalent as they are now. They just didn't take them up.[86]

A 1927 Los Angeles Civic Bureau of Music and Art pamphlet describes what changes occurred in Easterners and Midwesterners upon their arrival:

> The mental environment then includes the inspiring success of developing the territory, the romantic daring of the past, . . . widespread enthusiasm aroused by the new homeland, ambitious associates and changed living conditions, which all stimulated spontaneity of expression. . . . People, who come West from Eastern cities and farms, undergo a subtle spiritual change and find themselves in a state of mind from which the Pacific slope with its vast distances, cheerful living conditions, natural rather than traditional, mode of life had entirely released them.[87]

Peggy's first music jobs in Los Angeles were with well-known vaudeville performers Irene Franklin (1876–1941)[88] and entertainer and drummer Juanita Connors.[89] About playing in their bands, Peggy says, "There were a lot of things I thought should be done with those bands that weren't being done. They weren't keeping up with the times; they played the same things over and over, and the same licks. And I thought, it's a new field, and we ought to get with it."[90]

MUSIC STYLE AND FORM

Peggy's band in the late 1920s and early '30s played what we now call ragtime, along with popular songs, mostly from Broadway shows.

The songs are in strophic form, with the same phrase and chord structure repeated several times, often to accommodate the dancers. The first chorus usually introduces the melody; it is followed by additional choruses, during which the musical material is developed. The songs are usually thirty-two bars (AABA) song form, sometimes with elaborate introductions and "closers." Sometimes the band would sing a verse and chorus and then take turns on additional verses with instrumental solos, with the rest of the band playing accompaniment, ending with a chorus which everyone played. Sometimes there would be a modulation from the chorus into the verse or from a verse into a chorus. Peggy often started her arrangements with a hot, upbeat "closure" first and then lit into the song. This would help get the dancers on their feet and out onto the dance floor.

Peggy always played the most recent pop hits with her band. Keeping current and up-to-date was a great selling point for a band. She made sure her band could play the tunes audiences were most likely to request.

Bootleg song sheets were readily available, despite the efforts of the publishers to prevent their distribution. In 1929, there were song-lyric magazines. In 1942, George Goodwin initiated a subscription service called Tune-Dex, which promised bandleaders and music directors the latest popular tunes. They distributed three-by-five-inch cards that contained the pop-song melody, with lyrics and chord symbols. The back of each card identified the copyright holder and performing rights agency controlling the song's license. Peggy used these to make arrangements for use on the bandstand, without buying the sheet music or a commercially available arrangement. By 1949, "fake books"—a collection of lead sheets with lyrics, chord symbols, guitar tablature, and the melodies for popular tunes—were available.[91]

A photograph of Juanita Connors's band at the Egyptian Theater in Hollywood in 1928 pictures includes Pee Wee Preble, trombone; Edna Lewis,[92] saxophones; Margaret Packard, saxophone; Chela Perkins, saxophone; Helen Boyd,[93] bass.

Peggy's brother, Orval, worked nights in a ballroom and, during the day, rode a motorcycle, as a messenger for the *Los Angeles Times*. Later, he would get a job at MGM as chauffeur for child star Shirley Temple. Musicians' scale was five dollars per night plus tips in a "kitty." Only the higher class bars and clubs paid a living wage.

By the time Peggy moved to Los Angeles, Southern California had a rich tradition of all-women performing ensembles, which had begun in the late nineteenth century. The Los Angeles Women's Philharmonic was founded in 1893 and continued until 1961. Eva Anderson founded the Long Beach Women's Symphony in 1925; it was funded by the city tax. All-women concert bands performed regularly in the San Diego area, beginning as early as 1899 with The American Troubadours at the Hotel del Coronado, conducted by C. A. McClure. R. E. Trognitz conducted The Ladies' Concert Band in San Diego, beginning in 1904. Babe Egan started her band in 1924 and was well-known in Los Angeles.[94]

Eventually Peggy began appearing in movies, but before that, she toured on the vaudeville circuit with the largest presenter of vaudeville shows in the late 1920s, Fanchon and Marco.

EVA ANDERSON AND THE LONG BEACH WOMEN'S SYMPHONY

In 1940, the Long Beach Women's Symphony attracted a crowd of more than five thousand for the Municipal Auditorium concert to celebrate the fifteenth anniversary of the group, a fact which attests to the popularity of the organization in Long Beach.

Eva Anderson, founder and conductor of the orchestra, was born on a farm in northern Missouri, and made her musical début at age three in a country schoolhouse entertainment. At age seventeen, she went to the Beethoven Conservatory in St. Louis. After completing her studies, she signed on with the Old Redpath Chautauqua and Lyceum Bureau as a featured violinist, and toured the circuit, giving more than 3,500 concerts throughout North America. She settled in Long Beach in 1919. In addition to the Long Beach Women's Symphony, she also directed the orchestra of the First Baptist Church and had a violin quartet which carried her name.

An important artistic, social, and recreational organization in the cultural life of Long Beach, especially during the Depression, the orchestra offered young women there an opportunity to travel, to attend social functions, and to meet people throughout the state.

Many have said that Eva Anderson ran her women's orchestra more like a vaudeville show than a classical orchestra, and indeed she had a genuine gift for showmanship and a knack for engendering publicity.

Although the Los Angeles Women's Symphony often claimed to be the oldest women's orchestra in the country or the world, the Long Beach Women's Symphony promoted itself as the largest women's symphony in the world, with between 100 and 127 players. The orchestra was supported by the City of Long Beach through the Recreation Commission.

Fanchon and Marco. Photo courtesy of Sandra Holden.

Newspaper advertisement in Atlanta, Georgia, for the Fanchon and Marco production, "Jazz Temple Idea."

CHAPTER III
On Tour with Fanchon and Marco

Regarding the late 1920s, Peggy says, "It was during the time when motion picture theaters presented fabulous stage shows in conjunction with movies that 'all-girl bands' were in demand. . . . I knew every stage door entrance from coast to coast and back again."[95]

In the fall of 1928, she successfully auditioned for the vaudeville producers Fanchon and Marco. Fanchon "Fanny" Wolff Simon (1892–1965)[96] and Marco "Mike" Wolff (1894–1977) began their agency in 1926 with one touring show, and by 1929 had grown to an astounding fifty-two shows on the road. Originally a brother and sister vaudeville dance team, their act also included Fanchon playing the piano to accompany Marco's violin playing. They started their own production company after an accident in a show that severely injured Fanchon's hip.[97]

Fanchon and Marco got their start from Harry C. Arthur, Jr., manager of the West Coast Theaters, headed by the Gore Brothers, who asked them to provide a show for the Warfield Theater on Market Street in San Francisco, then operated for the Loew Circuit. From their immediate success in that theater, he gave them a three-month contract. They expanded to the Oakland West Coast House and then to Loew's State Theater in Los Angeles.[98] Moving their headquarters to Los Angeles, their units opened there and had a run of ten weeks on the coast. It is ironic that, by 1926, many felt that vaudeville was on the wane and that a touring company would not be financially lucrative. However, Fanchon and Marco had the perfect formula. Calling their shows "Ideas," they knew how to develop a theme for a touring company and carry it out in every detail, from the selection of the music, to the flamboyant costumes and sets, and the casting.[99]

Every Fanchon and Marco production had a stage band and master of ceremonies (emcee), often hired from the local community. They brought in specialty acts and headliners, frequently auditioning and rehearsing in Los Angeles. According to Arthur Ungar, part of Fanchon and Marco's success was that they "knew production from the performers' angles and how to accomplish it in what appeared [to be] style at a nominal cost."[100]

With Harry Bourne as their costumer, Fanchon and Marco established their own studios to build the sets under Marco's supervision. This design operation also made costumes and sets for films and rented out to picture houses and "tab" organizations. There also was a shoe department "which takes care of itself financially."[101]

Eventually Fanchon and Marco shows were placed in four Publix Theaters on the West Coast, extending the circuit dates to fourteen weeks, ending in Salt Lake City. In 1927 and '28, they expanded to the East, including Denver, Kansas City, and New York City, making deals with Fox New York, Fox Midwest, and Fox New England. By 1930, they were performing in sixty theaters, coast to coast.[102] Among those actors whose careers were launched by Fanchon and Marco are Cyd Charisse, Joan Crawford, Dorothy Lamour, Judy Garland (as one of The Gumm Sisters), Doris Day, and Bing Crosby.[103]

Another of their stars was saxophonist and composer Cornelius "Rudy" Wiedoeft (1893–1940). Born in Detroit of German immigrants, he started performing at a young age on violin and clarinet with his family orchestra, including his father, A. C. Wiedoeft, violin-leader; his sister Erica on piano; brothers Gerhard on bass, Herbert on cornet, and Adolph on drums; and Rudy on clarinet. When the family moved to Los Angeles in 1904, young Rudy began performing at the Imperial Cafe. The family orchestra played two seasons at the Redondo Beach Hotel and then at Lake Tahoe. Rudy went to Chicago to study clarinet with Joseph Schreurs, former first clarinetist with Theodore Thomas's orchestra, and then played in the U.S. Marine Band, under the baton of Bohumir Kryl. He joined Local 47 (AFM) in 1909 and was designated a Life Member on May 29, 1939.[104] One of Wiedoeft's closest friends in Los Angeles was the composer and conductor Ferde Grofé.

Wiedoeft began playing the C-melody saxophone in his early teens. In the 1910s, he made recordings for every major record label—Columbia, Edison, and Victor—including Edison Amberol cylinders, Pathé Freres vertical groove phonographs, and hill-and-dale discs. Credited with having popularized the saxophone in the United States with his electrifying performances,[105] Wiedoeft was particularly successful on radio.

Rudy Wiedoeft is considered a "pre-jazz" artist, and his music is best described as Ragtime. In the 1920s, performing both on radio and on the vaudeville circuit, he became known for a variety of humorous sound effects on the saxophone, including a laugh, slap, flutter tongue, and rooster crow. For a while, he worked in Rudy Vallee's (1901–1986) band, which toured in France. Some claim that Rudy Weidoeft died of a knife wound inflicted by his wife. This incident did not end their tumultuous marriage nor his life; he died in 1940 of liver disease, probably from alcoholism. His mother, Anna F. Wiedoeft, died three days after he did, although she had not been told of his death. After his ex-wife died in a hotel fire in 1963, his possessions and the royalties from his music went to his wife's sister, Gertrude.[106]

Peggy's first assignment from Fanchon and Marco was touring with Rudy Wiedoeft:

> Fanchon and Marco called me and asked if I would get together a sextet of saxophone players to back up Rudy Wiedoeft in a show called "Saxophobia Idea." And so I did. I got the girls together and we toured for about 30 weeks with that show.[107]

The back-up group included Peggy [Knechtges] Gilbert, Jackie Barton, Virginia Darnell, Ena Weckerling, Mildred Childres, and Pearl E.[108]

According to Peggy, Fanchon personally rehearsed each show, devised the choreography, and supervised the costuming and set design. Because she attended to every detail of the production, every show was indelibly marked with her sense of style. Having performed in vaudeville for many years, she knew instinctively what worked. The Fanchon look could be seen not only in the vaudeville shows she put together, but also in dozens of Hollywood films, which she also designed. Peggy recalls that Fanchon was tough, but fair. However, when one of the girls in "Jazz Temple Idea," bass player Dorothy Green, broke her arm in San Diego, Fanchon insisted that she perform the show before being allowed to seek medical treatment. Peggy describes Marco as the "business man and also final judge on all that goes out."[109]

The "Saxophobia" cast traveled by train, as did most vaudeville troupes. Oftentimes, after the last show in the evening, they packed and boarded a train for the night, waking in the morning at the next destination. They performed three or four shows per day, playing cards and sleeping at the theater between shows. Peggy recalls that sometimes the theater doorman would order food from nearby restaurants and have it delivered to the theater. The performers were treated as stars by the public and widely covered in the press. Fanchon and Marco had a particularly effective "advance man," who traveled ahead of the show, garnering publicity with enticing photographs, taken by some of the most talented photographers of the time. This was a great adventure for a young woman from Iowa—glamorous and well-paying.

"Saxophobia Idea": Rudy Wiedoeft and an all-girl sextet for the Fanchon and Marco show. Peggy Gilbert is on the left in the top row.

Peggy sent most of the money she earned to her mother in Los Angeles, keeping only enough to cover the cost of personal items.

Peggy enjoyed working with Rudy and said that he was always kind and generous to her. From him, she learned about reeds and techniques for playing the saxophone.[110] He had a beautiful, lyrical tone. Most of the arrangements they played were his own; occasionally, he would bring a new chart for them to try out. Rudy's wife, who traveled with them on the road, was jealous and resented it when Rudy wanted to talk to the girls about business or music, but that did not seem to dampen his generosity. During the week they spent in Vancouver, Rudy had kegs of beer brought in for each show for the entire crew and cast.

STANDARD EIGHT-ACT VAUDEVILLE BILL

1. Opening, silent act, which would not be interrupted by noisy latecomers. Getting booked into this slot was an insult to some performers.
2. Singing sister or singing brother act.
3. Comedy sketch or one-act play.
4. Novelty act or eccentric dance number.
5. Rising star or falling star.

Intermission

6. Big act, large set, novelty orchestra, choirs, or top animal act.
7. "Next to closing," reserved for the headliner ("top of the bill"), vocalist, or comedian. This was the longest act of the show.
8. Closing spot, short films, or annoying act to encourage patrons to leave the theater. Films were #8 on the bill. Some vaudevillians' film shorts were inserted here.[111]

"Saxophobia Idea" Itinerary

Although the exact itinerary for the "Saxophobia Idea" tour is not known,[112] it was likely similar to the other Fanchon and Marco tours. Shows would open in "break-in" theaters in Los Angeles, such as the Loew's State Theater or The Fox Manchester Theater.[113] "Saxophobia" opened near the end of October 1928. The route would have included San Diego, opening November 2; perhaps the Egyptian Theater, Hollywood; Pasadena; West Coast Theater in Long Beach; December 4–8 at the Wilson Theater in Fresno; San Francisco at the New Fox Theater; December 17 in Oakland at the Fox Theater;[114] the Senator Theater in Sacramento; then the Elsinore Theater in Salem, Oregon; Fox Broadway Theater in Portland; Fox 5th Avenue Theater in Seattle, Washington; Broadway Theater, Tacoma;[115] The Strand Theater in Vancouver; Tabor Grand in Denver; Wisconsin Theater in Milwaukee; Lafayette Theater in Buffalo; Fox Poli in Worcester, Massachusetts; Palace Theater in Hartford, Connecticut; Palace Theater in Bridgeport, Connecticut; Fox Theater in Brooklyn, New York; Fox Theater in Philadelphia; Fox Theater in Washington, D.C.; and Fox Theater in Atlanta. Peggy recalls that they then played in a couple of cities in the South, as they made their way back to Los Angeles.[116]

The *Newsette*, published by West Coast Theaters, in Fresno, describes the "Saxophobia" show, which included a screening of a "big Talkie," *Mother Knows Best*, starring Madge Bellamy, Louise Dresser, and Barry Norton.[117] It featured "son-of-a-saxophone, Rudy Wiedoeft," playing "the best liked of all saxophone solos, 'Saxophobia.'" Comedians Joe and Willie Hale were also on the bill, juggling and doing acrobatics. "Glorified Girl of the Follies, Murie Stryker" danced, including a "tap speciality" and an Oriental dance. June Knight, Radha,[118] and Natalie Harrison also danced. The article continues,

> The Saxophone Beauties accompany Rudy in the ensemble numbers and the way they play the saxophone is nobody's business. These pretty misses are all talented musicians and furnish a rich background for Rudy's numbers. Eugenia Reynolds, a winsome little singer, offers the latest songs most delightfully. Elaborate stage settings and costumes add to the magnitude of this act and make it one of Fanchon and Marco's best.

Often the musicians would play live at local radio stations, to promote the stage show. The December 3, 1928, issue of *The Fresno Bee* includes a famous photo of Rudy Wiedoeft and his all-girl backup band in feathered headdresses, with the caption: "This is Rudy Wiedoeft himself, the king of the saxophone, and also, but not least, his bevy of saxophone beauties now appearing at the Wilson Theater. Wiedoeft and the girls will be on the air on *The Fresno Bee* radio program tonight."

After the "Saxophobia" tour, Peggy returned to Hollywood and on May 27, 1929, transferred her musicians' union membership from the Sioux City Local to Local 47.[119] When the leader of an all-girl group performing at El Mirador Hotel in Palm Springs quit to get married, Peggy was hired as saxophone player and bandleader for four months in the spring and summer of 1929. One hundred miles southeast of Los Angeles, El Mirador Hotel was a popular resort, catering to the Hollywood movie community. The band performed during lunch and again during dinner and for evening dancing. Peggy did not know the women in this band before taking over the band and did not play with any of them again. "They weren't of the caliber of players I wanted to work with."[120]

However, Peggy did enjoy life at El Mirador: "That was a lot of fun, because at that time the stars all had their little cabins around the swimming pool. . . . I got acquainted with them. It was great. We'd play their private parties, as well as the hotel jobs. Well, it was an exciting period."[121]

Actress Marion Davies, paramour of William Randolph Hearst, met Peggy and heard her band at El Mirador. The beautiful blonde Davies was born Marion Cecilia Douras in 1897 in New York City and started in the entertainment business as a child. After briefly appearing in the "Ziegfeld

Follies," at age 20, she made her first film, *Runaway Romany* (Ardsley-Pathé, 1917). The following year, she appeared in a film backed by William Randolph Hearst, which launched a romantic relationship with him that lasted thirty years. She made nearly fifty films, her last at age forty in 1937, *Ever Since Eve* (Warner Bros.). She died of cancer in Los Angeles in 1961, and is buried in Hollywood Forever Cemetery, next to Paramount Studios.

Marion often engaged Peggy's band to play for her private parties at the Malibu beach house she shared with Hearst; later she helped Peggy get gigs for her band in films. "In one film, they put us all in long blonde wigs, and when Marion Davies saw me, she said, 'I need a stand-in right now—you do it.'"[122]

At one time Peggy was a "stand-in" for Marion Davies, and considered a professional acting career instead of music. This was one of her publicity photos, c.1930.

The "Jazz Temple Idea"

In October 1929, Peggy got another call from Fanchon and Marco.

> I got another big girl band together, about sixteen pieces, and we went out on another idea, called the "Jazz Temple Idea" and that's when the girls had to dance. They had to do everything. We came back from that tour, which was about fifty some weeks, almost a year.[123] Then we went into another rehearsal, a lot of the same girls who were with me were still in that band and we added some more and went out again with the "Busy Bee Idea," and that was another one where we all had to dance and sing and do everything.

Increasing the burden Peggy felt to support her family was the fact that her mother had suffered financial losses in the crash of 1929 and also was in poor health. The family continued to grieve the loss of Peggy's father and Orval's wife. Peggy said, "You don't cry working on the stand. You smile." She felt that work was the best thing she could do to get through the grief.

An undated newspaper clipping about Fanchon and Marco's "Jazz Temple Idea," describes the act: "The girl band . . . replaces Bert Green's orchestra when the latter goes on strike and does the jazz stuff great." The girls in the band danced and did routines, but at the end, revealed themselves to be jazz musicians. Wally Jackson was the leading comic with the show; Gus Elmore, "in black face . . . gives a hair-raising portrayal of a Zulu, spear and all, and is very funny."[124] The Four Van De Veldes, two girls and two men, "do foot juggling and balancing stuff." Nora Schiller and Sylvia Doree were also in the show and "The Movietone completes the bill."[125]

Another review states,

> What circus is complete without a wild man? A real, sure-enough, straight-from-the-jungle man-eating cannibal! That's what Gus Elmore looks like when he gets all dressed up in his cannibal costume, and talks Zulu to the India rubber man. And wait till the children see his tail! A real tail that wags, when he is mad, and which you can put salt on, if you're quick enough.[126]

According to Peggy, "We'd come out in costume and do a dance routine, and I'd have an argument with the male bandleader in the pit. I'd say, 'You're not playing our music right. We can't dance to that!' The bandleader would say, 'All right, if you think it's so lousy, play it yourself!' and they'd walk off. Then I'd say 'OK, girls, let's go!' And the scrim would go up, and we'd sit down and start playing. The audience would roar!"[127]

Variety writer Arthur Ungar provides the following description of the show:

"Jazz Temple Idea": Peggy Gilbert is in the front row on the far right.

Bound to click. A novelty. Has 15 girls, recruited from here and there, whipped into shape over four weeks' period by Fanchon as versatile stage jazz band. Girls are instrumental soloists, can sing, and also dance a bit. Act is bound to be one of the outstanding features turned out by these producers for the 1929–30 season. . . .

Setting is Jazz Temple of Mayan architecture. Nora Shiller [Schiller] opens in front of the temple singing theme song of unit, "Temple of Jazz," which Fanchon and Marco accredit themselves for so far as music and lyrics are concerned. While the songstress is unloading the lyrics the 12 line girls of house, attired in so-called barbaric costumes, do a native spear dance. The balance of the girls—15 of the unit—strut forth in hoop skirts. Sylvia Dore [Doree], who is violinist leader of the group, follows with bit of jazz stepping.

Gus Elmore in Zulu[128] make-up and raiment for comedy bit with George Stoll, house leader.[129] This is prelude to entrance of Wally Jackson for grotesque dance stepping. Jackson goals with trio of routines. Stoll then goes into comedy specialty with Red Corcoran that ends in a conventional blackout with a new tag, sure for laughs.

Kara [Karabaeff] Vieff, formerly with Pavolowa, on next for another stop-gap in show.[130] Starts with tap rhythm, using wing and pierrot side maneuvering, then into hock on toes to tap time, which is classic of its kind.

He uses full aluminum soles on shoes, and each of his tap beats is distinctive and timed for rhythm.

Unit girls next trip out in pastel party dresses, with picture hats to match. Go into dance routine, with house band cutting short on steps. Discourse between house leader and girls, with the house band deciding to take the air and leave the girls to their own resources. Of course, the old gag, "play this," "I play that." Then into shell for about 20 minutes of instrumental group, solo and quartet entertainment, with Miss Dore [Doree] specializing *à la Nonenette* on fiddle. Reed section as well as brass section well matched, with one girl in latter section triple tongue soloist, and scoring great. Foursome comes forth for bit of vocal harmony, and get by nicely.

They are young, good-looking girls, shapely, too, and far superior to average girl band aggregation one sees in vaude [sic] units. With plenty of rehearsal and combined playing, it is likely that by the time these girls hit east of the Windy City, they will be acclaimed another F. and M. sensation.

Finished with their musical work, girls make change to semi-negligee costumes, do bit group vocalizing and arm movements while stage band in upper shell picks up the melody. On a shell above them are Jackson and Elmore in jungle costume having a merry time surrounded by a group of statuesque maidens.[131]

One article states that the girls played classic, jazz, and singles trios that "led to a flash finish,"[132] a reference to the fact they were the "flash act" in the show. Another review describes the girls as dressed like cannibals in the opening of "Jazz Temple Idea."[133] This same review reports that "the girls played hot arrangements of 'He's a Good Man to Have Around'[134] and 'Here We Are.' . . . A couple of classic numbers were played, after which the girls completed their act by playing a red-hot number of Abe Lyman's 'Weary Weazel.'"[135]

In the *Oregon Daily Journal,* Harold Hunt writes:

Sam Jack Kaufman and his band boys did a "walkout" from the Fox Broadway stage Thursday; in fact, did several. But they found that Fanchon & Marco chorus girls could take their places and produce just as good melody and fun, so they walked back, to join their 15 pretty rivals in the finale of the current stage show. Of course, it was all in play, but the audience liked the stunt, liked the girls and showed a decided liking for hearty applause.[136]

In Wisconsin, a February 25, 1930, clipping headlined "Super-Saxes," with the caption, "An Added 'Kick,'" describes the show:

Two girls of the Fanchon and Marco "Jazz Temple" revue at the Wisconsin theater have speeded up their routine with "Playasaxs," the new type musical instruments being given by the *Wisconsin News* for two six-months' subscriptions. All you have to do is adjust the roll and turn the crank and you have all the melody of a moaning "sax."

The San Diego Fox Theater[137] Opening Night program, dated November 8, 1929, lists the "Fanchon and Marco Players": Karabaeff, Wally Jackson [dancing comedian], Lucille Page, Gus Elmore, Nora Schiller [blues singer],[138] Sylvia Doree [violinist], Temple Beauties, The Cheer Leaders, and Sunkist Ensemble. On the "Jazz Temple Idea" promotions, the girls' band was listed variously as: Sunkist Beauties, Sunkist Ensemble, Sunkist Musical Beauties, Mayan Temple Beauties, and Musical Maidens.[139] Guest stars included Jackie Coogan, Buster Keaton, George Jessell, and Will Rogers.

The members of the band in which Peggy played included[140]: Sylvia Doree, violin, leading the band; Annette Schiller and May McManus, violins; Eva Meyers, Jackie Barton, Virginia Darnell, and Margaret Knechtges,[141] saxophones; Dixie Dean, banjo; Helen Kaplan[142] [Kay?] and Enid Gleason, trumpets; Mary Anneberg, trombone; Helen Boyd, bass; Alice Oakason, drums; Rose Haber,[143] piano.

How much was Peggy paid for her performances with Fanchon and Marco? Her scrapbook contains a receipt, dated January 23, 1930, for taxes paid in Vancouver, Canada, to the Province of British Columbia, for her performance at the Strand Theater. Her net taxable income was $64.85, on which a tax of $1.29 was paid.

"JAZZ TEMPLE IDEA" ITINERARY[144]

October 17, 1929	**Fox Colorado**, Pasadena, CA **Emcee**: Slim Martin
October 24, 1929	**Loew's State Theater**, Los Angeles, CA **Emcee**: George Stoll **Film**: *Frozen Justice* (Fox Movietone)
November 8, 1929	**Fox Theater**, San Diego, CA [opening dedication of the theater] **Emcee**: Al Lyons **Film**: *They Had to See Paris* (Fox Movietone) **Local Band**: Al Lyons conducting the Fox Symphony Orchestra[145]
November 15, 1929	**Fox West Coast**, Long Beach, CA **Emcee**: Herb Kern **Film**: *The Thirteenth Chair* (MGM) **Local Band**: Herb Kern and That Band
November 21, 1929	**Egyptian Theater**, Hollywood, CA **Emcee**: Lou Erickson, drummer **Film**: *The Saturday Night Kid* (Paramount)

November 29– December 1, 1929	**Wilson Theater**, Fresno, CA **Emcee**: Milt Franklyn **Film**: *The Lady Lies* (Paramount) **Local Band**: Milt Franklyn[146] and His Band
December 2, 1929	**Fox California,** San Jose, CA **Emcee**: Jack Stanley **Film**: *His Glorious Night* (MGM)
December 6, 1929	**New Fox Theater**, San Francisco, CA **Emcee**: Walter Roesner **Film**: [not known]
December 13, 1929	**Fox Theater**, Oakland, CA **Emcee**: Herbie King[147] **Film**: [not known] **Local Band**: Herbie King and His Orchestra
December 20, 1929 (continuing through Christmas Week)	**Fox Senator Theater**, Sacramento, CA **Emcee**: Oliver Alberti **Film**: *Three Live Ghosts* (United Artists) **Local Band**: Oliver Alberti and His Band
December 28–30, 1929	**Elsinore Theater**, Salem, OR **Emcee**: "n.g." ["no good," according to Peggy] **Film**: *Halfway to Heaven* (Paramount)
December 31, 1929	**Fox Broadway Theater**, Portland, OR **Emcee**: Sam Jack Kaufman **Film**: *Untamed* (MGM) **Local Band**: Sam Jack Kaufman's Broadway Band
January 9, 1930	**Fox 5th Avenue**, Seattle, WA **Emcee**: Owen Sweeten **Film**: *Red Hot Rhythm* (Pathé) **Local Band**: Owen Sweeten's Band
January 20–25, 1930	**The Strand Theater**, Vancouver, BC **Emcee**: Jackie Souders **Film**: *The Painted Angel* (Warner Bros.) **Local Band**: Jackie Souders and His Band
January 30, 1930	**Tabor Theater**, Denver, CO **Emcee**: Art Reynolds **Film**: *Sally* (First National Vitaphone) **Local Band**: Art Reynolds and His Orchestra

February 7, 1930	**Fox Theater**, St. Louis, MO **Emcee**: Bert Frohman[148] **Film**: *Harmony at Home* (Fox) **Local Band**: Bert Frohman and His Merry Melodians Also the Fox Grand Orchestra, William Parson, conductor
February 21, 1930	**Wisconsin Theater**, Milwaukee, WI **Emcee**: E. Max Bradfield[149] **Film**: *Roadhouse Nights* (Paramount) **Local Band**: E. Max Bradfield and Joyboys
March 4, 1930	**Lafayette Theater**, Buffalo, NY **Emcee**: Stanley Meyers **Film**: *The Cohens and Kellys in Scotland* (Universal) **Local Band**: Johnny Lyons and His Lafayette Syncopators [also known as Johnny Lyons and His Boys]
March 22–28, 1930	**Fox Poli Palace**, Worcester, MA **Emcee**: Freddy Mack **Film**: *Montana Moon* (MGM) **Local Band**: Freddy Mack and Band
March 29–April 4, 1930	**Fox Poli Theater**, Springfield, MA **Emcee**: Bert Green **Film**: *Free and Easy* (Buster Keaton) **Local Band**: Bert Green's Band
April 5–11, 1930	**Palace Theater**, Hartford, CT **Emcee**: Don Gil[150] **Film**: *The Golden Calf* [unknown]
April 12–18, 1930	**Fox Poli Palace**, New Haven, CT **Emcee**: Barney Rapps **Film**: *The Rogue Song* (MGM) **Local Band**: Barney Rapps' band[151]
April 19–25, 1930	**Palace Theater**, Bridgeport, CT **Emcee**: Gus Meyer **Film**: *The Rogue Song* (MGM)
April 27–29, 1930	**Palace Theater**, Waterbury, CT **Film**: *The Rogue Song* (MGM)
[no exact dates]	**Fox Theater**, Brooklyn, NY **Emcee**: Rube Wolf[152] **Film**: *High Society Blues* (Fox)

	Local Band: Fox Concert Orchestra, conducted by Rube Wolf
May 9, 1930	**Fox Theater**, Philadelphia, PA **Film**: *Double Cross Roads* (Fox Movietone) **Local Band**: Fox Grand Orchestra, William A. Krauth, conductor
May 17, 1930	**Fox Theater**, Washington, DC **Emcee**: Alexander Callam **Film**: *High Society Blues* (Fox) **Local Band**: The Fox Grand Orchestra, conducted by Leon Brusiloff[153]
May 26, 1930[154]	**Fox Theater**, Atlanta, GA **Emcee**: Don Wilkins **Film**: *The Cuckoos* (RKO) **Local Band**: Don Wilkins and His Band; also Fox Grand Orchestra, conducted by Enrico Leide[155]

Peggy's next Fanchon and Marco tour, the "Busy Bee Idea," traveled for forty-five weeks throughout the United States and Canada in 1930 and 1931. Peggy earned the nickname "Bunky," because she was willing to sleep in the upper bunk in sleeper cars of trains. "Terry" was an acrobatic dancer on the tour. Jackie Barton, who was only seventeen or eighteen, played alto saxophone and clarinet. Her mother was the wardrobe mistress and chaperone. Other musicians included: Alice Oakason, drums; Rose Haber, piano and accordion; Helen Kay, first trumpet; Dorothy Green, bass; Ena Weckerling, saxophone and clarinet; and Dixie Dean, banjo. Nora Schiller was a singer in the show; the star was singer Liana Galen.

An article in *The Fresno Bee,* dated September 5, 1930, with the headline "Harmonists on the Air," includes a photo with the caption: "Here are two of the members of the girls' band of a dozen members who will be heard to-night on The Fresno Bee radio during the broadcast by Oliver Alberti and other entertainers from the Fox Wilson Theater." Most of the girls on the Fanchon and Marco tours autographed their portraits for Peggy, which she kept in her scrapbook.

Peggy Gilbert in her costume from the Fanchon and Marco production, "Busy Bee Idea," 1930–31.

Peggy admits to being a prankster on the road. She put garlic on the lamp on the conductor's podium in a theater in Canada because she disliked the conductor. At a theater in Washington State, she put limburger cheese on the conductor's stick, because he was mean to the girls in the band. Once, she put pebbles in the solo male tap dancer's shoes, when he went offstage for a quick change of costume, because, according to Peggy, "He was not very nice to the girls in the band." One show featured a girl violinist who would have nothing to do with the girls in the band. "I'll fix her," Peggy said, and put two pennies in her violin, which made her solo sound funny. "No one told on me, either."

On one occasion, Peggy was late returning from lunch and barely had time to get into her costume, so she left off her leotard. When she danced, everyone got a good view of her panties and made a point of letting her know all about it. "The musicians in the pit had a good laugh!" But Peggy was not the only joker on tour. In "Jazz Temple Idea," the girls in the band had a hand-bell routine, each playing a single bell. Someone rearranged the bells so the girls would play all the wrong notes during the routine. "We all got a laugh out of that!"

After Fanchon and Marco, Peggy explains, "We came back into town and the vaudeville was just about over and that time Los Angeles was still flourishing. We still had everything out here. I was doing an awful lot of work in the studios. MGM especially."

Fanchon and Marco Girls

May Annenberg, trombone

Jackie Barton, saxophone

Dorothy Green, bass

Rose Haber, piano

May McManus, violin

Annette Schiller, violin

CHAPTER IV
The Depression, the Movies, and the Hawaiian Tour

By the end of the "Busy Bee Idea" tour, the Great Depression dominated American life, making it more difficult to earn a living in show business. This was the worst national economic failure in United States history; half of all white families and 90 percent of all black families were impoverished. Even though motion pictures had become the chief American entertainment by the early 1930s, some of the studios discontinued contract musicians and only engaged musicians as needed. Many theaters disbanded pit orchestras, displacing thousands of musicians virtually overnight. In order to keep working, bands had to travel, often performing "one-nighters."[156] Jukeboxes eventually took over in the clubs.

Having learned about the power of publicity from the advance men on the Fanchon and Marco productions, Peggy started promoting herself as a bandleader, using photos of The Melody Girls. Through contacts she had made at El Mirador Hotel and through Marion Davies, she put together an all-girl band to appear in several movies.

Peggy's bands appeared in a number of movies as "sideliners."[157] This meant they appear as if they are performing in films, but others—usually the studio's union musicians—are recorded on the soundtrack. Peggy said, "In the late 1920s and early '30s, every time you saw a girl band in a picture, it was my band." Often sideliners are "acting" to a "pre-record": they have the music in front of them, so they can look authentic on camera. The irony was that the women sideliners were members of the Musicians' Union, perfectly capable of playing on both the set and the recording.

The Screen Actors Guild (SAG) was founded in 1933 to curtail exploitation of actors, including long hours at the Hollywood studios. Many high-profile actors would not join in the beginning. Actors without contracts suffered greatly during the Great Depression, due to cost-cutting measures taken by the studios. The producers refused to negotiate with SAG until 1937, after the passage of the National Labor Relations Act.

Sideliners and extras did not receive screen credit, so it is difficult to determine exactly how many films Peggy did at MGM. However, in 1931 she appeared in *Politics*, directed by Charles Reisner, starring the Canadian actress Marie Dressler (1868–1934).[158] An undated newspaper clipping with the headline, "Peggy Gilbert and Band Are in Movie," mentions *The Wet Parade* and *Politics*, featuring Marie Dressler,[159] and *That's My Boy*, a Columbia Picture with Richard Cromwell.[160] She and her band appeared in enough films that she started promoting herself as Peggy Gilbert and the Metro-Goldwyn-Mayer Girls, or variations on that name. A photograph of

Peggy Gilbert and Her MGM Orchestra. This is an example of the "advance" newspaper publicity used to promote her band while touring.

that band, taken on an MGM movie set, was reprinted in several articles about Peggy's orchestra; it included several women Peggy knew from Fanchon and Marco tours.

Peggy describes work for musicians in the movies:

> When you played, you went out there and really . . . they taped you just as you were. It was not like it is now, I mean, you can correct things, and correct errors. Just like early television. You know, when we were on early television you went on and whatever went over the air was it. There was no chance of getting it back and correcting it.
>
> A lot of [the movies] were collegiate type of things. Lots of them were musicals with the Doris Days and things like that. Sometimes they'd have a mixed band [which] at that time was starting to be acceptable. But most of the time, [we were] all-girl bands. I did an awful lot of that. I can't even tell you the number of movies I worked in. I was known as Peggy Gilbert and Her MGM [Metro-Goldwyn-Mayer] Orchestra for a long time out here. And booked and played theaters under that name.
>
> [Now] you tape everything first, then you do the side-line. You know, you do the acting afterwards. But at that time, they didn't do that. They did the whole thing at once, whether you looked well or not playing your horn or not, which was sometimes criticized by some of the people, 'Those girls didn't look pretty while they were blowing horns,' you know. So I would tell them, 'After all, how are you going to blow a horn and smile at the same time?' You can't.[161]

In discussing a 1930s photograph of her band on a large hay wagon, Peggy says,

> We were supposed to be playing in a big park for a big event that was taking place in a town. That happened at the old Republic Studios out here in the Valley. We played on the wagon while they were pulling it and it was recorded at the same time. So if the sound sounds funny, when you hear some of those old pictures, you'll know why. . . . They just didn't have the facilities for taping and for recording like they have now. So improved. But it was fun in those days, so much fun. Everybody loved it.[162]

Also in the photograph are drummer Alice Oakason, banjo player Dixie Dean, and trumpeter Mabel Hicks.

1932

In 1932, Amelia Earhart (1897–1937) flew her famous solo flight across the Atlantic Ocean. Charles Lindbergh's baby was kidnapped. The country was in deep economic woes. But, because Peggy had to support her family, she was determined to make a living as a musician and continued to take every music job available.

Her work often required Peggy to travel throughout California. For example, on May 25, 1932, an article in *The Diablo Beacon*, published in Concordia in Contra Costa County, announces that Peggy Gilbert and Metro-Goldwyn-Mayer Queens of Jazz were performing at the Martinez State Theater. The article states that Meta Moore[163] played trumpet, Peggy Russell was an impersonator, and Eubie Blackwell was the violinist.

The *Martinez Morning Herald*, dated May 27, 1932, carries the same photograph with the headline: "Girls' Recording Orchestra Appears Tonight at the State Theater." The caption states:

> Gilbert and Her Metro-Goldwyn-Mayer Girls' Recording Orchestra recently had a part in 'Politics' and have appeared in a number of feature pictures and comedies. Peggy Meal acts as mistress of ceremonies and directs. She also features HOT fiddle numbers and dances. She has the distinction of being the only girl Mistress of ceremonies at the Capital Theater, New York, where she had a long engagement as stage leader. Enbie [Eubie] Blackwell also does HOT fiddle numbers. . . . Meta Moore is the leading girl soloist on the West Coast and features some specialties. The girls do a number of 'impressions' in which they give some clever [impersonations] of [Rudy] Vallee, [Paul] Whiteman [1890–1967], Louie [Louis] Armstrong [1901–1971] and The Boswell Sisters. They have a very clever and versatile group and rate well up with the best male orchestras. [After] their stage performance at the State Theater tonight they will go to Oakland, where they will be special guest artists at the opening of the new Sweet's Ballroom.

A publicity photograph of Meta Moore's band includes Peggy Gilbert, among other band members, standing behind a piano. Peggy said that Meta Moore had hired Peggy's band and asked to "front" it. Peggy said, "I didn't care about that as long as we all got paid."[164] The band members include Lona Bowman, piano; Meta Moore, trumpet; Peggy Gilbert, alto saxophone, baritone saxophone, and clarinet;[165] Eubie Blackwell, jazz violin and viola; Crystal Harvey, banjo; Mabel Hicks, second trumpet;[166] Peggy Russell, drums;[167] Edna Lewis, alto saxophone;[168] Ena Weckerling, tenor saxophone.[169] Eubie, Crystal, Edna, and Ena had toured with Peggy in Fanchon and Marco shows.

About Eubie Blackwell, Peggy wrote,

> "[She] was hitting the trail with me in and around Los Angeles in the early '40s and her 'hot' viola playing was turning the music critics inside out, to say nothing of all of us who worked with her. She was a girl who inspired the rest of us to give a little more when it came to 'taking off' on a chorus.

> . . . We were going from theater to theater and then to 'after hours' spots and then getting up at the crack of dawn to make a sideline call at one of the motion picture studios. We never missed not having enough sleep. We were young. Do you suppose that had anything to do with it?"[170]

In August 1932, Vivian Duncan, of the famous Duncan Sisters, asked Peggy to organize an all-girl band to accompany them in a road show planned for California. The *Los Angeles Times* reports:

> Say what you like, there's just no keeping those Duncan Sisters from bobbing up serenely. Now Vivian Duncan is about to turn orchestra leader. That is, if she doesn't go on a vaudeville tour with sister Rosetta, to South America.
>
> Among the Olympic visitors, it appears, is an orchestra of twelve charming girls, fine musicians from various countries, including Spain, Italy, Sweden, Germany, France and other countries.
>
> Mischa Gutterson, violinist and orchestra leader, is training Vivian to direct, a feat not difficult, as Miss Duncan is an accomplished musician as well as composer.
>
> If the orchestra is taken out on the road by Miss Duncan as an act, she will, as director, imitate the various famous directors of history, from Wagner down to our own Sousa.
>
> One serious obstacle stands in the way of Miss Duncan's leaving home, it seems, and that is the small Evelyn. Nils Asther is not in favor of his wife traveling and objects strenuously to her taking their baby along. And Vivian objects just as hard to leaving her baby behind.
>
> Oh, well, there is still that clever musical on which Nina Wilcox Putnam [writer, 1888–1962] and Vivian have collaborated, called "Champagne" and which three film concerns are considering.[171]

At the time, Vivian Duncan (1897–1986) was married to actor Nils Asther (1897–1981). Born in Denmark and raised in Sweden, he moved to Hollywood in 1927 to appear in silent films. However, his foreign accent was an impediment for the talkies. In the summer of 1931, Vivian's husband announced that she would probably not work any more, now that they had a daughter. The following December to January found the Duncan Sisters, Vivian and Rosetta (1894–1959)—of "Topsy and Eva" fame on stage and screen—in bankruptcy court, trying to reorganize their debt. According to Vivian,

> Three years ago we had more than $1,000,000 and the money was rolling in. We were a big success and everyone with something to sell was plying us with propositions backstage while we were doing our act. We signed up for almost anything they had to offer, most of the time, without reading what we were signing. We listened to everyone. Now we're penniless. . . .

> Then I got married and went to Europe and left Rosetta all alone, breaking up our team. She worked a little, but the money hasn't been rolling in for more than a year. Now it's all gone and all we've done today is cry like a couple of babies. But we're starting all over again and we're going to do a comeback. We'll pay all our debts if they'll just give us a chance; watch and see.[172]

Touring with an all-girl band would be part of her "comeback." However, among the complicating factors was the husband who did not want his wife to work. While the band was traveling, Vivian often asked Peggy to sleep in her room, because she was afraid of her husband. In September 1932, *The Los Angeles Times* reports that "Vivian Duncan Denies Rumors of Separation":

> The fact that Nils Asther, motion-picture actor, has taken a bungalow at a hotel in Pasadena does not necessarily mean that he is separated from his wife and child. . . . Miss Duncan . . . declared that Asther is working at night in pictures and went to the hotel temporarily so that he might sleep during the day. . . . She explained that she is rehearsing a new act and that the only place she has to rehearse is at their home.[173]

However, by November 1932, Vivian had received a divorce:

> Too much mother-in-law disrupted the home life of Vivian Duncan, of the famous Duncan Sisters and Nils Asther, Swedish motion-picture actor, according to Miss Duncan's testimony yesterday before Superior Judge Bush, where she was granted a divorce and custody of their baby daughter, Evelyne Rosetta.[174]

Playing in Peggy's band on the Vivian Duncan tour were: Meta Moore, trumpet; Lona Bowman, piano; Peggy Gilbert, alto sax, baritone sax, and clarinet; Eubie Blackwell, jazz violin and viola; Crystal Harvey, banjo; Mabel Hicks, second trumpet; Peggy Russell, drums; Edna Lewis, alto sax; Ena Weckerling, tenor sax.[175] Peggy also recalls that Naomi "Pee Wee" Lawson (Preble) played trombone in that band. Peggy is certain that Vivian's daughter was not with them on the road.

A photo of Peggy in the *Hollywood Citizen-News*[176] bears the caption, "Peggy Gilbert, popular girl orchestra leader, who directs her own dance band, and who will be heard over KFWB tonight, 11:30 p.m. to 2 a.m. [980 AM]." This could have been anytime during the 1930s, when Peggy's band was often heard over KFWB. The chief stations in Los Angeles at that time were KFI-KECA (National Broadcasting Company) and KHJ (Columbia Broadcasting Company). For many years, KFI-KECA broadcast performances of the Metropolitan Opera, the Los Angeles and San Francisco operas, the Los Angeles Philharmonic Orchestra, the Hollywood Bowl, and other symphonic groups. The New York and Philadelphia orchestras were heard on KHJ. The local stations were KNX and KFWB, which did not have network facilities. According to pianist and music reviewer José Rodriguez,

> All Southern California stations have popularized and made familiar the Americana of music. A word here in favor of the much-praised and also much-maligned 'hill-billy' music, a genre of art which springs out of the heart of American and which holds, in its naïve forms, the germ of a future rich in possibilities. The same can be said for dance bands and their jazz music which, in its creative and instrumental style, is so pregnant with developments.[177]

Peggy was savvy about using radio broadcasts to build an audience for her band, because of her success with The Melody Girls back in Sioux City. She knew it would be crucial to her success in Los Angeles, too. Her bands were heard on radio in Los Angeles throughout the 1930s and into the '40s. Sometimes they were broadcast live from nightclubs and ballrooms; other times they performed in live broadcasts at the radio station.[178]

> I was always the leader or the manager of all these things—leader-manager. . . . However, I always liked to play. I didn't want to stand up in front. I never considered myself a glamour girl; I considered myself a musician. The glamour girls were the Ina Ray Huttons and the Ada Leonards and the Bobbie Grices and some of the other girls at that time that would front girl bands and sing, you know, and wave a stick in the air. I really liked to play and I liked to beat it out and I'm still doing it.[179]

Peggy's band appeared under a variety of names during those years:

> Everybody who booked our band wanted to name it. . . . So it was Peggy Gilbert and Her Coeds, Peggy Gilbert and her Metro-Goldwyn-Mayer Stars, Peggy Gilbert and Her Symphonics, Peggy Gilbert and her Nymphonics. . . . I don't know who thought up that one, but that was horrible! I can't even remember all the names that we were booked by.[180]

Peggy had copies of a large newsprint ad for the "Grand Opening of the La Salle Market Washington Blvd. at Normandie, Saturday July 23rd" [no year]. An old photograph of Peggy's band from Sioux City, Iowa, bears the caption: "Above is pictured the famous girls' band which was heard over the radio during the Chicago Convention. This popular musical aggregation will sing and play for your pleasure in the super entertainment program tomorrow at Washington and Normandie Ave." Other performers included The Troubadours, The Babylonians, and Grecian Girls Band. "You're invited to the Biggest Show in the World at Washington and Normandie from 10 a.m. to Midnight. Produced by Kathryne Campbell, Director of Special Events, and a complete and enjoyable International Entertainment Event in Honor of the Olympics."

Although this information implies that the year was 1932, it uses a photograph of The Melody Girls from many years before. Perhaps this was the only photograph Peggy had of her own band.

In late 1932 or early 1933, Peggy decided to go back to Sioux City, to take care of some unfinished business. Before she left for Los Angeles, Peggy had been engaged to saxophonist and bandleader Maynard Foster; she had broken it off before leaving Iowa. He married someone else in Sioux City, while Peggy was touring with Fanchon and Marco, but his wife contacted Peggy to tell her that Foster's continuing devotion to Peggy was ruining their marriage. So Peggy met with Maynard and his wife to clarify her intentions. Peggy told them that she admired Maynard and considered him a good man, but had no desire to marry him. Over the succeeding years, she remained in contact with Maynard's family.[181]

1933

In 1933, Prohibition was repealed in the United States. In Europe, Adolph Hitler became chancellor of Germany; the first Nazi concentration camps were established; World War II was soon to begin. President Franklin Delano Roosevelt launched the New Deal, a series of programs implemented between 1933 and 1937 designed to provide relief, economic recovery, and financial reform. It was a liberal coalition, involving the Democratic Party, big city machines, labor unions, Jewish and Catholic minorities, farmers, and Southern whites. Among the New Deal's creations were the Social Security Administration, the Tennessee Valley Authority, and the Federal Deposit Insurance Corporation.

While Peggy was visiting Sioux City, she heard a band from Lincoln, Nebraska, called Boots and Her Buddies. It included Peggy's old friend, trumpeter Sally Brown. They needed another saxophone player, and Sally invited Peggy to play with them. So she borrowed a saxophone from Maynard Foster and went on the road with Boots and Her Buddies.[182]

Boots and Her Buddies

Sally Brown joined Boots and Her Buddies sometime after The Melody Girls broke up and left the Martin Hotel in Sioux City. A newspaper clipping in Sally's scrapbook, published in the early 1930s, reads:

> Lincoln Girls Are on Tour of the South: Just recently having completed a six month's tour thru Nebraska, Kansas, Iowa, Colorado and North and South Dakota, the eight Lincoln girls shown in the picture are off again

Boots and Her Buddies *(before Peggy Gilbert joined the band)*.

> on another extended tour of the southern states. From left to right they are: Sally Brown, Helen Hard, June Protzman, Lulu Jo Hyland, Alta Nelson, Katherine McAuthor [Kathleen McArtor], Katherine Cruise and Sarah Jacobson. Their first engagement will be in Wheeling, West Virginia. Besides the orchestral numbers, different members will be featured soloists, while others will appear in tap dancing acts.

"Boots" was a nickname for Alta Nelson. On one flyer, Helen Hard is listed as an "eccentric dancer," and Lulu Jo Hyland as a piano and accordion player. Sally played trumpet; Kathleen McArtor was a drummer;[183] Katy Cruise played saxophone.[184]

Peggy tells this story about playing with Boots and Her Buddies:

> I borrowed a horn and joined them on the road—nine of us in a seven-passenger car, with our instruments and suitcases piled on top. The band was doing very badly, playing jobs all through the Midwest on a percentage basis. We'd drive 200 or 300 miles in all kinds of weather for a one-night stand, and maybe the weather was so bad that nobody showed up [to hear us], so by the time we split the money we had just enough for a hamburger and gas to get to the next job.
>
> Our costumes had these black satin pants, and we used to back along the walls onto the bandstands because all the seats of our pants had been patched. Those girls were such fantastic dedicated musicians, but they were starving to death.[185]

Sometimes the band would stay in the bandleader's large, comfortable home near Lincoln. They also toured South Dakota and had a longer stint at the Wichita Falls Hotel, Texas. One photograph shows Peggy with the band, on top of a hotel in Lubbock, Texas; another, taken at the Colorado State Fair, pictures them wearing sailor outfits. Boots had a routine where the band members would stand on chairs, playing with their backs to the audience, gradually turning around to create a big sound at that elevated level.

Peggy stayed with Boots and Her Buddies for about three months, but finally returned to Los Angeles. Because she was not making enough money, her family—mother, grandmother, brother, and his children—was having financial difficulties. As soon as Peggy returned to Los Angeles, she found work playing her saxophone. A few weeks later she got a letter from the other band members, saying that they were coming to Los Angeles.

> The band all left Boots and Her Buddies because they just weren't making any money and she was going to have to give up. They all came out here and I got a little apartment for them.[186] There were seven of them in a pull-down bed apartment . . . with a kitchenette. They slept all over the floors. I had several of them at my house. It was fun. I got them to work right away. I went down to the union; told them [at the Musician's Union] I had to have them in here. They were members of Lincoln, some from Chicago,

> some from New York. But they all wound up here, put their transfers in and away we went.[187]

By that time, the girls in the band included Katy Cruise, Sally Brown, Bunny Hart, Helen Hampton, and Kathleen McArtor. Peggy recalls that pianist Helen Hard may have been on that trip, but returned home, at her parents' insistence, to finish college.

"Boots and Her Buddies" was also the name of a newspaper comic strip, created by Edgar Everett "Abe" Martin (1898–1960), which first appeared on February 18, 1924, distributed by the Newspaper Enterprise Association.[188] This "Boots" character was a popular blonde college student. The "Buddies" were her competing suitors. It is not clear what college she attended, but in the comic strip she carried a pennant with an "M"—perhaps a reference to Martin's alma mater, Monmouth College in Illinois. "Boots" was known in the 1920s and '30s as the "Sweetheart of America": "an old-fashioned girl, holding herself chaste in the midst of the flapper era."[189] There were a number of spin-off cartoons and a novel. The comic strip appeared in more than seven hundred papers and continued until 1968. It is not clear which started first—the comic strip or the band. Some have suggested that the comic strip may have been a takeoff from "Polly and Her Pals." Peggy believes it is more likely that Boots borrowed the name from the comic strip.

After the band broke up, no one ever heard from Alta "Boots" Nelson again. Is it possible that she got a "cease and desist" letter from lawyers at the Newspaper Enterprise Association? In any case, the comic strip outlived the band by some forty years.

Trumpeter Sally Brown kept a diary of the girls' difficult car trip to Los Angeles:

> 1933[190]
>
> **My Trip to California**
>
> The Buddies bought car for $25.00. There were six of us altogether. Left Grandfield, Okla, 1:30 a.m. May 4, 1933. Kay (piano player) sick and crying. We all bid Boots good bye. Tonight was our last job with Boots. Arrived in Wichita Falls, Texas, 3:00 a.m. Hespersona (our car) had flat tire and bad brakes. Fellows' friends with us took Hespersona to be fixed and we all went to Hotel Holt to Howard's room (friend of Boots). A lot of people in his room so we went across street and ate breakfast. Katy-Mac-Helen-Andy and Jimmy spent rest of night on Mezz. [mezzanine] of Hotel until 6:30 when we bought a tire. $2.95. Left Wichita Falls eight a.m. Had flat tire 20 miles out of Wichita Falls.
>
> Truck load of men stopped to help us. Mac and Kay caught ride to nearest town to buy new tire. Men kinda tough. Got tire fixed and drove on till we met kids. They had to walk 2 miles. Drove on and boy did it get hot!

> Stopped in Haskell, Texas, at 12:30 and got cold drinks. Drove on a way. So hot and windy stopped again to get drink at 3:30 p.m. Drove on and stopped by creek and shade to cream our faces and are they sore? I think I'll burn up. Rested there an hour and drove on to Sweetwater, Texas. Stopped to have brakes tightened and to eat. Katy driving—ran into fender of another car and dent my small bag which was tied on side of car. Drove on after eating. Cooler now. Car from New York with two fellows in it passed us and stopped. Said they were going to California too so we gave them Peggy's address to call and tell her we were on the way. Generator broke about eight p.m. and had to buy new one. $4.75 and set us back three hours. Drove all night. Got along fine but was plenty chilly. Stopped twice for coffee.
>
> Stopped in Penwell, Texas, at filling station about 6 a.m. and creamed our faces. Stopped for gas at Kent, Texas. Some cowboys there wanted us to stay and play a dance there that night but it was too much of a proposition. Needed the money but couldn't run risk. Nothing doing. Ha! Drove on to Vanhorn, Texas, and ate there. Cleaned faces again. Sun getting hot and everybody's faces blistering. Lost my hat twice and had to drive back after it. Stopped at 3:30 p.m. in Sierra Blanca, Texas, and had brakes on car re-lined. The two fellows from New York drove up while we were there. Talked and they took pictures. Wanted to see us in El Paso tonight. Started on and at 6 p.m. arrived El Paso, Texas, out of sorts tonight. Ate 10¢ dinners because we are getting low on money. 1,014 miles yet to go. (5 a.m. Boy what a night. About froze. Freeze at night and burn up in day time. Stopped at half way house about 1:15 and drank coffee. 10¢ a cup. Were we mad!)
>
> Some tough looking Mexicans in these here parts. Left 6 a.m. Drove on through Arizona Mts. Pretty scenery. At Gripe, Arizona, State agriculture inspection of cars. Saw Wild Cat caged at filling station. Saw first palm trees in Safford, Arizona. Seeing lots of palm trees here. Went through Banan Mts. today in Arizona. Beautiful scenery. Ate supper in Mesa. Just 17 miles from Phoenix. Drove on thru Phoenix and Blythe. Stopped for coffee at Wickenberg and Salami. S. spent $.35 in slot machine at Wickenberg. Was I mad. Only 305 miles to Los Angeles now. Drove all day Tues. in desert. Oh, boy, was it hot. Burnt our faces. Terrible. Car broke down at Blythe, Calif. Was to cost us $1.25 so Katy and I looked for a pawn shop and hawked [hocked] her diamond ring for $5.00. Then the mechanic felt so sorry for us he did the job for nothing. Were we thankful? Arrived in Redlands, Calif. 7 o'clock Tuesday evening. Lights on car not good so stayed in tourist camp all night. Saw first oranges on trees. Drove on to L.A. Wednesday. Arrived at Peggy's house 5 o'clock. This was the Buddies' wild goose chase.[191]

The arrival of the "Buddies" in Los Angeles on May 9, 1933, struck Peggy as an opportunity to have her own big band, instead of leading a combo or playing in other bands as a sideman. The night they arrived, she was performing at the Paramount Theater. Orval brought them to see the show; they sat in the front row. Although they had showered and dressed up, their faces were so sunburned that Peggy said they looked terrible. They loved the show and were so impressed. That night Peggy told the contractor/bandleader that it was her last night with that band, that she was starting her own band. He told her, "You can't do that!" and Peggy answered, "Oh, yes, I can!" She knew this was her chance.[192]

Sally Brown wrote her sister and parents on May 12, 1933:

> With brains (Margaret) at the head of this band we will get some place. Boots and Buddies were pretty sore about us leaving . . . and with Peggy helping us we are getting along great. We are living in a darling apartment and living here is cheap. A dozen oranges 10 cents; six dozen $.25. . . . Last night Margaret took us all down by the ocean and that's about the biggest thrill I've ever had. Saw Marion Davies' (movie star) home on the beach which covers several blocks. We went thru Hollywood and saw all kinds of interesting places. Peggy's brother has a big Lincoln and that's what we ride around in. Tonight we are having a showing at the Santa Monica Elks Club, playing just three tunes and getting $1.00 a piece plus our transportation. That's just a tryout for future dates. Tomorrow night we have a job—$5.00 apiece and transportation. So you see how Peggy works. Tonight will be our first showing. Golly, we used to drive 200 miles with Boots sometimes and make $.50. Ha! Thank goodness, that's over.[193]

The girls from Boots and Her Buddies who made it to California were the lucky ones. The Dust Bowl began in November 1933 in South Dakota. The Dust Bowl was a series of dust storms in the mid to late 1930s caused by a massive drought and bad farming techniques. These storms ruined crops and left the land barren and dry. One of the worse dust storms took place on April 14, 1935, and was known as "Black Sunday." People fled Texas, Arkansas, Oklahoma, and the Great Plains, as the storms left more than a half a million people homeless. Many lost their homes and farms to foreclosures. Those who fled were called "Okies" and many of them came to California, documented by Farm Security Administration photographer Dorothea Lange among others. By 1935, the American Federation of Musicians had to lobby to secure relief for unemployed musicians through the Works Progress Administration. Peggy says that some of the former band members who worked for Peggy in California in the 1930s sent cash to their friends and family in the Midwest—including some girls from Boots and Her Buddies—to help them survive the Depression.

Peggy's All-Girl Band in Las Vegas

As a rule, Peggy accepted every playing job that she was offered, including one in Las Vegas. Although gambling had been going on for decades, it was legalized in Nevada in 1931. That same year, construction began on the Hoover Dam Project (then called the Boulder Dam) which, at its peak, employed 5,128 people. The dam was needed to stop the annual flooding of local farms from the Colorado River, and to provide a dependable source for water to Los Angeles and Southern California, through the creation of a hydroelectric power plant. Thus was the young town of Las Vegas insulated from the economic hardships that wracked most Americans in the 1930s. Jobs were plentiful because of Union Pacific Railroad development, legal gambling, and construction of the nearby Hoover Dam.

Peggy's band played at The Meadows Casino, at 25th Street and Boulder Road, on the road to the Hoover Dam. "Las vegas" is Spanish for "the meadows"; hence the name of the casino. Tony Cornero, also known as Tony Stralla and Admiral Cornero, was one of the early builders of the Las Vegas Strip. He got his start during Prohibition as a rumrunner, and was well known for unloading banned liquor from ships off the Southern California coast. After serving time for illegal activities, he went to Las Vegas to build The Meadows Casino with his brothers Frank and Louis; it opened on May 3, 1931. Cornero's vision of Las Vegas as a classy, elegant, glamorous place set the standard for the other casinos to follow. He built a landing strip near the casino for the small planes that delivered wealthy patrons.[194]

Two months after opening, the Cornero brothers sold the hotel to Alex Richmond, but kept the casino until early 1932.[195] A Labor Day fire in 1931 closed the hotel portion. The piano player in Peggy's band (who was also the daughter of the agent who booked the band) married Tony Cornero and left the band. After Peggy incorporated members of Boots and Her Buddies into her own band, she went back to Las Vegas with them. In addition to Mac, the musicians included Bunny Hart, guitar; Sally Brown, trumpet; and Katy Cruise, saxophone and clarinet.

Peggy's band performed for the opening ceremonies of the new Boulder Dam, on February 1, 1935, playing in one of the locks before the water was let in. The sound of the band echoed throughout the elaborate concrete tunnels. President Franklin D. Roosevelt spoke at the dedication. The name was changed to Hoover Dam in 1947.[196]

Costumes for the Band

According to Peggy, costumes were essential to a band's success, and she often designed the costumes for her group.

Peggy Gilbert's All-Girl Band in Las Vegas, at the Meadows Casino: Sally Brown, trumpet; Bunny Hart, guitar; Kathleen McArtor, drums; Katy Cruise, sax, clarinet, vocals; [unidentified], piano; Peggy Gilbert, leader, saxophone, clarinet, c.1930s.

> You had to dress more feminine in those days. When slacks first came in, they were acceptable. Then for a time, in order to get booked in theaters, you had to wear evening gowns. Everyone hated to work in them because they were a mess. Running up and down, standing up, coming down to microphones and performing, getting back and stepping up on platforms. Lifting them up and holding them up, while holding a horn in one hand. They really are not the most comfortable outfits to work in. But we had to.
>
> Then there was a time I dressed the entire band in tails. We had white satin tails and black satin trousers and big bow ties. And I had just the opposite of the girls when I fronted the band. We wore high silk hats. They were beautiful. But they weren't very practical, because we were constantly taking them to the cleaners.
>
> Then we had outfits that looked like Spanish outfits and I'll never know why. They looked like Spanish toreadors. They had nothing to do with the band or the way the band sounded. Then we dressed in all-white uniforms, right after the Olympics were here in California for the first time. I think that was 1933.[197] And so we wore all-white slacks and white tops. And they were very acceptable and red, white, and blue scarves and everything. We wore them for quite a while. When we were in nightclubs we wore white suits with black shirts and black little handkerchiefs in the pockets. From time to time, we graduated to different outfits. We'd use the fancy outfits for night time and slacks for days and it worked.[198]

It was important that the women instrumentalists were attractive. According to Peggy,

> That's always been one of the problems faced by women in music. You could play as well as any man in the business, but if you were fat or weren't passably good-looking, you didn't stand a chance. The girl bands were hired as attractions for the men, and club managers were always reminding us not to take the music so seriously, to smile more. How can you smile with a horn in your mouth?[199]

At one time or another, Peggy Gilbert's band played at all of the major theater chains, including Warner Bros. Theaters, Pantages Theaters,[200] and West Coast Theaters. A photograph taken at the Paramount Los Angeles shows: Sally Brown, trumpet; Ronnie Adell, trumpet; Bunny Hart, banjo; Dorothy Green, bass; Kathleen McArtor, drums; Katy Cruise, first alto sax; Peggy Gilbert, tenor sax, clarinet, leader, vibes; Helen Hampton, alto sax, clarinet. The pianist may have been Kay Warren. Several of the musicians had been members of Boots and Her Buddies, and some are from Peggy's Fanchon and Marco days.

An article under the headline, "Peggy's Nymphonics Hit in Days of Don," reports Peggy's band played in Santa Barbara August 3, 4, and 5 [probably 1933]. It lists the band members as: Katy Cruise, saxophone; Helen

Hampton, saxophone; Bunny Hart, guitar; Ronnie Adell and Sally Brown, trumpets; Kathleen McArtor [sic] drums; Kay Warren, piano; and Dorothy Green, bass.

In September 1933, Peggy Gilbert and Her Famous Coeds performed at the Coconut Grove in Bakersfield, California. An article in the local newspaper, dated September 21, 1933, reports that Peggy's band was "fresh from Fox Theater engagements in San Diego and many other sections of the west and had recently been seen on Pioneer Mercantile Company's big television station. It mentions that her band appeared in films, *The Wet Parade*, *Politics,* and *[That's] My Boy.*"[201] The performance was broadcast over a Bakersfield AM radio station, KERN, from 10 to 10:30 pm on opening night.

The Coconut Grove, one of Bakersfield's most popular nightclubs, was located above the Post Office Market building at Eighteenth and H streets. It was "completely renovated and redecorated as owners of the pavilion and managers of the three-times-a-week programs of dance music prepare it for the most lavish fall opening in its history."[202]

The article also states that Peggy's band had appeared the week before at the Fox Theater in San Diego and had recently completed a ten-day engagement at the Hippodrome Theater in Bakersfield. It mentions their recent appearance on the "Pioneer Mercantile Company's big television station."

> Her 10-piece orchestra includes such stars as Bunny Dare, guitar and banjo specialist,[203] who last spring had screen test in Hollywood, then changed her mind and stayed with what she believes to be one of the finest musical organizations in the country; Kathleen McArthur [McArtor], drummer for the orchestra, who was featured in that role with the Ingenues of RKO and Paramount Public circuits and with Babe Egan's band which toured Europe; Patsy Lee, lovely mistress of ceremonies, a group of vocal specialists and many others.
>
> The orchestra is billed to play here for two weeks, beginning Saturday, Tuesday, and Thursday program of dances. Sunday and Monday nights it is slated to play the Fox Hippodrome theater in Taft, and October 6 is billed as one of the major attractions planned by the American Legion of Visalia.[204]

W6XAH-TV, Bakersfield

When Peggy Gilbert claims her band was the first all-girl band on television, she may be right. An article by Frank B. Smith, Jr., excerpted from "Smith Family Odyssey," tells about this early attempt at television broadcasting in Bakersfield:

> In 1932 my good friend Jasper McCrillis and I worked in the laboratory of a longtime friend who had a license to build and operate an experimental television station in Bakersfield, California, whose call letters were W6XAH. This station was licensed to broadcast both video and audio signals aimed toward all of Northern California.
>
> I was officially designated the announcer and my friend, Jasper, the technician. Since we both had extensively listened to radio, we naturally considered ourselves highly skilled in our respective professions. . . .
>
> We broadcast video by means of a mechanical scanner—a swiftly whirling disk perforated with slots that would pick up visual images. Our music library considered of only one platter and when we went on the air, we would play our single recording, "Goofus,"[205] a catchy popular tune performed by a nimble fingered pianist. The title expressed all there was to say about our early project. We gave the venture our best though we were mostly uninformed about what we were doing. . . .
>
> W6XAH was the first TV station to broadcast into Northern California.

Mark D. Luttrell provides the following information about W6XAH-TV:

> The owners of television station W6XAH were brothers Frank, Leon and Charles Schamblin, residents of Bakersfield, CA. These men were owners of the Pioneer Mercantile Company in Bakersfield, which held the F.C.C. license required for broadcasting. . . . The Schamblin brothers were able to produce basic television images but they were only able to be received in the vicinity of the studio and only a few homes had televisions receiving signals in those days. People gathered on the sidewalk outside the studios to watch the experimental broadcasts on television monitors that had been set up. . . . Broadcasts varied and included musical groups such as local dance bands. My grandfather, Al Randour was a member of the "Moonlight Serenaders" band that Mr. Frank Schamblin had organized which was one of the groups appearing on W6XAH. . . . Because of limited funding and technical problems with these television experiments, efforts were discontinued that same year. However, the Schamblin family then started KPMC (the PMC was for Pioneer Mercantile Company) radio in 1933.[206]

In Peggy's collection are copies of newspaper ads for performances at the Hippodrome Theater in Taft: "On Stage, Peggy Gilbert and Her Famous Co-Eds, In Person, 10 Gorgeous Stars of Radio, Stage and Screen." They appeared along with a screening of the film *Another Language*, starring Helen Hayes and Robert Montgomery, released in 1933.

WHAT'S IN A NAME?

Peggy Gilbert's band appeared under the following names:

All-Star Girl Dixieland Jazz Band
The Early Girls and Three Chirps
Jacks and Jills
Jacks and Jills of Jive
The Melody Girls
Peg Gilbert and Her Femmes
Peggy Gilbert and Her All-Girl Orchestra
Peggy Gilbert and Her Band
Peggy Gilbert and Her Coeds
Peggy Gilbert and Her Famous Co-eds
Peggy Gilbert and Her Four Femmes
Peggy Gilbert and Her Hollywood Femmes
Peggy Gilbert and Her Melody Misses
Peggy Gilbert and Her Metro-Goldwyn-Mayer Girls' Recording Orchestra
Peggy Gilbert and Her Metro-Goldwyn-Mayer Orchestra
Peggy Gilbert and Her Metro-Goldwyn-Mayer Stars
Peggy Gilbert and Her Nymphoniacs
Peggy Gilbert and Her Nymphonics
Peggy Gilbert and Her Radio Girls
Peggy Gilbert and Her Six Farmerettes
Peggy Gilbert and Her Symphonics
Peggy Gilbert and Metro-Goldwyn-Mayer Queens of Jazz (MGM Queens of Jazz)
Peggy Gilbert and The Dixie Belles
Peggy Gilbert Girls
The Peggy Gilbert Orchestra
Peggy Gilbert's Studio Band
Peggy Gilbert and Her 41 Cuties
Peggy Gilbert's All Girl Band
Peggy Gilbert's All Girl Orchestra
Peggy Gilbert's Girl Band
Peggy Gilbert's Orchestra
Peggy Gilbert's Symphonics

The Hawaiian Tour

Late in 1933, Peggy booked her band to go to Hawaii with E. K. Fernandez.[207] Known as the "Barnum and Bailey of the Hawaiian Island," he began in the entertainment business in Hawaii in 1903. With many of the girls who had been with Boots and Her Buddies, now members of Peggy's band, they took the S.S. Lurline to Honolulu, arriving on October 5, 1933. It was a great opportunity, especially as the Depression was worsening in Los Angeles. The Lurline (III) was launched by Mrs. William P. Roth, wife of the president of Matson Navigation Company, on July 18, 1932; her service route became San Francisco–Los Angeles–Honolulu. The ship held 475 first-class and 240 tourist-class passengers, with a crew of 359.[208]

While onboard the ship, Peggy discovered that they actually had been booked to play for a circus. She ascertained this after meeting circus performers aboard ship who had also been hired by E. K. Fernandez. "If we could have walked home, we would have," she recalls. "But when we got to Honolulu the girls said, 'It's so beautiful here, let's give it a try.'"[209]

Peggy Gilbert's Band in Hawaii, 1933–34. Peggy is holding the "Aloha" sign.

Peggy describes the tour:

> We had a 'work-or-play' contract. We were paid a weekly salary, no matter how many days a week we worked. Sometimes we worked a lot and sometimes we worked not very much. But we worked all the islands, every one of them, including Moloka'i where at that time they had a special part set aside for the afflicted people. . . .[210]
>
> We wound up doing an entire show singing and acting. We had one act with us, only one. That was a high wire act. I learned how to be a part of that act. I had to go up and perform on one of the ladders. This man held two ladders, one on each side and they were ten feet high. I was the same

height and weight as his wife. And I had never done anything like that before in my entire life. So we would practice until I could climb the ladder and hang by my knees and by my feet from the bottom of the ladder and go through motions up there to music. The girls were playing "Stairway to the Stars" and were scared to death that I was going to fall off the ladder.[211] But that was a delightful year over there.[212]

On the Hawaiian tour were: Katy Cruise, saxophone; Kathleen McArtor, drums; Caryl Agnew,[213] piano; Sally Brown, trumpet; Ronnie Adell, piano; Eva Meyers and Helen Hampton, saxophone. The year in Hawaii was a fabulous adventure for Peggy and the band.

SOME ALL-GIRL BANDS OF THE TWENTIETH CENTURY*

(in alphabetical order)

Ada Leonard's All-American Girls
Aileen Shirley and the Minoco Maids of Melody
Alive!
Babe Egan and Her Hollywood Redheads
Bee Palmer Orchestra
Bee Turpin and Her Orchestra
Beryl Booker Trio[214]
The Biltmore Girls
Blondes on Parade
Bobbie Grice's Fourteen Bricktops
Bobbie Howell's American Syncopators
Count Berni Vici Orchestra
D'Artega's All Girl Band[215]
The Darlings of Rhythm (Margaret Backstrom and Josephine Boyd)
Dixie Rhythm Girls
The Dixie Sweethearts
Dr. Stallcup's All-Girl Orchestra
Eddie Durham's All-Star Girl Band (a.k.a. Eddie Durham's All-Stars)
Edna White's Trombone Quartet
Four Star Girls
Frances Carroll & Her Coquettes
Gibson's Navigators
Gladys Beatty Girl Band
Green's Twentieth Century Faydettes
Harry Waiman and His Debutantes
The Harlem Playgirls
Helen Lewis All-Girl Band[216]
Hip Chicks[217]
Hollywood Sepia Tones
Hollywood Sweethearts
Ina Ray Hutton and Her Melodears
The Ingenues

Mary and Her Platinum Blondes, with whom Fern Spaulding Jaros played trombone in Chicago, 1932.

International Sweethearts of Rhythm
The Lil Armstrong All-Girl Band
Maiden Voyage (a.k.a. Ann Patterson's Maiden Voyage)
Mary and Her Platinum Blondes
The Maxwell Girls
The Melody Maids
Mildred Myers and Her All-Girl Orchestra
Nellie Jay and Her Jay Birds
The Parisian Redheads (from Paris, Indiana)
Phil Spitalny and His All-Girl Orchestra (a.k.a. Phil Spitalny and His Hour of Charm Orchestra; Phil Spitalny and His Musical Queens)
Pollyanna Syncopators
Prairie View Co-Eds
Queens of Swing
Red Stanley and His All-Girl Band
Rita Rio and Her All-Girl Band
Swinging Rays of Rhythm
Thelma White and Her All-Girl Orchestra
Tiny Davis' Hell Drivers
The Twelve Vampires
Vi Burnside Combo[218]
Virgil Whyte's All Girl Band[219]
Virgil Whyte's Musicgals

*This is a list of bands which Peggy Gilbert did not lead or play in. Her bands' names are found on page 65. There may be as many all-girl band names as there were "girl" musicians—everyone seemed to have her own band at one time or another. Girl bands were so popular, in fact, that they were spoofed in the RKO Radio Pictures short *Twenty Girls and a Band* (1938), featuring bandleader Nick Stewart and male musicians dressed as women.

Another novelty all-girl band, with whom Fern Spaulding *(2nd from right)* played trombone.

CHAPTER V
Peggy Gilbert's Big Band and the Hollywood Nightclub Scene

By the time Peggy's band returned from the Hawaiian Islands, they had a "tight" sound and were ready for the big time. The girls got along well and Peggy had gained additional confidence as a bandleader and performer. But were there jobs in Los Angeles in 1934? For musicians, yes—even girl musicians—mostly in nightclubs, and especially in Hollywood. According to Peggy, the secret to keeping the band working was that whenever she had a gig at one club, she would line up the next one, because it was hard to get gigs if the band wasn't working. She would invite club owners and bookers from other clubs to come, as her guest, to see the band. They played at all the popular nightspots in Los Angeles in the 1930s.

At that time, evening entertainment in Los Angeles was centered mostly in Culver City (near MGM and Columbia Pictures), as well as in the big Los Angeles hotels. Peggy remembers "following" Bing Crosby at the Cocoanut Grove at the Ambassador Hotel, which opened in April 1921 and attracted movie stars and the social elite. In addition, Peggy appeared at the Hollywood Roosevelt Hotel, which continues its jazz tradition today in the Cinegrill. Ballrooms, located all over Los Angeles, were also extremely popular.

The Plantation Club, opened by comedian Roscoe "Fatty" Arbuckle, on August 2, 1928, was in the 11700 block of Washington Boulevard; its décor was created by Cedric Gibbons, head of MGM's Art Department. Other Culver City clubs included Frank Sebastian's Cotton Club, King's Tropical Inn, The Green Mill, The Hot Spot Cafe, Barton's, Ford's Castle, Moonlite

Gardens, The Hoosegow, Casa Mañana, and the East End (at Adams), the latter owned by the parents of U.S. billionaire businessman Kirk Kerkorian.

By the late 1930s and '40s, Los Angeles nightlife had moved to Sunset Strip, including the Zamboanga South Seas Club, Don's Beachcomber, Don Dickerman's The Pirates Den, Carmel Gardens, and Hollywood Casino. The Brown Derby, started by Herb Somborn, Wilson Mizner, and Sid Grauman, was famous for inventing Cobb salad and Steak Diane. The first Brown Derby opened in 1926 on Wilshire, across the street from the Ambassador. Another club, La Bohème, was closed in 1932 for liquor violations. Café Trocadero opened in 1934 and closed in 1946. The Clover Club was on the 8600 block of Sunset Boulevard, but was closed in 1938 by the L.A. Vice Squad. Ciro's (originally Club Seville), at 8433 Sunset, operated from 1939 until the late 1950s. The Brazilian-themed Mocambo Club opened in 1941 and closed in 1959. All of these clubs had live music; some of them hired women musicians.

Peggy Gilbert's band at the Club New Yorker, Hollywood, 1935 *(left to right):*
Bunny Hart, guitar; Naomi Preble, trombone; Mabel Hicks, trumpet, flugelhorn;
Jerrie Stanley, sax, clarinet; Kathleen McArtor, drums; Katy Cruise, alto sax, baritone sax;
Nellie Sandahl, piano; and Peggy Gilbert, tenor sax, singer, leader.
Note the hanging microphones for live radio broadcasts.

Peggy had learned the basics of music arranging from her father when she first started playing professionally, and recalls that,

> Whenever a big band came into L.A., we'd get acquainted with them and sit up all night copying parts; that's how we always had the most fantastic arrangements. Of course, I would be sure to announce, "This is by special permission of so-and-so." Anyway, we weren't really competition to them, because a girl band was considered a novelty. The only competition we had were bands in the East, like Ina Ray Hutton's. The Peggy Gilbert Band was the West Coast girl band.[220]

Peggy and her band members would take food to the hotel where the men's band stayed, and cook for the men, while copying out the arrangements for their own use.

Among Peggy's signature methods was starting a tune with its last chorus, rather than with a slow introduction. She found it more exciting for the audience. She also developed a preference for quick modulations—that is, jumping from one key to another and skipping the "modulatory" passages.[221] Her management style was also very smart: rather than confront a band member about excessive drinking during a performance, she told the musician that the club owner didn't want her glass visible to the audience. Peggy got the results she wanted. She always presented her band members to their best advantage. For example, she hired two musicians who had suffered from polio, and made sure that they were placed on the stage, and costumed, in such a way as to hide their disabilities.

According to Peggy, club managers were always worried that her band would alienate the women in the audience. So she had a policy that, if a couple were sitting at a table, the band members would look at the woman, not the man. "It worked—the women didn't get mad then. It was a case of survival."[222]

Peggy describes the band's gigs in the mid 1930s:

> We did the Club New Yorker on Hollywood Boulevard, which was also a big restaurant. We played out at the Cotton Club—at that time that was a big club, in Culver City. . . .We played the Monte Carlo Club [including Katy Cruise, Audrey Hall, Bee Turpin, Kathleen McArtor, Mabel Hicks]. We played Las Vegas, of course, several times, and we played clubs in San Francisco. We played clubs in San Diego and all over Southern California. . . . The group that I finally wound up with was a fantastic band. We were playing in all the clubs, nightclubs here, jamming in the after-hours spots with the fellows after we finished. . . .Then we wound up playing ballrooms. We played the Zenda Ballroom for two years, then we went to the Figueroa Ballroom.[223]
>
> After we played all the theaters, there were no more theaters to play, because they had no more pit bands and had no more shows. That was the end of them. We saw that finished. I think we finished almost everything out here.[224]

As Peggy observed, the entertainment business underwent many changes in the 1930s. Vaudeville theaters closed; movies began to dominate. During the Depression, many restaurants and supper clubs cut back on live music performance. For a while in the 1930s, Peggy's brother Orval had his own ballroom on Western Avenue in South Los Angeles. He took it over because the previous owner would not pay the musicians performing there. However, the ticketman and doorman Orval hired let people in for free, when his back was turned. Eventually, he had to close the ballroom for good.[225]

THE BIG BAND

When Peggy and others talk of a "Big Band," they are referring to an ensemble developed during the Swing Era, which included between twelve and twenty players.* Peggy led the band as the first tenor saxophone player. Standard instrumentation for a Big Band is:

Reeds or Sax Section:

- Alto saxophones (2), with possible doubling on clarinets, flutes, soprano saxophone
- Tenor saxophones (2)
- Baritone saxophone

Brass Section:

- Trumpets (4) (could include cornets, flugelhorns, mellophone). Usually, lead (first) trumpet plays the highest, most strenuous parts; second trumpet is usually jazz soloist.
- Trombones (3 tenors)
- Bass trombone (could be a tuba)
- (French horn could substitute for tenor trombone or bass trombone)

Rhythm Section:

- Drums (in Latin jazz, there is often a second percussionist)
- Bass (double bass and, later on, electric bass)
- Piano
- Guitar

From 1935 until 1945, Big Band jazz was synonymous with commercial dance music and many of the jazz elements were diluted. Smaller groups, called "combos," had more freedom to improvise.

*A combo could consist of bass, drums, piano, and at least one other instrument, like saxophone. In the 1930s and '40s, Peggy often had a violin in her combo. Usually a soloist (saxophone or trumpet, for example) started out with the melody; then one or two others played solos, then the leader took over again for one or two more choruses. In the '30s, the rhythm sections were generally lighter, with more of a swing feel. Peggy says that, although she was the leader, she was more flexible and allowed the other girls in her group to solo and lead musically.

1935

Throughout 1935, the situation in Europe continued to deteriorate. Germany issued the anti-Jewish Nuremberg Laws; Jewish refugees arrived in the United States by the hundreds, including musicians, looking for work in Hollywood. Although this was the height of the Great Depression, the Hollywood scene continued to flourish, with music performed live at nightclubs, theaters, cafeterias, dance halls, and heard round-the-clock on radio.

An article in the *Los Angeles Herald Examiner* by Ray De O'Fan, dated June 19, 1935, "New All-Girl Orchestra Will Invade South," announces that Peggy's band was being broadcast over KFWB, KFOX, and KFXM:

> It is her boast that the girls of the orchestra can play both sweet and hot, as musicians describe it. The only string instrument in her band is the guitar. For sweetness she relies on the saxophone section, and for the "heat" on three charming misses who play anything in the way of brass. "There is no reason why girls should not produce as good an orchestra as any," says blonde Peg Gilbert. "In our tours throughout the country and in Hawaii, we found people looking at us as if we were freaks or something, but in time the novelty passed away. The test, in the long run, lies in the quality of the music."

The 1935 radio show listings in the *Los Angeles Times* frequently include Peggy's orchestra on KFOX, heard at 11:45 p.m.[226] That year, her band also played regularly at the Italian Village, located at 425 West Eighth Street in Los Angeles, appearing nightly from 3:30 to 5:30 p.m., the time designated as the cocktail hour.[227] One newspaper article reports, "The Cocktail Dansant featuring Peggy Gilbert and Her Farmerettes of vaudeville fame, is providing a decided hit at the Italian Village Café . . . and is drawing capacity crowds daily. A floor show is also being presented, including Mele Darlo, acrobatic dancer and accordion star; Dave and Elizabeth, Adagio Dancers, and many others."[228]

During a strike of unionized kitchen workers, Peggy and her band could not cross the picket line because they were union musicians. Afterward, the owner refused to have Peggy's band back, even though she had a contract. She complained to the Musicians' Union and was told that this was the price she and her girls had to pay for doing what was right by the union kitchen workers.

One of Peggy's best jobs was at Club New Yorker in Hollywood, advertised as "The Smartest Café in Town."[229] Hollywood at that time was "a stay-up town," meaning that it had an active nightlife. An article from *Variety* in 1935, "Night Club Reviews," dated July 27, states that, "Peg Gilbert's troupe of eight does a first rate job of *dansapation*" at Club New Yorker in Hollywood. Other announcements describe them: "Peg Gilbert and Her Femmes play hotter than hot rhythm music." Another announcement reads, "Peggy Gilbert and her band, currently at the Club New Yorker, made some test recordings during a matinee at the café, may get a contract with a major recording company. The test recordings were made by Allan Gordon."[230] Club New Yorker was located at 6728 Hollywood Boulevard. The band was heard over KFWB at 11:30 p.m.

Members of the band that summer were Katy Cruise, sax; Jerrie Stanley, sax and clarinet; Mable Hicks, trumpet; Naomi Preble, trombone; Nellie Sandahl, piano;[231] Kathleen McArtor, drums; Bunny Hart, guitar; with Peggy Gilbert as saxophone and leader.

A notice in the "News of the Cafés" column of the *Los Angeles Times*[232] of September 28, 1935, announces:

> Next Sunday night marks the opening of the fall and winter season with a week of gala entertainment at the Club New Yorker. Manager Frank Kerwin announces that no expense has been spared to provide his patrons with the finest food, the music of Peggy Gilbert's orchestra, new and clever entertainers, with one and original B.B.B. acting as master of ceremonies.

Another article published with a photo of Peggy's band at Club New Yorker (c. 1935?) has the headline: "Peg Gilbert and Her Femmes." Band members are listed as Bunny Hart, [Naomi] Pee Wee Preble, Mabel Hicks, Jerry [Jerrie] Stanley, Katharine McCarter [McArtor], Katy Cruise, Lona Bowman, and Peggy Gilbert. The caption continues,

> For eleven months, these girls were a featured attraction in Hawaii. The reason for their popularity is understandable. Every one of them radiates personality and ability. Besides holding the distinction of being the only femme band on the belt, they are considered as the "best bet" over the air. Their half-hour dance music is a haven for many a listener-in. Bunny Hart, Katherine Cruise and Peg Gilbert create a trio that is outstanding in harmony and rhythm. As far as the patrons are concerned, at the Club New Yorker, where they are holding forth nightly, Peggy Gilbert and Her Femmes can stay just as long as they care to.[233]

Also on the bill were B.B.B. ("Entertainer to the Stars"), Russ Cantor, June Marlowe ("Blonde Syncopator of Song"), Deena (Interpretative Dances), Gloria Martin ("The Inimitable Songstress"), Ibi Engle ("Dancer Moderne"), Roberta Smith ("Debutante of Song"), Mary Lane ("Voice of the South"), and Leonard Stevens ("At the keys"). Peggy remembers that "B.B.B." was a very clever comedian and good singer. He started his act wearing an especially tall hat with a rounded point at the top. Then he would put the hat in front of his body and turn sideways, giving in silhouette the image of a very large penis, a gag that always drew laughs from the audience. With a large following, he even had his own club for a while, but he told Peggy, "It's too hard to do your act and watch the cash register," so he gave up his own club to be an emcee and comedian.[234]

Peggy Gilbert and Her Melody Misses appeared October 25, 1935, at the Dinner and Entertainment California Section American Water Works Association at Hotel San Diego, billed as: "10 piece orchestra, direct from the Club New Yorker, Hollywood and Featured over KFWB."

A small article announces, "Zenda Dance Ballroom, 936 W. Seventh Street, L.A. invites service station operators, and others to come hear and enjoy the enthralling strains of Peggy Gilbert and her all-girl orchestra, which has been held over indefinitely by popular demand." The Zenda Ballroom, located near South Figueroa Street in downtown Los Angeles, was called the Zenda Dancing Academy in the 1930s, under the direction of Harold T. Zulawinski. It was also known as the Zenda Dance Café or Zenda Café.

1936

In March 1936, Peggy put together "Peggy Gilbert and Her 41 Cuties" for the 41 Club's 35th anniversary celebration. Located on the second floor of 833 South Spring Street, the club advertised "Hawaiian Days and Hula Nights, Continuous South Sea Island Festival of the torrid tropics."[235] The club was owned by Tommy Jacobs; club "members" used a special card to access a back room, where there was continuous gambling. Peggy remembers that, when her saxophone player was ill, she hired a man for the band who could not sight-read the charts; it caused quite an uproar among the band members.

> The entire institution has been redecorated in the South Sea Island motif and the songs, dance numbers and costumes will suggest the torrid tropics. Fun, favors and leis for the ladies are to be featured. Two orchestras will furnish dance music and the continuous floor show includes a cast of forty artists, with the feminine element predominating. . . . Chef Adolf Ackerman presides over the kitchen of the club; John Alexander is in charge of beverages and service; the Six Counts of Rhythm and Peggy Gilbert's 41 Cuties alternate in furnishing sizzling dance music.[236]

Peggy Gilbert and Her Co-eds performed April 25, 1936, at the Annual Dinner Dance of the California Yacht Club, "The Royal Order of Clams."

Peggy's band was often in demand for such social occasions in private clubs and fraternal organizations.

A press release dated August 29, 1936, announces that Peggy Gilbert's band was performing at the Albert Sheetz Circus Café, 6656 Hollywood Boulevard:

> And speaking of music—this orchestra is out-of-the-ordinary. Blond, petite, Peggy Gilbert and her four brunette femmes bring rolling, modern rhythm in their inimitable fashion. On a raised platform, clad in yellow and black satin outfits, 'gainst a sparkling, colorful background, make them a pleasing eyeful.

Another article about Peggy's band performances at the Penn Albert Hotel states that her band had an eight-month engagement at the Circus Café in Hollywood. A ticket-size ad for the Circus Café states: "Peg Gilbert's All-Girl Orchestra. Five Charming Misses who were featured attraction in Hawaii for eleven months and who are well known and liked in the radio world today. Come. Eat, Drink, Dance, and Be Merry!"

1937

John Albert Sheetz (1873–1941) founded the Albert Sheetz Mission Candy Company and restaurant chain. In the late 1930s, he owned and operated the Beverly Café, located at Burton Way and Cañon Drive in Beverly Hills; it included a candy counter, cocktail bar, fountain, and restaurant.[237] Peggy recalls that his establishments always had flower stalls in front and that he always had fresh flowers on the bandstand. She remembers him as a nice man, who was very good to his employees.

In 1937, Sheetz arranged for Peggy's band to play at the Penn Albert Hotel, which he owned, in Greensburg, Pennsylvania, just west of the Appalachian Mountains. They appeared in the hotel's Chrome Room, with the performances broadcast over radio station WHJB. Peggy still has some of the fan mail from those appearances. The band included Kathleen McArtor, drums; Bunny Hart, guitar; Mabel Hicks, trumpet; and Caryl Agnew, piano. Peggy and Mabel drove from Los Angeles in Mabel's car, spending one night in Chicago, where they visited the Three Deuces Night Club.

An article about the Penn Albert appearances states, "Miss Gilbert's aggregation is rated tops as exponents of modern harmony and swing rhythm. They played an eight-month engagement at the Circus Café, Hollywood and appeared in *Melody for Two* with James Melton and Patricia Ellis, Warner's Picture."

Melody for Two (1937) was directed by Louis King. A Warner Bros. production, it was originally called *King of Swing*. Melton, a famous operatic tenor of the day, plays the role of "Tod Weaver," leader of an all-girl band. He tries to resist their charms, but falls in love with the band's assistant conductor, "Gale Starr," played by Ellis. The featured song, "September in the Rain," written by Harry Warren, with lyric by Al Dubin, was originally heard in *Star Over Broadway* (1935). In *Melody*, Peggy recalls that the girls were not side-lining, but they actually played.

While at the Penn Albert, Peggy met Eleanor Roosevelt (1884–1962), who was also staying there. On several occasions, Mrs. Roosevelt invited Peggy for iced tea and conversation in the hotel dining room. Nicknamed "the Flying First Lady," because she traveled extensively on White House business, Mrs. Roosevelt was in Greensburg to tour coal mines and observe the working conditions of the miners. Donning a hard hat, she went into the mines with the workers, despite the dangers. "The miners go into the mines every day, risking their lives for our country. The least I could do is to go there with them just once," she said. Peggy recalls that Mrs. Roosevelt said she felt obligated to travel on her husband's behalf, because he was not well enough to travel and do things that needed to be done for the nation.[238]

An ad in a local newspaper (May 1937) states, "Peggy Gilbert and her Four Femmes say Goodbye to Greensburg and Hello to Hollywood. Gala Farewell Party tonight in the Chrome Room. New Floor Show, with a photo of Peggy." There are fan letters from people throughout Pennsylvania who heard Peggy's band on the radio every day.

A newspaper photo of "Peggy Gilbert and Her Girls" (c.1937?) has the following caption: "Will provide music for the R.P.D.A. [Retail Petroleum Dealer Association] Big Party November 9. The girls are: Berea, bass violin; Mac [Kathleen McArtor], drums; Helen, cornet; [Mabel] Hix [Hicks], trumpet; Pee Wee [Naomi Preble], trombone; Lona Bowman, piano; Katie [Cruise] saxophone, violin; and Jerry [Stanley], saxophonc." Peggy's picture appears on the cover of their publication, *Dealer News*, dated November 9, 1937.

This Week in Los Angeles, August 8, 1937, announces the Peggy Gilbert Orchestra at Zenda Dance Café. An ad states, "This ad and 15 cents good any night except Saturday." A brief article in the same publication says,

> And now for real dancing novelty in a ballroom, Zenda introduces Peggy Gilbert and Her Orchestra, reputed to be one of the finest bands of its type in the country. There is no doubt but what the regular young patrons of Zenda are going to find this band indeed interesting, and marvelous to

> dance to. With its elaborate café, delicious cocktails, this is really one of the pleasure spots in Los Angeles. After one visit, you'll come again and again.

Peggy's band played the Zenda five nights a week, Tuesday through Saturday. They were broadcast live from the Zenda on KFI Radio.[239]

On August 1, 1937, Peggy's band[240] appeared in the second Hollywood Swing Concert at The Palomar, located at Third and Vermont in Los Angeles. This was the site of Benny Goodman's famous appearance in 1935, which marked the beginning of the "Swing Era." *The Big Broadcast of 1937* (Paramount, 1936) was filmed there. The Palomar burned down in 1939.

A letter, dated August 9, 1937, from Dr. Leonard B. Stallcup, chairman, Second Hollywood Swing Concert, reads:

> Dear Peggy:
>
> Please permit me, on behalf of the A.F. of M. Local 47, Musicians Post No. 424 of the American Legion, to extend their most sincere thanks for the assistance you gave us in making the second Hollywood Swing Concert a huge success. I am sure you will be interested in knowing that the profits from this event were ample to assure our California State Championship Band of sixty pieces the necessary funds to transport them to Stockton this week, in order that they may defend their championship. I've heard nothing but praise for the splendid manner in which you and your organization performed, and would appreciate your extending to each member of the organization my personal thanks for appearing at the concert.

The magazine *Dancing Topics* includes an article with Peggy's picture, under the headline, "Peggy Gilbert Popular," announcing the seventh week of their engagement at the Zenda Dance Café:

> From all indications, greatly increased nitely patronage proves the colorful appeal of these mistresses of melody whose delightful brand of "Swing" definitely places them among the top-notch bands. It is interesting to note that Miss Gilbert developed the first band ever to play for television, the result of which brought her fan mail from such distant corners as South America, Africa and other remote places. Later she accepted an eleven months' engagement in the Hawaiian Islands. Returning to the United States and the stage, the popularity of her band soon brought her into contact with the motion picture studios. Many of the late Marie Dressler pictures bore witness to the musical aptitude of her colorful group of players, and only recently she was signed for a current Warner Bros. production. Miss Gilbert's engagement has been extended indefinitely.[241]

BANDS APPEARING AT THE SECOND SWING CONCERT

August 1, 1937, at The Palomar
presented by Local 47 of the Musicians Union and
Post 424 of the American Legion

Peggy Gilbert and Her Orchestra
The Four Play Boys
Les Hite and His Orchestra
Hal Kemp and His Orchestra
Louis Prima and His New Orleans Five
Carl Hoff and His Orchestra
Benny Goodman Quartet
Floyd Ray and His Orchestra
The Four Squires
The Stomp Shop Rug Cutters
Nick Lucas and His Guitar
Benny Goodman and His Orchestra
The Five Jones Boys
Jimmy Grier and His Orchestra
Stuff Smith and His Famous Door Five
Bobby Sherwood and His Orchestra
Harriet Wilson and Her Singing Strings
Finale: David Broekman, His Orchestra and His Ensemble

1938 and *The Great Waltz*

The strife continued in Europe in 1938. Hitler annexed Austria and, on November 9 and 10, made a brutal attack on Jews throughout Germany, now known as *Kristallnacht*. European Jewish émigrés kept on coming to Hollywood. To make a movie called *The Great Waltz,* celebrating the life and music of Johann Strauss, MGM recreated Austria on the set in Culver City.

Based on a Broadway musical which opened in 1934, *The Great Waltz* was directed by Julien Duvivier, assisted by Victor Fleming and Josef von Sternberg (both uncredited). It stars Luise Rainer, as Strauss's wife; Fernand Gravey (1904–1970) ("Gravet" in the credits) as Johann Strauss II; and coloratura soprano Miliza Korjus (1909–1980) as the operatic diva, "Carla Donne," who steals Strauss's heart. A fictionalized account of the composer's life, it features music of both Strauss and his father, adapted and arranged by Dimitri Tiomkin and orchestrated by Paul Marquardt. The Russian violin virtuoso Toscha Seidel was hired to dub solos on the soundtrack, thereby launching his Hollywood studio career.

Of this movie, Peggy says,

> I got a hundred girls together for that scene in the beer garden and that was where I became acquainted with a lot of the string players and lots of the "legit" players. They are still showing that picture, by the way, every now and then, *The Great Waltz*, and you'll see all these girls, one hundred of us sitting in the beer garden. And I worked a lot of pictures then . . . at all the different studios.[242]

Besides the Los Angeles Women's Philharmonic, founded in 1893, there were several other all-women symphonic orchestras in Los Angeles. The Hollywood Woman's Symphony Orchestra, founded in July 1932 and conducted by Anna Priscilla Risher, performed its first concert in the Greek Theater in Griffith Park. They performed regularly in La Cañada and at the Hollywood Woman's Club Auditorium.[243] The Glendale Women's Symphony was founded in 1931 by William C. Ulrich; that same year Bessie Chapin founded the Women's Little Symphony Orchestra of Los Angeles.[244] Members of all of these ensembles participated in the orchestra for *The Great Waltz*. It took several weeks to set up and rehearse that shot, before it was actually filmed. Peggy's band played every night at a club or ballroom and spent every day at MGM.

Among the musicians in the beer garden scene are: Mabel Hicks, Audrey Hall,[245] Katy Cruise, Bee Turpin,[246] Kathleen McArtor, Marie Ford,[247] and Peggy Gilbert.[248]

Another violinist who played with Peggy's band was Fern Buckner[249] (1910–1981), who became a close friend. According to Roy Ringwald, "Fern was the spark of any party she attended . . . witty, beautiful, enormously intelligent. Fern was the most talented woman I've ever known."[250] Peggy tells this story about Fern:

> We were playing the Paramount Theater stage show in L.A. Between shows we talked about how thrilling it would be to play the Bowl. The violinist in the orchestra glanced in my direction and said, "Why not?" So . . . the night was cool and beautiful after the last show and Hollywood wasn't that far away. I found myself climbing over fences and up and down hills with clarinet in hand. The two of us stood on center stage and we played "Bach." The acoustics were astoundingly good. Our audience was an occasional fawn strolling down from the hills—a rabbit or two—and the sounds of the night. Shortly after this incident Fern Buckner joined Fred Waring in New York, where she had a long and successful career as the featured soloist with the orchestra.[251]

In 1938, Peggy put together a "Western" group of women musicians for *Rhythm of the Saddle*, a Republic picture with Gene Autry ("The Singing Cowboy") and Smiley Burnett (who plays "Frog Millhouse"). An actress pretends to conduct the all-female band and act as emcee in the nightclub owned by the sinister "Jack Pomeroy" (played by Le Roy Mason). Gene Autry (1907–1998), one of the leading recording artists of the day, plays foreman of a ranch owned by the wealthy rodeo owner "Maureen" (played by Peggy Moran). Despite Autry's charisma, most of the songs in the film are lackluster. A great stagecoach race features Republic's famous stuntmen. The band members had beautiful hairdos and makeup.

Peggy's Article in *Downbeat*

In 1938, an anonymous author published an article in the well-known national jazz publication *Downbeat*, entitled "Why Women Musicians Are Inferior." Peggy was so outraged that she responded her own thoughts. Published in the April 1938 issue of *Downbeat,* her article appeared under the degrading banner headline, "How Can You Blow a Horn with a Brassiere?" Here is Peggy's article, in its entirety:

How Can You Blow a Horn with a Brassiere?*

"Sissy!" Pens Skirt Swinger to Writer Who Said Women Are Inferior

Los Angeles, Calif.

Dear Father Superior:

You get up, make a lot of unintelligible noise, and expect the people to shout, "Bravo!" or echo in reverential tones a deep "Amen." You are like a small boy pulling his sister's pigtails when you think she hasn't a chance to fight back. You are the little boy who yells "Sissy!" from the second floor.

If Gene Krupa[252] were a woman, how long do you suppose he would be an ace drummer in Benny Goodman's band? In evening gown, he might still be sensational even hampered by brassiere straps, girdle, skirt, and high heels—but Mrs. G. K. or Miss Anybody couldn't make a one night stand with bags under her eyes. She could be good, but no matter how good, the public, especially the men, would not tolerate an unattractive, second-hand stage prop. And that's one of the superficial reasons women are inferior to men as musicians *(if they are)*: their inability to make a career of music because, for women, as a profession it can last at best only a few years.

Put Women on the Pan

Ha! We admit it, you say. You're absolutely right, but your line is as old as time. You think you have put women on the pan. You have. But it has been done for ages, Father Superior—even since Eve—and far better than you could ever do it. Your weak, illogical, ineffectual argument is hardly

*Courtesy *Downbeat* magazine.

resented. It's your attitude we resent, because it expresses the attitude of all professional men musicians toward all professional women musicians. A woman has to be a thousand times more talented, has to have a thousand times more initiative even to be recognized as the peer of the least successful man. Why? Because of the age-old prejudice against women, that time-worn idea that women are the weaker sex, that women are innately inferior to men.

So you actually think that because men have had centuries of musical education behind them that the present masculine generation has inherited that knowledge, that talent? That's not worthy of you, Father. We expect better arguments than that. Knowledge is not hereditary, and whether or not talent is present in the chromosomes is still a matter of conjecture. But even if it were wouldn't a daughter, being a child also of a talented musician, be just as likely to inherit that characteristic—as the son? If we were ladies, of course, we should ignore that thrust and tactfully help you, to forget that you rambled a bit out of your sphere. Now, if you had said environment, perhaps we should have agreed. It's a man's world, admittedly. You would be right without having to prove yourself right. You think what millions of men musicians think—and it may be you are justified. But at least establish a true premise from which to argue (or gripe).

Why Sex—Not Ability?

But after all, that's not the issue, is it? Or isn't it? It seems that you, like all the rest, have judged musicians according to sex rather than ability. You have generalized no end to prove your point, always adding in your liberal way "with few exceptions." "Women Musicians Are Inferior"—that's your point, isn't it. You were a bit vague even about that, but the editor kindly clarified the subject in the headline. And why are women musicians inferior (*if they are*)? Since you [are] not particularly enlightening as to the reasons such a broad statement might be true, we'll hand you a few tips—if you give us an audience and don't rush for the exit because a woman is speaking. We'll use a low, well-modulated voice, and powder our nose and comb our hair.

And then, too, as we have inferred, women are never hired because of their ability as musicians, but as an attraction for the very reason that they are women, and men like to look at attractive women. Consequently, the manager is continually reminding the girls not to take the music so seriously, but to relax, to smile. How can you smile with a horn in your mouth? How can you relax when a girdle is throttling you and the left brassiere strap holds your arm in a vise? If we quaver a little on the high notes, it's because we are asked to do a Houdini—and if we hit an occasional blue note, it's because we play with *too much* feeling, and mascara gets in our eyes. On the other hand, men's orchestras are usually hired because of their ability as musicians. Their good looks, their present-ability other than neatness rarely will enter the question. Even the best girl bands in the country have to have an S.A. artist fronting them to captivate the audience while the musicians in the band indulge themselves in that orgy of facial contortions which seems so important to you, Father Superior.

> Men have always refused to work with girls, thus not giving them the opportunity to prove their equality. This is especially true of wind instrument players, obviously one of the foci of your attack, Father. Girl violinists and stringed instrument players have had breaks. Descending to the personal for a moment, I wish to add that I have a few girls in my band, who could hold first chairs in the best men's bands, if given the privilege. But what men's orchestras would consent to such an experiment? A great many men musicians have highly complimented my band saying it was as good or better than their organizations, but if the question of actually giving us an opportunity to establish our equality arose, we should immediately be relegated to an inferior plane and given the form answer A: "It's not being done."
>
> You say that women musicians are inferior because of lack of practice. If that's true, it's because there is no future in music for girl musicians for the reasons previously mentioned. Wood-shedding would be fun if we could see there was anything to gain by it—other than personal gratification. However, even you should agree as an "artist" that that is an admirable motive in itself. Oddly enough, Father, they take just as much pride as men in their work, and they woodshed as much as men and perhaps more, because of the obstacle of prejudice to be overcome and because of the harsh criticism fired at them from all sides such as that in your article. As for the point you noted that women are not compelled to support themselves, we urge you with apologetic banality to go West, young man. Evidently, you haven't gone farther in that direction than Chicago. Now, in California, it's different. The women support the men—as well as themselves. Step around a little more, Father, and have a looksee. There are several Misses Prima, Eldridge, Musso, and Trumbauer[253] in circulation—and if you are a fair-minded gentleman, be gallant and respond to their "cries for help."
>
> Very humbly yours,
Peggy Gilbert

The response to her article was overwhelming: Peggy received letters of support from women musicians from all over the country. She began to see herself as not only a bandleader and contractor, but also as an advocate for women musicians.

However, having reached her thirties, Peggy feared that her career might be coming to an end, because she thought she was losing her youthfulness and beauty. It was so important to look young and attractive. Peggy didn't show her age and, like many women, she guarded that secret with care. At that moment, she would never have guessed that she would continue to play professionally into her nineties.

In 1938, Peggy and her band appeared in a film called *Reckless Living* (Universal), directed by Frank McDonald. This comedy is about a pair of mismatched lovers (Robert Wilcox and Nan Grey), passionate about horse racing, who get involved in a get-rich-quick scheme. The legendary Broadway comedian Jimmy Savo (as "Stuffy") appears in this film, doing pantomime and musical numbers. Some girl singers in this film are uncredited, including Mary Brodel, Eleanor Hansen, Marilyn Stuart, and Constance Moore. The score includes songs by Jimmy McHugh.

A flyer announces Peggy Gilbert's All-Girl Band, "Direct from the Paramount Theater," in a return engagement at The Zenda Ballroom, starting January 14, 1938. "Peggy came to the Zenda unknown to our patrons, and as the first all-girl band to play at the Zenda during its thirty-two years of dancing. After coming in on a two weeks' contract she stayed for four months, from August 1 through New Year's Day. That in itself speaks for the way in which the Zenda patrons enjoyed her music." The gig was eventually extended to two years.

1939

When World War II began in Europe in 1939, people in the United States still believed their country would stay out of the conflict. That year also marks the first year of commercial airplane flights over the Atlantic from America. The New York World's Fair, in Flushing Meadows, captured the imagination of Americans, helping them focus on possibilities for the future. The Fair highlighted industrial advancements and new inventions, including television, and works of art. On opening day, April 30, 1939, the RCA Pavilion was the site of the television broadcast of a speech by President Roosevelt, considered the first commercial TV broadcast.

By this time, Peggy Gilbert is listed in *The Overture* as a "licensed booker, license no. 1978."[254] *The Studio News*, dated January 26, 1939, announces that Peggy and Her All-Girl Orchestra would appear at "The New Hollywood Café," 6916 Santa Monica Boulevard, "supported by a Grand Array of Singers and Dancers."

On March 17, 1939, the *Arizona Republic* in Phoenix announces, "Police To Give Ball Tonight," with a photograph of Peggy holding a baton. The caption reads: "Peggy Gilbert's Studio Band will swing out tonight and tomorrow night at the Shrine Auditorium for the policemen's ball, sponsored annually by the Phoenix chapter, Fraternal Order of Police. Miss Gilbert is pictured here at the microphone at a recent performance of her band."

Another article, dated March 8, in the *Phoenix Gazette* also announces her band's appearance at the Police Ball, stating, "The band, consisting of 10 members has appeared in several motion pictures, including 'The Great

Waltz' and 'Reckless Living' and will come to Phoenix from the Gay White Way Night Club in Hollywood." Proceeds of the ball were to benefit the "death and sick benefit fund" of the Fraternal Order of Police.

A publicity shot for the policeman's ball pictures: Bee Turpin, piano; Katy Cruise, saxophone and clarinet; Audrey Hall, saxophone, clarinet and violin; Helen Ireland, saxophone, clarinet; Peggy Gilbert, saxophone, clarinet, vibes, vocals; Mabel Hicks, trumpet, flugelhorn; Dorothy Sauter, bass; Bunny Hart, guitar and banjo; Kathleen McArtor, drums; Naomi Preble, trombone; and Helen Kay, trumpet.

A large cartoon (see illustration) in the March 12 issue of the *Arizona Republic* pictures Peggy, along with a comic-character policeman, and the

Cartoon by Reg Manning, published in the *Arizona Republic*, 1939.
Courtesy David C. Manning.

caption, "Cops will become jitterbugs when they stage their 15th annual St. Patrick's Day Policemen's Ball. This year the Ball will be held two nights; Friday and Saturday." One cartoon character asked another: "How does an all-girl orchestra increase attendance at th' policemen's ball? The other answers, "It brings out all th' wives!" Next to the drawing of Peggy is a sign, "Clear Traffic for the Siren."

Later that spring, an announcement in *The Sportlight*, published in San Diego,[255] states, "The Peggy Gilbert Girls are to start an engagement at Blue Lantern Café, Columbia Street, just off Broadway, according to Scardina Bros., proprietors of the new establishment. They also appeared at the Hollywood Café in 1939 and at the Gay White Way (on the site formerly occupied by the 'Barn' at Cahuenga and Sunset." A review states, "These gals play nice, and they are handling a tough show that would have many of youse guys stumbling all over the joint in search of notes."[256]

KMPC

In 1939 and 1940, Peggy's band was broadcast on KMPC (710 AM), "The Station of the Stars." The performers were called "The Early Girls and Three Chirps,"[257] having been named in a contest held by the show's sponsor. The band included Dot Sauter, bass, Katy Cruise, alto, clarinet, vocals; Audrey Hall, alto sax, clarinets, violin, vocal; Grace Pappalardo,[258] vibes and accordion; Della Anderson,[259] guitar and banjo. In addition to being leader, Peggy played tenor sax, clarinet, and bongos, sang vocals, and made the band's arrangements. She describes the show:

> I had the only all-woman staff band. . . . I had the staff band at KMPC when we were in Beverly Hills. . . . We did an hour and a half show in the morning from 9 to 10:30 a.m. We had to get there at 7 o'clock in the morning and get the show set up. We did another half-hour show from 1 to 1:30 in the afternoon and that was five days a week.[260]

Not only did they do the regular morning and afternoon programs, but they also were on call to do additional programs, as requested by the commercial sponsors. These early mornings followed late nights of playing in clubs. The musicians also managed to do sidelining work in motion pictures.

From a surviving air-check of this band, it is clear that they had a very sophisticated sound.[261] The recording opens with a selection featuring Audrey Hall on violin, on a Gypsy-style piece called "Deep in the Forest." After a lengthy slow section, clearly showing what an accomplished violinist she was, it breaks into an up-tempo dance section with pizzicato violin. The next selection is "Blue Skies," by Irving Berlin. Sung by the vocal trio of the group—called "The Three Chirps"—it demonstrates exquisite, close harmonies with splendid intonation and beautiful tone. This song also features Peggy on vibes, introducing the tune and playing a lengthy solo. The announcer, a man named "Ken,"[262] gives the exact time, in the 8 am hour, and tells the audience, "If you're not up and ready and off to school, you certainly should be." The next tune is "South of the Border," also featuring "The Three Chirps."

The final selection is "Swing, Little Indians, Swing," a jazzy version of the children's counting song, "Ten Little Indians." The announcer mentions the "six gals and one guy" on the broadcast—meaning the all-girl band and himself. Peggy could easily have announced the broadcast, too, in addition to singing and playing, having done so for more than a decade. However, Ken's announcing allowed the band members time to prepare for the next tune.

The Early Girls and Three Chirps, on KMPC Radio *(left to right)*: Audrey Hall, Peggy Gilbert, Della Anderson, "Ken" the announcer, Dorothy Sauter, Grace Pappalardo, and Katy Cruise.

CHAPTER VI
God Bless the Girl Who's Got Her Own [Band]

By the late 1930s, there was such demand for all-girl bands that it is difficult to keep track of them all. The most famous was Ina Ray Hutton and Her Melodears; her international success inspired many female musicians to create their own all-girl bands. The musicians had to be young, beautifully dressed, and led by a glamour girl. Peggy encouraged her band members to be stylish, attractive, and youthful-looking, so they could keep working. Bandleader Babe Egan, now in her forties, was still performing occasionally, at places like the Million Dollar Theater in Los Angeles. She attempted other businesses, as well, and during World War II, had a company to manufacture sexier nurses' uniforms "for the troops." Peggy never liked the image of the "glamour girl" bandleader; she always put the music first and sometimes had to refuse club owners' requests to do some "stunts" to make the show sexier and more risqué. She was discouraged to see bands succeed that were led by women who were not musicians, when there were so many qualified women players seeking work. However, Peggy was astute enough to know how to play the game and keep her band working. From photos of her during this period, it is clear that she was beautiful and always had "a class act."

According to George T. Simon (1912–2001), "Without a doubt, the sexiest of all the big bandleaders is Ina Ray Hutton. Fortunately for her sake and that of the rest of the band she had a good deal more to offer. For Ina Ray is a charming, gracious, intelligent, and talented gal."[263] Simon proceeds to say that Ina Ray's early career with her all-girl orchestra was not memorable, "for her all-girl orchestra was like all all-girl orchestras. 'Only God can make a tree,' I remember having written in a review of some other such outfit, 'and only men can play good jazz.'"[264] Although Peggy did not play with Ina Ray's band, they knew each other and Peggy did play with some of Ina Ray's band members.

In her August 1979 column in *The Overture*, Peggy answers Simon's comment:

> His reference to all girls being unable to play jazz caused my toes to curl. I happen to know that there were many top musicians in her [Ina Ray Hutton's] orchestras, including trumpeter Jane Sager, who has not only played with the best of the men's bands around the country but has taught them how to play their instrument and is now considered one of the finest trumpet teachers and coaches in the country. There were many others of equal talent who backed up this "sexy front"—and they deserve more than a statement which degrades and humiliates their expertise in musicianship. George, if you are reading this, it will be my pleasure to enlighten you on the facts about girl musicians. They made history, too, and are still making it.

Ina Ray Hutton, born Odessa Cowan on March 13, 1914, was the daughter of pianist Marvel Ray. Her mother was a jazz and blues pianist in Chicago.[265] Her older half-sister was June (Rae Cowan) Hutton, a vocalist with Charlie Spivak in *Pin Up Girl* (Twentieth Century Fox, 1944) and with Tommy Dorsey's Pied Pipers. Ina Ray may have begun her career as early as age eight[266] as a dancer and singer in musical revues in the 1930s, including the Gus Edwards revue on Broadway, with George White's "Melody '34" and "Scandals," and "Ziegfeld Follies 1934." Trained as a pianist, she did not play a musical instrument in her shows, but her alluring gyrations on stage were cause for fascination. Her movements are in tempo, but she is definitely not conducting the band. Rather, she "fronted" her band, being neither music director nor bandleader.

Irving Mills, who was Duke Ellington's publisher and Cab Calloway's manager, decided to help build an all-women orchestra around Ina Ray called The Melodears, which was active from 1934 to 1939. He added Hutton to her name, because of all the publicity at that time attached to Woolworth heiress and socialite Barbara Hutton (1912–1979), dubbed "a poor little rich girl" by the media.[267] Mills hired arranger-composers Alex Hill, Eddie Durham, and Will Hudson to make charts for her band and had them recorded on Vocalion and Victor, making them the first all-girl band to record for major American labels.[268] He promoted Ina Ray, with her bleached platinum hair, as the "Blonde Bombshell of Rhythm."

The Melodears appeared in two shorts: *Feminine Rhythm* (1935) and *Accent on Girls* (1936),[269] as well as in *The Big Broadcast of 1936* (Paramount). In the short *Swing, Hutton, Swing* (1937), made at the Paramount News Lab in New York City, the cue sheet states that it features "Ina Ray Hutton and Her Orchestra," probably meaning The Melodears. The tunes include "Organ Grinder's Swing" by I. Mills, Mitchell Parrish, and Will Hudson; "Bugle Call Rag" by Pettis, Mills, and Schoebel; "Star Dust" by Hoagy Carmichael; "Doin' the Suzi-Q" by Benny Davis and J. Fred Coots; and "Melody of Swing" by Will Hudson.

Among the excellent musicians who played with Ina Ray Hutton's all-girl band in the 1930s were: Mardell "Owen" Winstead, trumpet; Betty Sattley, saxophone; Alyse Wells, trombone, among other instruments; Betty Roudebush, piano; Ruth Loew, piano;[270] Gladys Moser, piano; Nadine Friedman, saxophone; Marjorie Tisdale, saxophone; Kay Walsh, trumpet; Estelle Slavin, trumpet; Fy Hesser, trombone; Jessie Bailey, trombone; Marge Rivers, bass; Marion Gange, guitar; Lillian Singer, drums; and Virginia Myers, drums.[271] A photograph taken at the Chicago Theater in Chicago, probably in 1939, shows Ina Ray with trumpeter Marnie Wells and guitarist Marion Gange.[272]

In 1939, Ina Ray severed her relationship with Irving Mills. The following year, she started an all-male band, with saxophone player and arranger George Paxton as director-leader.[273] She often appeared in a tight, sexy gown and waved an extra long baton in a manner that resembled baton twirling, more than conducting. Ina Ray Hutton and her men's band appeared in *Ever Since Venus* (Columbia, 1944). Directed by Arthur Dreifuss, it is a musical about selling kiss-proof lipstick. Ina Ray has only a few scenes in the film.

Another Paramount short was entitled *Ina Ray Hutton and Her Orchestra* (1943). Directed by Leslie M. Roush, it features her men's band playing four swing numbers, on two of which Ina Ray is vocalist. The cue sheet, dated March 10, 1943, lists "My Silent Love" by Dana Suesse, with lyric by Eddie Heyman; "Knock Me a Kiss" by Louis Jordan; "Angry" by Henry Brunies and Jules Cassard, with lyric by Dudley Mecum; and "Smiles" [also known as "There Are Smiles"] by Lee S. Roberts, with lyric by J. Will Callahan. They also play eleven seconds of "Yankee Doodle." The mono short is nine minutes in length. Stuart Foster is also credited as a vocalist.

In 1950, Ina Ray made another short for Columbia Pictures, entitled *Thrills of Music: Ina Ray Hutton and Orchestra*. With her all-male orchestra, it begins with her standard tune, "Angry," also in the 1943 Paramount short, followed by "Three Little Bears" and a rumba number.

Ina Ray's television show began broadcasting live from the Santa Monica Ballroom on May 18, 1950, on KTLA-TV, whose program director was Klaus Landsberg. From 1952 until 1956, the program was broadcast live from the Melrose Theater, across the street from Paramount studios. For six weeks in the summer of 1956, it was broadcast nationally on NBC. Her band included: Mickey Anderson, clarinet; Jackie "Zackie" Walters,[274] saxophone; Deedee Ball,[275] piano; Helen Blackburn, trombone;[276] Lois Cronen (Magee),[277] trombone; Janie Davis, trumpet; Peggy Fairbanks, trumpet; Helen Hammond, trumpet; Helen Kay, trumpet; Evie Howeth Campbell,[278] saxophone; Margaret Rinker, drums; Judy Van Euer, saxophone;[279] as well as instrumentalists Helen Smith, Zoe Ann Willy, and Helen Wooley. Jane Sager also played trumpet with Ina Ray's band.[280] Peggy recalls that there was a jazz violinist on the show, who rode a motorcycle.

According to Peggy Gilbert, many of the girls found it difficult to work with Ina Ray, because she was generally very diffident and would not speak to them outside of the gig. Peggy felt that Ina Ray did not want her in the band, because Peggy "was Joe Union."

Ina Ray Hutton may have married four times. Her first husband was Lou [Parris] Parisotto, a saxophone player in her band, whom she married in 1944; she married trumpet and bandleader Randy Brooks in 1949, whom she divorced in 1957; her third husband was Michael Anter, a Las Vegas hairdresser; and her fourth husband was businessman Jack Curtis. She retired from show business in 1968, but appeared in the 1974 film *Brother, Can You Spare a Dime*—a compilation of Depression-era film clips and newsreels—singing "Every Man a King." She died on February 19, 1984, of complications due to diabetes.

Ina Ray Hutton's was a big name in the music world from the 1930s until the late '50s. Every "girl" bandleader was compared to her; she set the standard, particularly related to dressing beautifully. Peggy was not a glamour girl, but rather, she was an accomplished instrumentalist who struggled to be taken seriously as a musician. She could have hired someone glamorous to front her band, but she decided instead to focus on the music. For this reason, Peggy was greatly respected by the women who played with her.

1940

According to the "Los Angeles Band Directory" in *The Overture* issue of September 1940, Peggy's band was then performing at Bud Taylor's Café.

It lists Audrey [Barnett],[281] [Peggy] Gilbert, Kathleen McArtor, and Jennie [Genevieve] Howell[282] as band members. Other women performers listed in that month's band directory include: Jeanette Ward at Brittingham's; Vivian McKenzie at Broadway Ace; Lucille Silverstone[283] at California Cocktail Lounge; Vivian Oliver at Club La Valle (with Mickey Hein, Estelle Gerard and Antoinette Maggio); Margaret Johan, organ; Helen Miller, piano, at Melrose Cavern; Thelma Rogers at Cinegrill (with two men in her band); Dixie Dean at Silver Dollar (with Kay O'Grady, Shirley Sidney, Natalie Robbins [Robin], and Doris Pressler);[284] Myrtle Bittner at Diana Ballroom with O. Dombrowski, Leon Ladd, Bob Houseman, and Max Pedrini.[285]

After-Hour Clubs

Peggy recalls that in the late 1930s and '40s, the girls in the band often went to after-hour spots after their gigs:

> The most famous of these was probably on Central Avenue down in the black district of Los Angeles in those days, which was perfectly great. There was a place called Ivie's Chicken Shack [at Vermont] where you could go and meet all the musicians who were in town. It didn't matter if they were black or white or what. I mean, that's where everybody went. That was just the thing to do. We went there specifically to jam and sit in with the black musicians because they played so great. We appreciated them. They were nice enough to give us a chance to sit in with them. You couldn't do that unless you were invited.
>
> We'd go down there after we finished work at night at 2 o'clock in the morning, after the club closed, and take our instruments. A lot of girls [went] without escorts, a strictly black district. You wouldn't do that today, but we had a ball and we were never in any trouble down there. Never. Everybody treated us just beautifully. We'd stay there all night. We'd jam. We met all the greats that would be coming through town. All the musicians, because they all wound up down there. And the musicians played all night long, until morning. We called it "The Breakfast Club" because we'd all have breakfast.[286]

Asked if she knew any of the black women jazz musicians, Peggy said,

> I heard about several of them like Vi Redd[287] and Clora Bryant[288] and a lot of the girls, the trombone player [Melba] Liston[289] [1926–1999], who would be around. But we would never meet at that time, until the Sweethearts of Rhythm got together, which was a mixed band.[290] It was everything, all nationalities. [Then] we finally got to know some of them.[291]

> It was segregated at that time. . . . At that time there were two Locals [of the Musicians Union]: Local 767 and Local 47. They amalgamated in the early 1950s. The only whites that went down there were people in show business or musicians. It was a separate little thing we had going on there. I didn't realize that there was such a separation. It's unfortunate that we didn't all get together in those days. We missed a lot. I will always feel that we missed a lot, not knowing each other and working together.[292]

The Sweethearts of Rhythm, a racially integrated band, was formed in 1939 at the Piney Woods Country Life School in Mississippi and made its debut the next year at the Howard Theater in Washington, D.C. In 1941, vocalist Anna Mae Winburn joined The Sweethearts and became their leader. Eddie Durham, Jesse Stone, and Maurice King were among their arrangers/coaches. Members of the band included Ernestine "Tiny" Davis,[293] trumpet; Ray Carter, trumpet; Thelma L. Lewis, trumpet; Johnnie Mae Stansbury, trumpet; Edna Williams, trumpet; Marge Pettiford, saxophone; Amy Garrison, saxophone; Helen Sine, saxophone; Grace "Gracie" Bayron, saxophone; Viola "Vi" Burnside, tenor saxophone; Willie Mae Wong, saxophone; Judy Bayron, trombone; Helen Jones, trombone; Ina Bell Byrd, trombone; Lucille Dixon, bass; Roxanna Lucas, guitar; Johnnie Mae Rice, piano; and Pauline Braddy, drums. Vocalists included Evelyn McGee and Carline Ray. In 1945, they had a successful USO tour in Europe, but disbanded by the end of that decade.[294]

Local 767 Clubs in 1940 included: Bal Tabarin Café; Bill and Virginia's in Eagle Rock; Cabrillo Café in San Pedro; Club Capri; Club Bali; Dreamland Hall; Elk's Club in Long Beach; Jim Otto's Club Menio; Club Santa Fe; High Hat; La Cabana; Little Harlem Club; Louie's Café; Manchester Club; Merry-Go-Round; Mosby's Cocktail Lounge; Frock Café; Wagon Wheel; The Tropics; Harow's Lake Café; Paradise Hall, Rainbow Club, Radio Room; Shanghai Red Café; Shep Kelly's, which listed Dorothy Broil and Band; Silver Spray; Strangler Louis, Swanee Inn; and The K-9 Club.[295]

The Early Forties

By the early 1940s, Big Band jazz dominated American popular music and there were hundreds of big bands around the nation. Approximately fifty of these had national reputations, recording regularly and playing dance halls and theaters year round. Some of the big bands—like Ellington, Basie, Goodman, and Charlie Barnet—played jazz. Others—like Guy Lombardo, Kay Kyser, and Sammy Kaye—played very little jazz or a mixture of jazz and dance music.

Throughout the 1930s, awareness was growing that black Americans could no longer be treated as second-class citizens in a democracy. Part of this consciousness was created by the tremendous success of black jazz musicians and other performers. By 1940, many black musicians were highly respected in jazz, but still paid less than white band members. A further indignity was the fact that the family and friends of black musicians were often denied admittance to the clubs where black musicians were playing.

Peggy continued to seek opportunities for her band in films, although film production in Hollywood slowed in 1939 and 1940. In 1940, Peggy contracted a group of women musicians to appear in *Lillian Russell* (Twentieth Century Fox), an Oscar-nominated film about that great beauty of the American stage and vaudeville. Directed by Irving Cummings and starring Alice Faye, Don Ameche, and Henry Fonda, Peggy and others from her band can be seen in a still from that film, as a marching band during a Women's Suffrage march.

Every month, *The Overture* published listings under the banner of "Los Angeles Band Directory."[296] Peggy's band appeared often—playing at The Rice Bowl, Club La Valle, among other places—along with listings for other girl bands with girl leaders. For example, the March 1941 issue mentions that Virginia Massey led a group at George's with K[aty] Cruise, saxophone; Sandra Page, accordion; and Dot Sauter, bass. Bee Turpin, piano; and Frances Faye, accordion, were playing at Randini's. Peggy's band was at Club La Valle and included A[udrey] Barnett, guitar; G[enevieve] Howell, piano; and K[athleen] McArtor, drums. Other women might have been among the bandleaders, but most are listed only with a first initial.[297]

Sally Banning led a band in July 1941 at the Waldorf Cellar, which included Cay Due, piano; N[atalie] Robin, saxophone; D[ody] Jeshke, drums;[298] M[arion] Elzea [Wells], trumpet; and R. Knight, bass.[299] In September 1941, saxophonist Evelyn Pennak[300] led a band at Club La Valle with Lillian O'Poole, piano; Betty Pope, drums; and Doris Pressler, trumpet.[301] In December 1941, Kathleen "Mac" McArtor is listed as bandleader at The Rice Bowl. The women instrumentalists were interchangeable, band-to-band. Peggy had Mac lead the band at The Rice Bowl when she had other gigs, so that women musicians could keep the job.

Peggy Gilbert's Band at The Rice Bowl: Kathleen McArtor, drums; Audrey Barnett, guitar; Peggy Gilbert, saxophone, leader; Lona Bowman, piano.

Family Losses

When she was only sixteen years old, Peggy's niece, Darlene Maryland Knechtges (b. 1923) died from a fall off a cliff in Griffith Park. This occurred on March 19, 1940, during the Easter weekend, only a few weeks before her high school graduation. The local paper reported: "Death stalked a gay school holiday hiking party yesterday when Darlene Knechtges, 16, of 1341 S. Union Ave., fell 100 feet from the rugged slopes of Bee Rock, high in Griffith Park."[302] The article reported that, as Darlene and her two friends, Dick Spencer and Frank Murawski, were descending from Bee Rock,[303] Darlene slipped and fell. Peggy's family was devastated. Nothing could have prepared them for such a loss.

Darlene's brother, John Darwin Knechtges (b. 1925), was an accomplished drummer, like his father. Despite the family's efforts to dissuade him, he enlisted at age sixteen as an apprentice seaman in the United States Navy, when the United States entered World War II. He was posted to the Solomon Islands, and was on the USS Vincennes (CA-44), when it sank from Japanese torpedoes on August 9, 1942, during the Battle of Savo Island. John Darwin was declared missing in action.

One-Night Stands

In 1940, Peggy took her band on tour throughout Northern California. The July 11 issue of *The Searchlight*, the daily newspaper of Redding, California, announces that Peggy Gilbert's band is being heard on KVCV at 8:30 p.m. An ad states, "Opening at Benton's Café, May 17th, Peggy Gilbert and Her Radio Girls." Benton's Cafe was located a half mile North of Redding on Highway 99. The ad continues:

> They have just finished a long engagement at Paramount Theater in Los Angeles. Previous to that they were a sensation air feature on KMPC for a full year. They were also delightful features in MGM picture, "The Great Waltz" and in Twentieth Century Fox's latest release, "Lillian Russell." Two of their latest extended engagements were at the beautiful Club Capri in Beverly Hills and Merrill Jones Hotel in Santa Monica. These versatile girls all play a number of different instruments featuring electrical steel guitar and vibraharp and also offer the latest up to the date numbers in vocal selection.

These are the only references to Peggy's band performing at the Club Capri in Beverly Hills and the Merrill Jones Hotel in Santa Monica. Peggy seemed to have the knack for turning every gig into another.

A photograph taken at The Open Door shows Peggy Gilbert playing with jazz trumpeter, singer, and bandleader Joseph "Wingy" Manone (1900–1982),[304] who had moved to Los Angeles in 1940. Natalie Robin is on clarinet; Dot Sauter, bass; Kathleen McArtor, drums; Annis Elliott, piano.[305] Wingy, originally from New Orleans, earned his nickname when he lost an arm in a streetcar accident when he was ten years old. Using his artificial arm, he was an outstanding Dixieland style trumpeter. His band began touring in the 1920s. In the late 1930s and '40s, he recorded with sidemen Bud Friedman, Matty Matlock, Chu Berry, Eddie Miller, George Brunies, Jack Teagarden, Joe Marsala and Brad Gowan. Wingy appeared in a Bing Crosby movie, *Rhythm on the River* (1940), directed by Victor Schertzinger.

"Count" Berni Vici was originally a violinist. He formed an all-girl band in Hollywood to do a USO tour of the Philippines during World War II.

According to Lois Robbins Isaacs,[306] all he did was sunbathe on the beach in the Philippines. All of the girls were teenagers or in their twenties.

About Rita Rio's band, Peggy wrote:

> Rita Rio and her all girl band was a featured star attraction. She conducted, sang and danced and the audience was excited and charmed, not only because of her explosive personality but because she was backed up by top musicians who increased the magic of a great performance. Yet . . . when our "friend" [George T.] Simon, who wrote THE book about the Big Band Era, touched upon her in one short statement, he said, "Rita Rio, a very sexy looking lass, led a band that had a radio commercial, played ballrooms and was staffed by a bunch of rather unattractive girls who looked as stiff in their imitation tuxedos as their music sounded."[307]

Current Local 47 secretary-treasurer, Serena Kay Williams, talks about Peggy in the 1940s:

> I first met Peggy Gilbert back in the forties. My husband joined the Local 47 in 1942. Peggy was always at the union. Whether she worked there or served on a committee, I didn't know at the time, but that's when we met. He went to war and I went to work for Local 47. It was the only place I was assured. It was my first job. I worked for a while as a telephone operator, then for the financial office and Peggy used to come in there every week. We met and hit it off and became really close friends. I got married in late 1942 and my husband, Peggy, and I have always been friends. She's been my idol. I've always looked up to her.[308]

SERENA KAY WILLIAMS

Serena Kay Williams was born in 1921 in Kansas City, Missouri. Her father came from Liverpool, England, and her mother from Russia; they owned a delicatessen in Kansas City. When Serena was four, her family moved to Los Angeles for her mother's health. She graduated from Los Angeles City College.

Beginning at a young age, she sang with bands in vaudeville and acted in theaters; she also appeared as an extra in films, including Paramount's *The Ten Commandments* (1956). She met her husband, Earl Williams (1917–2006), a saxophone/clarinet player and orchestra leader, and became a singer for his group, "Sweet With a Beat" Orchestra. Earl worked for Local 47 from 1960 until 2000.

Serena studied the bass with Nat Gangursky. She played and sang in the female trio "The Coquettes" with Doris Crane and Chickie Fortina. After serving as a director on the union board, she became, in 1984, the first female officer of Local 47. In addition to serving as secretary-treasurer, she is also editor of the union's monthly publication, *The Overture*. Widely recognized as a Los Angeles trade union movement leader, she also serves on a number of community boards and councils.[309]

In those days, the musicians' union had an "advancement fund." Musicians would get a voucher on the job which they cashed at the union's Financial Office. Then the union would collect the money from the employers. Oftentimes, musicians would hang around the union office waiting for their vouchers to be disbursed. Serena worked in that office and Peggy came in regularly, to drop off contracts and cash her own vouchers.

Women Musicians during the War Years

In answer to the question of how the war affected her music career, bandleader-vocalist Ada Leonard, said, "Work became plentiful."[310]

Danny R. Johnson described the situation,

> In early war two the draft was ruining our band in the northeast. We started using gals and the business picked up three fold, our band improved four fold, and we ended up letting a very talented gal front the band, do the arranging, and hiring and firing as we handled the MC chores and promotion. We never had it so good.[311]

In the 1940s, Peggy's band played often at The Rice Bowl, a quality Chinese restaurant in Los Angeles's Chinatown. Located at 949 North Broadway, it was owned by two Chinese men, Ray Lewis and his brother. They had a band, sometimes with a singer and a dancer, for their floor-show entertainment. A dressing room, "the size of a phone booth," was shared by the acts and band members. A photograph of Peggy's band at The Rice Bowl shows Genevieve Howell, piano; Audrey Barnett, guitar; Kathleen McArtor, drums; and Peggy on saxophone. Pianist June Derry sometimes played with Peggy's band. According to a 1945 ad, "It's steeped in Oriental and Exotic atmosphere and the 'Temple Bar' is fast becoming the favorite bar of the city." In 1946, it was promoted as "America's most exotic Chinese restaurant in 'New Chinatown.'"

A photo of Peggy's band with a male ventriloquist and his "dummy" was taken in 1941 at The Club Hacienda in San Diego.[312] Mabel Hicks on trumpet and flugelhorn; Audrey Hall on saxophone, violin, vocals, and clarinet; Katy Cruise on saxophone, clarinet, vocals; piano was Patricia Olsen; Peg played sax, clarinet and vibes; Kathleen McArtor played drums; Dorothy Sauter, bass. The ventriloquist remains unidentified.

Just as Peggy's band might have been considered for recording sessions, the so-called Petrillo's War began. James Petrillo (1892–1984) was elected national president of the AFM in 1940. He was concerned that the popularity of sound recordings threatened the ability of musicians to make a decent living. Petrillo's War began in 1942 with a strike of musicians. They demanded not only to be paid for recording sessions, but also to receive royalties on the sale of the recordings. Beginning July 31, 1942, Petrillo instituted a national ban on phonograph recordings. AFM members refused to perform live on radio, except in connection with the war effort or government-sponsored broadcasts. The ban continued for two years, until record companies finally agreed to pay fixed royalties to the AFM.

These royalties were paid into the Music Performance Trust Fund (MPTF) and used to support live public music performances. This fund still exists today, supporting numerous performances in the community.

By 1942, the United States' involvement in World War II was well under way, and more women's bands were playing around Los Angeles. Because gas rationing limited most citizens to two gallons of gas weekly, one wonders how these musicians managed to play all over town in those years. Joyce Brown's orchestra played at the Morris Café; Ethel Sharpe's orchestra was at Rocky's Café; The Dixie Dean Orchestra was at the Chickadee Café; The Dody Jeshke Orchestra was at the Waldorf Cellar; The Dot Sauter Band was at the Wooden Shoe; The K. McArtor Band was at The Rice Bowl. The "leader" was the woman who got the gig and served as contractor for the rest of the band. Peggy said they often shared charts ("books"). There were also a number of individual women playing in clubs on piano, organ, or guitar. Pianist Lucille Silverstone, for example, performed with pianist Judy Winsor at the Brown Derby, and pianist Vivian McKenzie played at the Broadway Ace.[313]

Most of the men's bands were "second string," led by older men who could not perform military service. The union women instrumentalists who wanted to work during the war had many opportunities. These women knew one another and played together, including on tour in other parts of the country or in Canada. Although there was healthy competition among them, cooperation was the norm, due to the long-term friendships and camaraderie of being female in the male-dominated entertainment business.

For administrative purposes, Local 47 divided Los Angeles into districts: No. 1 was Metropolitan Los Angeles (Downtown); No. 2, Hollywood and Glendale; No. 3, South and Southeast Los Angeles; No. 4, Pasadena, the Alhambra area, and Chinatown, and the Plaza area; No. 5, Beverly Hills, Culver City, and Santa Monica; No. 6, the Los Angeles Harbor area, Redondo, and Catalina Island. The Local 767 "district" encompassed all the black venues, including many jazz clubs and Central Avenue, regardless of location. In those days, Los Angeles was very much a segregated city.

Peggy Gilbert, c.1935.

Women in Symphonic Music

The Pan-Pacific Woman's Orchestra was founded by Englishman Dr. Leonard Walker in 1941. The Los Angeles Women's Symphony, under the direction of Ruth Haroldson in the 1940s, was giving seven or eight concerts a year. Dr. Walker started an orchestra from among professional women musicians working in film and radio orchestras, with the help of violist Mae Gates Pepper. They made a special arrangement with the Musicians Union to give four concerts, in order to build its reputation. The first concert took place on October 22, 1941, at the Ebell Theater, presented by the Ebell Club's Music section. The program included works by Coleridge-Taylor, Berlioz, Rossini, Respighi, Rimsky-Korsakov, and Handel.[314] After doing a series of concerts for the Los Angeles Public Schools, the orchestra folded. Many of the musicians who played in this orchestra were among those Peggy had contracted for films, including *The Great Waltz*. The orchestra's demise may have been due to the fact that women were replacing men in the city's orchestras, as the war began. According to Ruth Haroldson, "During the war years women were admitted to symphony orchestras in a ratio of one to seven."[315]

In the early 1940s, KFAC radio had a program called "Women Today," that regularly interviewed women in classical music. There were several successful women composers in Los Angeles, including Radie Britain (1897–1994), Elinor Remick Warren (1900–1991), and Mary Carr Moore (1873–1957); well known to the community, they were writing for orchestra and opera.[316]

CHAPTER VII
The Victory Belles and USO in Alaska

Peggy Gilbert went to work for Local 47 in 1941, where she was involved in the war effort. The Japanese attacked Pearl Harbor on December 7, 1941, and the next day the United States declared war on Japan. On December 11, 1941, Germany and Italy declared war on the United States. However, the first "peacetime" draft in the United States began on October 29, 1940.[317] Local 47 helped open the Hollywood Canteen to entertain the troops, sold war bonds, organized blood drives, took care of musicians from Local 47 in the armed forces with mail and care packages, and helped musician-soldiers take care of personal business before they went off to war. Grieving over the loss of her niece and nephew, Peggy found her work at Local 47 comforting.

Peggy staffed Local 47's War Bond Booth. The campaign for War Bonds, also called Defense Bonds, started in 1941 to help finance World War II; in five years the effort raised $185.7 billion. These zero-coupon bonds were sold at 75 percent of their face value in denominations from $10 to $100,000. The extensive advertising campaign to promote war bonds involved contributed ad space and airtime by many American companies, especially newspaper and radio stations.

It was part of Peggy's war-related duties at the union to place men musicians into military bands.

> Getting back to the job situation . . . the men were all in the service and a lot of them were playing in bands in the service. Because I happened to be the person down at Local 47 when that first started, that was getting the men jobs in the bands. I would go down there and sit all day long and contact bands all over town here. The bandleaders and everybody who were in the

> service and ask if they had room for a trumpet player, if they had room for a brass player, and then they would send a request in for him and they would get right in there. You see, otherwise, they did not go through this business and take their chances.[318]

Each month, *The Overture* published a list of "Members of Local 47 in Military Service," as well as letters from members in the service, under the title, "Impressions of Enlisted Members." Covers of the magazine often had pictures of men in uniform. Local 47 mailed copies of *The Overture* to their servicemen members, including those overseas.

For the past seven years, Peggy's boyfriend and steady date was a man from the radio station that broadcast her band. He joined the military and, just before he was sent to the European front, they decided to get married in Las Vegas. The union magazine carried an announcement of the marriage in the "Personals" column, written by editor Frank D. Pendleton:

> Peggy Gilbert (sax, clarinet, vibs [sic]), member of Local No. 47 since May 27, 1929, and who has been even more favorably known for the past year as the pleasant little person in charge of the Directory Desk at headquarters in the Recording Secretary's Office, was not kidnapped, but on the spur of the moment, after a short courtship for only seven years, suddenly found herself in Las Vegas, Nevada, at 9 A.M. Sunday, June 28, 1942, the bride of James G. Wright.
>
> Mr. Wright has been radio technician for several years at KFI-KECA. He may be enlisted in the Navy Communications Division (radio) shortly.
>
> Peggy stands high in the music profession and had her own very successful girl's orchestra in Los Angeles and on the road for several years.
>
> The entire office personnel of Local 47 wish Mr. and Mrs. Wright the acme of happiness, and hope that Peggy will remain in the office as one of us "for the duration."[319]

Soon after the wedding, Jim went off to Europe, and Peggy continued to live with her mother, grandmother, and brother. The house seemed terribly empty without her niece and nephew. However, Peggy's mother loved to play cards, bingo, and other games, and managed to maintain a busy social life. Even during the war, there were parties and other social events at the family home.[320]

The Hollywood Canteen opened on October 3, 1942. It was founded by Bette Davis and John Garfield, with Jules Stein of the Music Corporation of America, for servicemen whose uniforms were their ticket into the club. According to *The Overture*, the Hollywood Canteen was "the House That Labor Built," having been created by a cooperative effort among fourteen local trade guilds and unions.[321] It was modeled after the Stage Door

Canteen in New York and visited by 20,000 to 30,000 servicemen each week. Located at 1451 Cahuenga Boulevard in an old red barn, it offered food and entertainment to servicemen. Hollywood stars volunteered to cook in the kitchen, wait on tables, and clean up. In 1944, Warner Bros. made a film about the Hollywood Canteen with an all-star cast, written and directed by Delmer Daves.[322] The Hollywood Canteen closed after V-J Day.

Peggy describes the fortuity for women musicians in the early forties:

> World War II probably offered a lot of opportunities to women musicians that they didn't have before because of prejudice.[323] I must say it. Women musicians were not used on radio stations much, even before television. They weren't in the staff bands, except for violins or something, harp, piano. So we finally had a little chance for recognition during . . . World War II. I was fortunate enough to have my band working. We worked ballrooms, we worked nightclubs. We worked everything. We were working all the time.[324]

Reveille with Beverly (1943)

Reveille with Beverly was a film made by Columbia Pictures in 1943, directed by Charles Barton and produced by Sam White. It starred Ann Miller as "Beverly Ross," along with William Wright, Dick Purcell, Franklin Panghorn, and Tim Ryan. "Beverly" hosts a 5:30 a.m. radio show with swing music, dedicated to local servicemen. Two friends of her brothers meet her and both fall in love with her: one is a wealthy man who sponsors the radio show and the other his chauffeur. Before she can decide whom to marry, they are both called up for active duty and go off to war.

The story is based on the real life of Jean Ruth Hay, who from 1941 until 1944 had such a radio program, six days a week. She played 78 rpm records of swing bands, awakening the servicemen with her sweet voice and music. As a young woman in Boulder, Colorado, she had heard friends stationed at Fort Logan, near Denver, talk about how they hated the buglers' morning wake-up at camp. So she went to the manager of Denver radio station KFEL 950 AM and offered a morning show for the troops. When she began broadcasting on October 21, 1941, it was an immediate success. She was featured in *Time* magazine and hired by KNX-CBS 1070 in Los Angeles. Beginning in May 1942, the Armed Forces Radio Services picked up her program and sent it to bases all over the world, waking up eleven million GIs in fifty-four countries.

After the war, Jean Ruth had a radio show in Santa Barbara and was the "Pillsbury Homemaker," eventually replaced by the "Pillsbury Doughboy."

She lived with her attorney husband, John Hay, in Northern California, and was a volunteer with Direct Relief, which sends medical supplies around the world. She died in 2004 at the age of eighty-seven.[325]

The film version of Jean Hay's radio career included cameo appearances by Bob Crosby and His Orchestra, Freddie Slack's Orchestra, vocalist Ella Mae Morse, Duke Ellington and His Orchestra, Count Basie and His Orchestra, Frank Sinatra,[326] The Mills Brothers, and The Radio Rogues. It was a low budget, high-grossing film. Among the songs heard in the film were "Night and Day," "Big Noise from Winnetka," "One O'Clock Jump," "Take the A Train," "Cow-cow Boogie," "Thumbs Up and V for Victory," "Lielito Lindo," and "Sweet Lucy Brown."[327]

Another program geared to the servicemen was Ona Munson's radio show for KNX, presented on Saturday evenings at 6 p.m. before a live audience. A smaller version of the Hollywood Canteen, her audience was packed with GIs and their families. Also appearing on the show was Jean Hay, as "Beverly Revielle," who at the time was also broadcasting on CBS in Los Angeles. The program was hilarious and very popular; one of its writers was actor and comedian Morey Amsterdam (1908–1996). Ona wanted an all-girl band, so she contacted Peggy to put a group together. Both the show and the band were called *The Victory Belles*.[328]

Ona Wolcott Munson was born in 1903 in Portland, Oregon. She earned fame as a singing and dancing ingenue in the original Broadway production of *No, No, Nanette* in 1925. She was also known for introducing the song, "You're the Cream in My Coffee." She enjoyed a successful radio and stage career in New York in the 1930s. Her first film was in 1928, and she continued her acting career through the forties. She played the tainted "Belle Watling" in *Gone with the Wind* (MGM, 1939), and was well-known for her deep, sexy, throaty voice. Many believed she was a lesbian, because of very public affairs with other Hollywood starlets, including Marlene Dietrich,[329] despite being married to director/songwriter Edward Buzzell in 1927 and to Stewart McDonald from 1941 to 1947. In 1949, she married the Russian-born neoromantic and surrealist painter Eugene Berman (1899–1972), with whom she lived in New York, until she committed suicide with an overdose of barbiturates.

> Among wartime contributions from CBS came an all-girl show called the Victory Belles in which girls would perform for troops at scattered military locations in California. As the bus carrying the Victory Belles arrived at a high desert training post some 5000 men gave us a warm heartfelt reception. After Beverly introduced the girls on the hurriedly constructed stage they each performed for our boys who would soon be shipping out. For the

> finale that Saturday night under the stars, Margaret Whiting performed a favorite song that she had been the first to record for Capital Records. To a hushed audience of homesick men she did "Moonlight in Vermont." What followed is the highest compliment a performer can earn . . . total silence for a long moment before wild applause rang out through the night. These memories would accompany our American troops to North Africa, now that their desert training was complete. The KNX Victory Belles also filled a Saturday night slot on the CBS Pacific Network. When broadcasting from studios or military bases all shows were sparked by the remarkable all girl Victory Belles band.[330]

Peggy Gilbert gives the following account of the Victory Belles:

> Ona Munson who was a movie star; she was in *Gone with the Wind*, you remember? And she had quite a little reputation at that time as a star and she had her own show on CBS. She wanted an all-girl jazz orchestra on it and so we got together. . . . There was actually no leader. A bunch of us just got together and said, "Here we are and this is it." . . . I was one of them and we were on that for a year. We had a weekly program. 1942, I think, right after the war started. We were at CBS in Hollywood. And what terrific audiences . . . they would bring the fellows in from all over the place around here, in uniform. And it was just a terrific show. I loved it. The girls were such fine musicians. They would cut the stuff. They'd put the arrangements in front of us just before we went on. We'd be lucky if we had time to go through it before the show started. We'd talk through it, usually, and maybe go through a couple of parts of it. And then, away we'd go. Accompanying acts and doing our own thing.
>
> We had some fine musicians. We had Jane Sager on trumpet; and we had Pee Wee [Naomi Preble] on trombone; . . . Katherine Cruise on first alto; I was on first tenor, clarinet, and vibes; Dody Jeshke, on drums; and Bee Turpin on piano. We had six or seven pieces, but all fine musicians. And we just cut those arrangements like nothing, sight-read them, right on the show. . . . I was real proud of that group. They were the best available in town at that time. We were there for a year. Besides playing shows, we'd go around to all the camps around town with that group. . . . And then finally we decided that we would go for some USO stuff.[331]

Peggy did not perform with the Victory Belles for many of their jobs, because she was working days at Local 47, but she did perform on the Saturday night broadcasts for nearly a year.[332] One of the air-checks from the Victory Belles, from December 12, 1942, is available from several sources.[333] It features "Victory Belles, Lurene Tuttle; Mabel Todd; Martha Mears,[334] Wilhelmina Gould, The Music Maids, Bee Turpin and Her Musical Jills of Jives.[335] Peggy says that it was not her playing the saxophone solo on the air-check recording from the December 1942 show; instead, she was playing vibes for The Victory Belles, and it was Audrey Hall playing the sax. The conductor and arranger was someone they called "Woody"; she thinks his last name was Woodman.[336]

Lurene Tuttle (1906–1986) is best known as the notorious busybody in 1950s and '60s television and film. She had her roots in vaudeville and went to radio during the Depression, known as "First Lady of Radio" and "Effie, Girl Friday" on *The Adventures of Sam Spade*. Later she was the sheriff's wife in *Psycho* (1960) and in the title role of *Ma Barker's Killer Brood* (1960). Mabel (Loomis) Todd (1907–1977) was a baby-voiced comedic radio actress who appeared in a variety of films in the 1930s and '40s.

Peggy remembers that Ona Munson was not in good health while the show was on the air, presumably in the beginning stages of the cancer that eventually caused her to take her own life. "Ona was a good person and very good to people who worked with her. She was a good boss." Peggy remembers that in 1945 or '46, Ona called her to visit her at the home which she shared with her mother, near the Pantages Theater in the Hollywood Hills. Ona gave Peggy all the transcription discs from the Victory Belles broadcasts. After helping to load them into the backseat of the car, she said, "Peggy, I'm going to say goodbye. I won't see you again. I know that," and then hugged her. Ona went to Italy with her husband, painter Eugene Berman, and died on February 11, 1955, at the age of fifty-one.

1944 USO Tour with Thelma White

By 1944, Peggy's husband was in Europe. She missed him, wanted to see him, and thought that if she signed up for the United Service Organization (USO), she could go to Europe and be with him, at least briefly. She turned her band over to Kathleen McArtor and prepared to leave town. According to Thelma White, they had to have twenty-one inoculations and several medical examinations before they could leave.[337]

Peggy provides the following account of the tour:

> So in 1944, six of us girls got together and we went to USO. . . . We did our whole show. They shipped us back to New York. We played a lot of camps [at] stations around New York and then we were supposed to be sent over to Europe where my husband was stationed at the time, in the signal corps and I thought, well, we'll get to see him, you know. Well, something happened over there and they shipped us all the way back here and then they sent us to Alaska . . . in the worst of winter. Terrible. Just before Christmas until the next spring, for six months. It was one of the most fantastic experiences of my life.[338]

A newspaper article entitled, "Six Maids in Review Due Here," announces that "Sweethearts in Review," would arrive next week "to entertain Ladd GIs." It lists members of the group as singer-comedienne Thelma White; singer-guitarist Frances Shelly[339]; acrobatic dancer Mitzie Martin; and a three-piece band with Peggy Gilbert, clarinet and saxophone; Peggy Russell, trumpet and drums; and June Derry, piano and accordion.

USO troupe in Alaska, 1944–45 *(left to right)*: Thelma White, Peggy Russell, Peggy Gilbert, June Derry, and Frances Shelly.

In the article, "Coming from Toronto, Canada to New York City, Miss Shelly stepped right into some of the best shows on Broadway," Mitzie Martin is described as "a tall, attractive dancer with brown eyes and auburn hair." About the band, it says, "Sweet and swingy tunes are the specialty of one of the best little bands touring, with Peggy Gilbert, Peggy Russell and June Derry giving with the jives. Peggy Gilbert has been on the stage since the age of eight, first as an actress and later as a performer on reed instruments, clarinet and saxophone." It goes on to describe Peggy Russell as "drummer and trumpeter, [who] has been actress, writer, and musician for nearly 20 years, starting as a small child. She has led her own all-girl band." It states that June Derry "got her start with Chicago school musical organizations . . . and has been playing in hotels, club and motion pictures on the West Coast for about 10 years."

Thelma White wrote in her memoirs that while they were "in camp" in Brooklyn, waiting to be deployed, "Peggy Gilbert let me slip in the middle of a burlesque dance routine. I landed on my right arm with a thud, breaking it at the wrist. For the next few weeks, I performed in a cast, which was extremely uncomfortable and chafed the skin until I bled, but it proved to be a wonderful prop for hospital shows."[340] Peggy tells the story differently: she says that Thelma had berated her for not "throwing" her hard enough during a routine, so Peggy gave it her best shot.

Peggy Russell, also known as Liz Rowland, was a trumpeter and drummer with Meta Moore's band and Peggy's big band, and also had her own band in Long Beach. On the Alaska USO tour, she was also Thelma White's "secretary-companion . . . giving me more loyalty and understanding than anyone I had ever known, except Mother."[341] She did a Louis Armstrong imitation, as part of her performance,[342] singing his signature piece, "I Can't Give You Anything But Love, Baby." After years of a severe drug problem, she died in jail.[343]

An undated newspaper article by Clifford Denny entitled, "Thrills, Tears Mingle in White Troupe's Tour of Aleutians," describes Thelma White's USO group as it was in 1944–45, having traveled more than 18,000 miles. Thelma is quoted as saying, "When they saw us . . . they placed their hands over their eyes and gasped. 'Oh, no, it just can't be. It's the loneliness that's getting us.' Never have I played before such an appreciative audience."

They traveled by train, jeep, truck, and small planes, one pilot and one girl musician in a plane. Peggy remembers that, at least once, they could not land in Anchorage because of bad weather and had to wait out the bad weather in a small cabin on an island, sitting on benches near a stove to keep warm. She was not afraid, because she knew that these were some of the best pilots in the world. Having had a pilot boyfriend in the 1930s who often took her, as well as her mother and grandmother, up in his two-seater plane, Peggy was comfortable in the air and loved flying.

Thelma White describes their Christmas tree: "We finally managed to salvage a mangled, moth-eaten tree. From colored paper, spangles from a dancer's costume, light bulbs lacquered with nail polish, and soap flakes, we made a Christmas tree that anyone would be proud of." Peggy drew a picture of this tree (see illustration) and commented, "That was the most unique Christmas I ever had!"[344]

This same article tells of the troupe's attempt to smuggle a Husky puppy back to the United States. They slept in a barracks which had been built on ground formerly used as a Japanese graveyard. "When the girls awoke each morning they would go to the door and view the grave marker of a Japanese colonel. According to Miss White, each girl would inspect the sign bearing the lettering, 'Col. Yamasaki,' and greet him with a cheery, 'Good morning, Colonel! Restful up here, isn't it?'" The article includes a photograph of Thelma wearing GI "longies," referred to as her "Aleutian Pin-Up Girl" picture.

Peggy's drawing of her trip to Alaska, Christmas 1944.

As part of the act, Peggy played the "Beer Barrel Polka" on two clarinets. She also sang and performed skits with the girls. It was such a small troupe that they all did a little of everything, constantly changing the show to ward off boredom, especially on days when they did six shows. The versatility of each member of the ensemble was its strength.

Actress and comedienne Thelma White had a long career in vaudeville. Born Thelma Wolpa in 1910 in Lincoln, Nebraska, her parents were Midwest carnival performers. By age two, she had become a member of the family act, billed as "Baby Dimples." At ten, she was part of The White Sisters, a popular singing and dancing group that toured the vaudeville circuit with Ziegfeld Follies and Earl Carroll Revues. In 1928, she signed with RKO and appeared in some two-reel talkies. In 1936, she was in two films at Paramount: *The Home* and *Forgotten Faces*. However, her appearance as the blonde vixen, "Mae Coleman," who pushes marijuana onto school children in *Tell Your*

Children (1936, later renamed *Reefer Madness*)[345] ruined her screen career. She claimed that on her USO tour, she contracted a rare form of polio which left her crippled, forcing her to retire, although some doubt the credibility of this story.[346] In her autobiography, she admits to a severe drug problem in the 1940s and '50s. Eventually, she became a Hollywood agent—representing such stars as Robert Blake, James Coburn, Ann Jillian, Robert Fuller, and Delores Hart—and a film/TV producer. She died at the age of ninety-four on January 11, 2005, in Woodland Hills, California.

Peggy Gilbert describes their USO experience:

> That was one of the most fantastic trips; I think I should never forget what happened—six months entertaining the boys that were stationed up in Alaska during World War II. It was a challenge as well as a wonderful experience. I think how we ever got through it and made it was remarkable. They didn't have girls up there before that. . . . There were six of us and no men. We put on the whole show. The reason we did that was because we played a lot of hospitals as well as auditoriums and we talked to the boys. We ate with the GIs. We went to the auditoriums with the GIs and played games with them sometimes.
>
> When we first got to Alaska, I had never ridden in a dogsled. Naturally, what did I know? I had come from California! What would I do with a dogsled? A guy came and he said, "Here's a sled. Would you like to take a ride?" The sled was only large enough for one or the most two people. He looked at me and said, "Are you game?" I said, "Sure," and he gave me a ride and he let me get out and stand on the runners. It was just a wonderful experience and more comfortable than you'd ever think. . . . That was my first dogsled ride and I think my last. I never got to do it again.
>
> We reached Anchorage, Alaska, just before Christmas and we had a couple of days off. We had been entertaining all the way up there from Edmonton, Canada. We had been playing for the boys in hospitals and camps. Anchorage was our home base. So, we reached Anchorage and we had a house instead of a Quonset hut[347] for the first time. . . . It didn't have much furniture in it but it looked great to us.
>
> So we said, "What are we going to do for Christmas?" Some of the girls said, "Let's go get a Christmas tree." So we got one of the fellows, a GI, to get a tree. There weren't any trees. It was Christmas time and we couldn't find any. So we cut a tree and we took it back. We got it home and we didn't have any decorations, so one of the girls—an acrobatic dancer [Mitzie] who practiced all the time on top of the table—said, "I'll make some things to hang on the tree, and practice at the same time." So that's what's she did. Thelma White, herself, who was the star of the show, sat on the floor and made out of jewelry little things to hang on the tree and stuck them with tape or anything she could find. We finally got a tree. We had a good Christmas. We entertained about six different hospitals on Christmas day. And that was fun. We ate with them. We had to stand in line with them.

But, I'll tell you, it was getting cold. Snow. We were more or less closed in and we were snowed in and couldn't go anywhere except where they'd take us, hospital ships or where the injured people, GIs were. . . . It took us about a half hour to dress because it was so cold our clothes weighed 40 pounds. They'd have to lift us in and out of the planes, because we couldn't walk up the steps, there was so much heft in the clothes. We had a wonderful time there. We met a lot of people we hadn't known were there. I kept bumping into musicians from Los Angeles all the time, who were in the service, every place we played. . . .

Alaska Nell[348] had a home there, a very modest home. She had a fishing line in the kitchen and she had a bell on it. And she threw it out to the dock and threw it out and when the bell would ring she had a fish on it. She'd go out and bring it in. . . . She was the first and only woman who delivered mail by dogsled. No matter what the day was, how much snow, how bad it was the mail had to be delivered. She did it, herself with her own dogs. She thought the world of those dogs. She worked for the government for years until she retired. She stayed there, she didn't want to go anywhere else, and she loved it. We met her and I got her book and she autographed it and I was so proud of that.[349]

My birthday was January 17. We just happened to have a Saturday night off. So we got one of the drivers to take us into town and they had planned a birthday party for me. They had it all set up in a special room. And we had a ball. They fixed a real nice dinner for us. We didn't realize that some of us were eating reindeer, and I had never eaten reindeer in my whole life. We had a good time. The girls all chipped in and got me a pair of earrings. It was fun.

Looking at this picture . . . sometimes we would be snowbound, for awhile in the Quonset hut, especially on the Aleutian Islands where it was very bad. We'd be snowbound for two or three days. We'd always got to the mess house. They would come and get us. They would have to shovel the snow to get to our door. One time they came and the door was solid snow so we called them. . . . They came to shovel us out. So we waited. Thelma thought she would warm us up so she started up the stove. There was an oil stove, some kind of oil. It ran out of oil. We didn't have anything to do with it. . . . The fellows took care of it. Thelma found a bunch of newspapers, tore them up and threw a match in there and we had a fire. It was the worse thing. We all got scared. We threw on some clothes real fast. The fellows got through and cleared the entrance. He came in with two buckets of water and slipped and fell and spilled the water on the floor and it froze because it was so cold by that time in there. That was an experience, I'll tell you.

We were hardly able to get to the mess room by ourselves. Sometimes they would have to come with three or four fellows and hold ropes and the wind was so bad and the mud was so bad and we'd hang onto the ropes and have to hold our head down, hold out mukluks and everything on. It was an experience. One time we made it into the room with the GI. We always separated when we got in. We all went to different areas, where we could

> talk to the fellows because they didn't see many people up there. Nobody would speak to us. And we wondered why. We finally found out that they were mad at us because we had come in late at night by plane and the officers took us to their house to rest and to have breakfast and then took us to our Quonset hut. They wouldn't talk to us because we were Officers' Material so they wouldn't talk to us. They banned us; however, they came to the show. That was OK.
>
> We had a drummer who played trumpet and sang like black jazz musician Louis Armstrong. We had a piano player. . . . The piano player was June Derry—pretty young girl, blonde, blue-eyed girl. She played a wild piano. She played the whole show, start to finish. Then they had me. I played two clarinets at the same time. Believe it or not. The "Beer Barrel Polka" with two clarinets. . . . This hand I had sprained my wrist and I couldn't hold my clarinet. I looked at the mic and saw a metal band on the bottom. It stuck out enough that I could put my clarinet against it. So, after my introduction, I ran out and put my clarinet on top of the mic, where this band was, and got a shock. It almost knocked me down. I stood there and played it and did the whole thing. I'll never forget that! That same night, we left for home and we left one of the instruments in the snow. A fellow forgot to put it in the van that he was driving. We got halfway there and looked over all the instruments and my sax wasn't there. I played sax and two clarinets and they were all in one case. I said we'd have to go back and, there it was, sitting there in the snow. So we got it. It was OK.[350]

Most of the girls on the USO tour did everything they could to sidestep the sexual overtures from officers. The officers would offer them unlimited alcoholic beverages, which Peggy says the girls often passed on to the enlisted men (who were restricted to soft drinks), by exchanging glasses with them. The girls managed to avoid the officers who themselves became too inebriated. She remembers several occasions when officers canceled performances for the troops and insisted on private parties with the girls. She also recalls playing pool, and often beating the Russian pilots who came to Alaska to pick up U.S. military planes.

PEGGY GILBERT'S ALASKA USO TOUR ITINERARY[351]

October 19, 1944	Hollywood to New York (by train); stayed at Century Hotel
December 9, 1944	Arrived in Edmonton, Alberta, Canada (by train, through Chicago and Winnipeg)
December 10, 1944	Railhead
December 11, 1944	Signal Corps Hospital

December 12, 1944	Edmonton Air Base; after evening show, flew in transport plane to Namao Air Base
December 13, 1944	Grand Prairie Air Base Fort St. John Air Base
December 16, 1944	Fort Nelson Air Base
December 17, 1944	Day off, rest at Watson Lake
December 18, 1944	Watson Lake Air Base; then to White Horse 2 days there, playing hospitals and camps
December 22, 1944	Arrived in Anchorage; stayed in comfortable little house
December 23, 1944	Bought Christmas tree in downtown Anchorage
December 24, 1944	Performed late Christmas Eve show
December 25, 1944	Christmas Day Show in Anchorage Went to Seward for 2 shows
January 1, 1945	Fort Richardson Hospital; USO Log Cabin in Anchorage
January 1–3, 1945	Hospitals in Anchorage area met Alaska Nellie
January 4 or 5?, 1945	Left Anchorage for Whittier
January 8, 1945	Whittier Fort Raymond Big Delta Tanacross Northway
February 6, 1945	Adak
March ?, 1945	Attu (stayed in Quonset huts) Snowbound there for weeks
March 22, 1945	Flew to Shemya
March 29?, 1945	Kiska
March 31, 1945	Last show before going to Amchitka Fort Meers Fort Randall

	Fort Greeley Naknek Fort Morrow Yakutat
May 12, 1945	Juneau
May 19, 1945	Annette Ketchikan Prince Rupert Seattle [8-day delay] Los Angeles

War in Europe ends; three months later Japan surrenders.

After she returned from the USO tour, Peggy had little to do with Thelma White and Peggy Russell.[352] However, she appeared in a "Soundie" with Thelma White's All-Girl Orchestra, recorded in 1946, performing "Hollywood Boogie."[353] "Soundies" were produced between 1940 and 1946, usually two to three minutes in length. They were intended for "visual" jukeboxes—16 mm rear-projection machines called Panorams—in bars, nightclubs, restaurants, and other public places.

Kay Boley

In October 1944, before going on tour with the USO, Peggy met contortionist Kay Boley at The Rice Bowl. Kay was performing on a bill with large marionettes, a Spanish dancer, and singer Wilma Wescott, a former child star and New York follies girl, with Peggy's band.[354]

Born in Chicago in 1917, Kay had gotten free dance lessons and dance shoes at the Flo Moray Dance School; by the time she was a teenager, she had begun a professional career as a dancer and contortionist. When they met, Kay and Peggy instantly became friends, as Peggy describes in 2005:

> Marriage, everything. Love. I was very fortunate. I met someone who was a very wonderful dancer and I played for her act here in Los Angeles. Her name was Kay Boley. When she first came out here I had seen her act. And she was a wonderful contortionist and worked on a table. I was playing a show and opening the first night. We were having rehearsal. And here comes Kay and she had no place to stay. All of her folks are from New Orleans and she had no one out here, except a good friend of hers who wasn't going to stay, who was married. I said, "Why don't you come to our house," and she's

> been my partner ever since. I mean, we have lived together almost 60 years. It's almost unbelievable. She's been through all of this with me, practically. . . . I think friendship is one of the beautiful things you can be lucky enough to have. I think friends are so important to your life, but in order to have friends, you have to be one. That goes both ways.[355]

In the band were Audrey Barnett, guitar; Kathleen McArtor, drums; and Annis Elliott, piano.[356] While Peggy was in Alaska, Kay toured Hawaii with E. K. Fernandez's organization.[357] While there, she bought Peggy the brooch seen in a photograph taken in 1945 *(see page 129)*. When Peggy returned from the USO tour, there was a big party to celebrate.

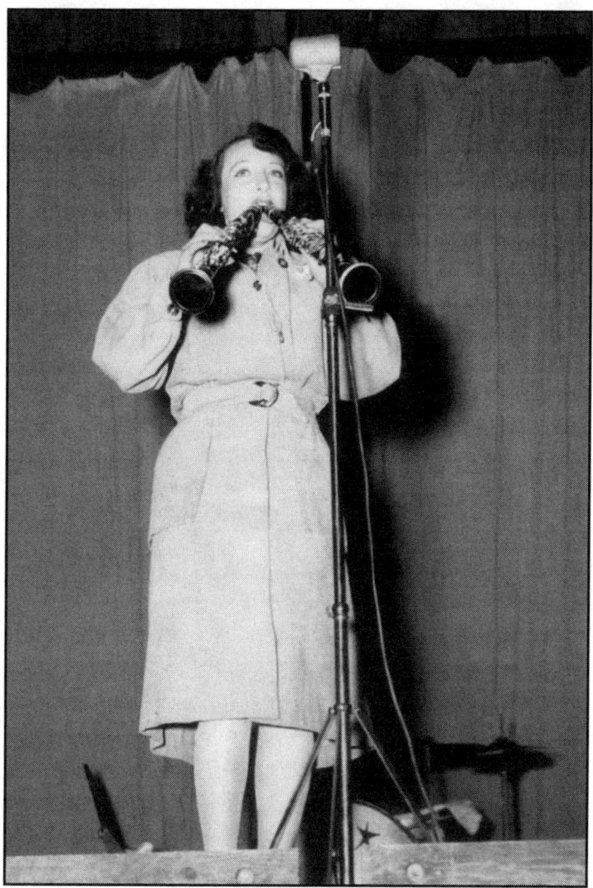

Peggy Gilbert playing two clarinets at once in her USO show.

Peggy Gilbert's partner of more than sixty years, Kay Boley, wearing costumes from her stage show as a dancer *(above)* and as a contortionist *(below)*, early 1940s. Courtesy Kay Boley.

CHAPTER VIII
Back to Work at Local 47

When the United Nations was founded at a meeting of fifty nations in San Francisco on April 25, 1945, the United States Senate promptly ratified the plan. More than 16 million Americans had served during World War II; 600,000 returned wounded and the country was anxious to recover. The Cold War became the most important political issue in the postwar period. Although the United States and Soviet Union of Socialist Republics had been allies during World War II, antagonisms surfaced at war's end. Germany was divided, with the East put under the control of the Soviets, and the West under British, French, and American occupation. In the spring of 1948, the Soviets sealed off East Germany from the West, a blockage that lasted until May 1949. Containment of the Soviet Union became a U.S. priority and focus of the Truman Doctrine. The Marshall Plan created the North Atlantic Treaty Organization (NATO); arms control became the main thrust of U.S. national security policy. The United States got involved in the problems in Asia; the Korean War (1950–53) involved armed conflict between the United States and China. Although Americans were more optimistic in the postwar years, everyone realized that the nation was not quite "out of the woods."

By war's end, Peggy was back in Los Angeles, trying to find work for her all-girl big band. She describes the postwar situation for women in music:

> But when the boys came back, that presented another story to the life of the girl musician, because we had to move over and let them take over where they left off. It was very evident to me, because I had my big band at the Figueroa Ballroom and I came to work one night and found the band in disarray. There had been somebody up there and the music was all over and

> the instruments were all out of order. Everything was a mess. I went to the owner of the Figueroa ballroom and said, "What happened?" And he said, "Oh, we just had Jimmy Grier's band in here. They are out of the service now and we're going to give them a job." I said, "I know, but we've got a contract." But he said, "They did their stuff for us, so now we have to do our stuff for them." So I said, "OK, girls, good-bye, we're out." We finished that week out and that's it. No notice. That's it. So Jimmy Grier's band came in. That's one of the things that presented itself. But at the time, everybody was feeling patriotic, so we did it. But that ended the era of a lot of work for girls, because the men had to have the jobs back.
>
> But it started another feeling. The men then realized that there were girl musicians who could play and sit on the bandstand with them. And play as well as they did, for the first time. Now the men's bands were taking in gals, exceptional musicians who were fine and they thought could hold up. They were giving them a chance to play in men's bands, which never happened before. And that's the result of all the work that the girls did while they were gone, where they came to the front and they heard them for the first time. They really heard them.[358]

The Figueroa Ballroom, located at Figueroa and Washington boulevards, was advertised extensively in 1945 and 1946 with the offer of "Free Cartons Cigarettes Every Tuesday."

> When we were thrown out of the Figueroa Ballroom, I was incensed to a certain extent and I thought that isn't right. So I thought I'd go to the musicians union. At that time, we were down on Georgia Street. I went before the board and said, "They can't do this." And they just laughed at me. And they wouldn't do a thing about it. They said, "That's all right, Peg. You know, after all now, that's ok, you gotta go along with it." So I didn't get any place. . . . Spike Wallace was the president at that time, a wonderful guy, terrific guy; he was also a marvelous trombone player, by the way. Well, anyway, so I went and spoke my piece down there, but I was still reminded of the fact that I wasn't considered a musician, but I was considered a woman first. A girl first. Now it's time to move over and let the men in. You see, that's it. That's the whole attitude of women musicians in the jazz field. It's not bad today, you've got a lot more going.[359]

Like "Rosie the Riveter,"[360] Peggy Gilbert and thousands of other women musicians lost their jobs after World War II. There is no doubt that the war changed the way in which women participated in American society, because they were called upon to fill roles not previously open to them. For the first time in American history, women joined the military.

However, after the war, a national propaganda campaign eased women out of the job market. What was a "girl" to do in mid-life, after a couple of decades of being independent and self-supporting? Some of them married and began families. Others found menial jobs in other fields.

Many women musicians gave up playing altogether. Women in symphonic music were also affected. According to Ruth Haroldson, "This year [1948] finds fewer women employed in major orchestras, with managers indicating that the ratio will soon be 1 to 20. . . . In a cross-country survey, managers give no definite reason for the current return to a 95 per cent male symphony except that, while their own particular conductors 'have no prejudice against women, naturally they will employ men instead if there is a choice.'"[361] Some women musicians could not handle the drastic changes in their lives and sank into depression, drug addiction, and alcoholism.

Those most affected by postwar discrimination against women were not the women in their teens and twenties, but rather those of Peggy's generation, who had lived independently and had successful careers before the war. This had prepared them for wartime duty, whether in the military or the USO, or working in factories. Peggy's generation was old enough to remember the sacrifices made during World War I; they knew how serious wartime duties could be.

For the first time in her life, Peggy could not find enough work to support herself. Jobs for women musicians continued to diminish. Further changes in the music business in the late 1940s and '50s aggravated the situation, as the Swing Era came to a close. Although she continued to play whenever possible and to organize her all-girl band to appear in films, Peggy went to work full-time for Local 47 of the musicians union, doing clerical work.

1947

Peggy expressed her concerns at the musicians' union, which responded in 1947 with a special issue of *The Overture* to celebrate the accomplishments of women in music. The cover featured "Evelyn and Her Violin," the wife of Phil Spitalny.[362] Next to a photo of Peggy Gilbert, the issue announced that, "*The Overture* plans another series of 'Women in Music' for a forthcoming issue. Those desiring to be represented in this feature, will please mail glossy prints to this magazine." In a two-page spread are photos of:

Elisabeth Waldo, violin

Kathryn Julye, harp

Henrietta Carrick

Pescha Kagan

Ted Bacon's Golden Strings: Georgia Mehra, Vivian Pesco, Janice Simmons, Thelma Beach, Ethel-Ann Reinig, Olga Mitana, Margaret Duncan, Gladys Johnston, Louise Friedhofer, Marion Bacon, Elizabeth Peterson, June Wiland, Dorothy Sauter, and Pearl Powers

Margit Hegedus, violin

Lora Temple, violin

Eileen Schaefer, harp

Women Musicians from the Los Angeles Philharmonic: Shibley Boyes, Phyllis Ross, Julia Malloy, Olga Mitana, Viola Wasterlain, Helen Tannenbaum, Doriot Anthony, Thelma Beach, Dixie Blackstone, and Geraldina Peterson

Lora Temple, violin, and Eileen Schaefer, harp

Women Musicians in Janssen Symphony Orchestra: Elizabeth Peterson, Claire Sheftel, Sylvia Ruderman, Harriet Payne, Davida Jackson, Barbara Putnam, Hilda Chazin, and Marcia Francis

Kathleen McArtor, Marie Ford, violin; Audrey Barnett, guitar; and Annis Elliott, piano,[363] at the Rice Bowl as "The 4 Graces"

Rangerettes: Cathy Redman, bass; Boots Lamoreaux, accordion; LaRaine Jensen, violin; Sally Salerno, guitar

Meryle Holmes, guitar; Ula Nainoa, guitar, uke, or steel guitar; Joyce Nainoa, bass

Nancy Barnes Kinsell, accordion

Betty Swanson; Joan Goddard, violin; and Barbara Murray, piano; as a classical trio

Irene Randall, violin; and Alice Nelson, accordion

A photo of a band called the "Hot Stove Five" was published in the May 1949 issue of *The Overture*: Dot Sauter, bass and leader; Audrey Hall, saxophone and violin; Audrey Barnett, guitar; Kathleen McArtor, drums; Dee Lane, piano; along with a photo of the Jacks and Jills, with Peggy Gilbert and Marnie Wells, trumpet and bass.

Peggy remembers that around 1947, she put together an all-girl band for Danny Thomas's first radio show in Hollywood, just after he arrived from Chicago. She believes it was on NBC, sponsored by a coffee company. She remembers a sixteen-piece big band in which she played bass clarinet; the conductor was Eliot Daniel, who later became president of Local 47.[364]

The Jacks and Jills

Because "of the lack of girl musicians available," Peggy organized the Jacks and Jills, a band with both men and women. An attractive photo of the group in front of a fireplace Peggy labeled at the Boise, Idaho, Officer's Club in 1942; however, the back of the photo is stamped: "Professional Photography by Witzel Studios, 1011 West Seventh Street, Los Angeles, California." The band included Marian "Marnie" Wells, trumpet and bass; Orval Knechtges Gilbert, drums; Gary Simmons, piano; and Peggy on vibes, clarinet, and vocals. It was booked throughout the 1940s by the William Morris Agency.

Peggy called her band "Jack and the Jills" whenever she had men playing in her band. She said she couldn't always get quality women musicians to play her gigs. This explains why the personnel is different in surviving photographs. For example, another photograph of the Jacks and Jills, dated April 7, 1944, taken by the house photographer at The Romantic 7-Seas Club in the Nevada Biltmore Hotel, in Las Vegas, shows Marnie Wells on trumpet; Phil Stewart on piano; Orval on drums; and Peggy on saxophone and vibes. The folder from the hotel states, "The romantic, alluring setting of the tropical 7-Seas Club featuring rain on the roof, exotic rum drinks, splendid music, dining, dancing and gaming."

Peggy Gilbert's The Jacks and Jills: Marnie Wells, trumpet, bass; Orval Gilbert, drums; Gary Simmons, piano; Peggy Gilbert, vibes, tenor, clarinet, vocals, c.1942.

The *Riverside Enterprise* of November 16, 1946, carries an advertisement for "The Jacks and Jills, Radio and Screen Artists featured on CBS 'Victory Belles' appearing at The Mission Inn. Dancing nightly except Sunday in Lea Lea Room." This photograph of the Jacks and Jills with palm trees shows Orval, Peggy, and Marnie. A photograph owned by Marnie Wells pictures: Lucille Hopper, guitar; Jack Kay, emcee; Orval Gilbert, drums; Marnie Wells, trumpet; G. Sharkey, piano; and Audrey Hall, saxophone and clarinet.

The Jacks and Jills played the Garden of Allah for nearly a year.[365] It is described in "Long Beach Pleasure Guide" for November 14–21, 1945:

> The mystic setting of the beautiful Garden of Allah brings after-dark pleasure seekers to within its walls for gay dinner-dancing and to pay homage to Peggy Gilbert and her "Jacks and Jills" who reign supreme in the art of supplying dance tempos to the enthusiastic customer. Continuous entertainment by versatile Phil Stewart at the "Novachord." No federal tax from 5:00 til 8:00 pm. 8th and Coast Highway. Seal Beach. Phone 802-19.[366]

One of her last gigs with the Jacks and the Jills was at the Mission Inn in Riverside. They played there in the 1950s, while she had a full-time job at Local 47.

Peggy remembers appearing in a 1949 United Artists film, directed by Gregg C. Talis and produced by Seymour Nebenzal Productions, called *Siren of Atlantis.* Maria Montez (1912–1951) stars as "Queen Antinea of Atlantis." In this film, based on Pierre Benoit's fantasy novel, *L'Atlantide,* Atlantis was located inside a mountain in the Sahara Desert. Peggy wore a dark wig and played an instrument like a marimba, but made with large bones, that sounded "absolutely horrible." When she came home from the shoot, it took hours to remove the Coppertone makeup. Maria Montez, born in the Dominican Republic, was known as "The Caribbean Cyclone." She was exotic and beautiful and appeared in many fantasy films in the 1940s, mostly at Universal.

Jazz was changing in the late 1940s. Charlie Parker (1920–1955) and Dizzy Gillespie (1917–1993) wanted to develop an alternative to big band swing music and came up with a "new jazz," called "bop" or "bebop," creating melodies from notes of the extended tertiary harmonies. Peggy's band seemed to be old-fashioned, when compared with bebop. Audiences stopped dancing to jazz and, instead, sat down to listen. Big bands began to disappear as small combos played smaller, more exclusive jazz clubs.

Further Changes in the Music Business

The Golden Age of Hollywood lasted from the late 1920s through the 1940s. The "studio system" involved thousands of people on salary—including actors and directors, stuntmen and cinematographers—and near assembly-line production of films. The studios owned theaters across the country that showed their films.

Two forces in the late 1940s converged to end the studio system. First, a federal anti-trust act separated film production from film exhibition. As a result of the anti-trust suit, the studios ended their staff contracts and began to make each film with a separate creative and technical team. Second, television's growing popularity ended film's dominance of the entertainment business. As the per-picture budgets increased, the number of movies being made decreased.

Peggy witnessed the studio system at work in Hollywood and, although she never was on contract at a studio, she often appeared as a sideliner, and contracted other women musicians to appear with her. Paramount Pictures' music contractor Phil Kahgan, for example, called Peggy whenever he needed women musicians on camera. Few women worked in the studio orchestras, with the notable exceptions of Eleanor Slatkin, Louise Steiner, Aida Muliera-Dagort, Dorothy Wade, Liliane Covington, Eudice Shapiro, and Dorothy Remsen. However, as the number of films made in the late 1940s and into the '50s decreased, there were fewer opportunities for Peggy and other women musicians to work, even as sideliners.

AFM president James Petrillo threatened another strike over television in 1948, when it appeared that the musicians would be paid only for the time spent recording, despite the fact that TV shows were distributed nationally and were recorded and rebroadcast. The recording companies stocked up on music to outlast the strike.

By 1949, however, Peggy was working full time at Local 47.[367] With her outstanding shorthand skills, she was much in demand as a secretary. She served on the Local 47 committee that built the Vine Street Building.[368] According to Serena Williams,

> In 1949, she was on the committee that decided to build this building [817 North Vine Street, Hollywood]. They had enough money in the union to pay cash for everything. They bought the land, and they put up this building. She was in on every plan. Spike Wallace was the President and he called her a little girl: "You don't know anything, little girl, sit down."[369]

Serena describes the day the building was dedicated, January 21, 1950:

> That was an amazing day. We had every known actor, musicians. There were twelve hours of intercontinental radio broadcast. Every room was filled with music. It was going on day and night. That's why the auditorium was built, in fact, for transcontinental radio broadcasts.[370]

Among those at the dedication were Bob Hope, Bing Crosby, Jimmy Durante, Phil Harris, Jack Kirkwood, Madelyn Russell, Hy Averback, Pat McGeehan, Ernie Newton, Jeff Alexander, and Lionel Barrymore. The American Federation of Radio Artists Chorus and a fifty-piece orchestra were conducted by Roy Bargy, Les Brown, Ferde Grofé, Paul Nero, Henry Russell, Walter Scharf, and John Scott Trotter. Dimitri Tiomkin conducted his "March [of the] Champion." A wide assortment of politicians was also on hand, along with two hundred Boy Scouts and fifty United States Marines.

The program booklet read:

> We dedicate this beautiful building not only to the advancement of music and musicians, but dedicate ourselves, as well, to that unity of purpose that alone safeguards our gains through unselfish service to our Local, our great American Federation of Musicians, and to the wonderful community in which we live.

Peggy was listed as one of the many masters of ceremonies for the dedication of the new building. Her all-girl band for the event, billed as the "All-Star Girl Dixieland Jazz Band," included Doris Pressler, trumpet; Annis Elliott, piano; Naomi "Pee Wee" Preble, trombone; Lenore Holcomb,[371] trombone. Jam sessions were presented throughout the building, including one led by Peggy Gilbert.[372]

LOCAL 47 PRESIDENTS, 1940–2007

1925–1932	J.W. Gillette
1933–1937	Frank D. Pendleton
1938–1939	Jack B. Tenney
1944–1950	J. K. "Spike" Wallace
1950–1956	John te Groen
1957–1958	Eliot Daniel
1959–1970	John V. Tranchitella
1971–1972	Keith Williams
1973–1982	Max Herman
1983–1984	Bob Manners
1985–1990	Bernie Fleischer
1991–1992	Max Herman
1993–1998	Bill Peterson
1999–present	Hal Espinosa

Los Angeles was growing rapidly, as a direct result of the Servicemembers' Readjustment Act of 1944, commonly known as the GI Bill of Rights. Thousands of homes were built in the San Fernando Valley to accommodate the veterans and their families. The GI Bill did much to reinvigorate U.S. economy throughout the country; its low-interest, zero-down-payment home loans for servicemen enabled millions of Americans to move out of urban apartments to the suburbs. The focus was on postwar recovery and renewal, rebuilding, and expansion. Between 1945 and 1960, the median family income in the United States doubled. More than two million veterans went to school on the GI Bill, leading to an expansion of universities across the country.

Peggy Gilbert, 1945.

Ada Leonard's band, early 1950s. Peggy Gilbert is in the front row on the far left. Courtesy of Frank J. Leonard.

CHAPTER IX
The Fifties and Sixties

Many women continued to find it difficult to adjust to postwar America, especially those who had worked and had been financially independent during the war years. The average annual salary in the 1950s was around $3,000; the U.S. population was 151,200,000. There were five men for every two women in the labor force. Many women musicians could not find work after the war and had to start new careers in more traditional "female" jobs. According to Peggy, "Many women I had performed with had drug and alcohol problems in the fifties. I guess they had trouble coping. Sometimes I had trouble coping . . . but at least I had a job at Local 47 and a home with Kay. I continued to perform evenings and weekends when asked."

In 1953, Peggy went to work for a barbeque manufacturing company in Burbank, California, as secretary to the president. Local 47 gave her a farewell party on September 11, 1953, and published an announcement in *The Overture* of her departure, "in order to accept a very fine position with a manufacturing and sales organization." However, she did not stay long in that position, returning to Local 47, where she worked until 1970. At the union, there were male jobs and female jobs. Men were officers, department heads, and supervisors; women were in clerical and secretarial positions.

Peggy and Kay moved from the Ardmore house that Peggy owned with her brother to Bloomfield Street in the San Fernando Valley. Eventually Peggy and Kay bought a house on Valjean Avenue in Van Nuys. They also invested in other real estate, including some rental properties and did quite well financially.

In her seminal book, *Women and Madness,*[373] Phyllis Chesler describes the rapid rise of the American psychiatric profession and expansion of the mental health system in the 1950s, primarily in an effort to help women through the adjustments made necessary by the new attitude about "woman's place" in society. Few women jazz musicians would fit the definition of "normal for a woman," during these decades.

The 1950s brought phenomenal economic growth and American society tried hard to develop a sense of uniformity. The transistor, invented in 1947, revolutionized communications. Additional technological advances in the 1950s and early '60s which improved life for Americans include penicillin, oral contraceptives, microwave ovens, audio books. In 1952 a polio vaccine was created by Dr. Jonas Salk. Also called infantile paralysis, polio was one of the most notorious diseases of the early twentieth century. The epidemic began in 1916 with 9,000 cases in New York City and 27,000 nationwide; by 1952, there were 57,628 cases of polio in the United States. The intense dread of polio was culpable. Public health officials imposed quarantine on homes where people were diagnosed with the disease. Peggy knew several musicians who had suffered from polio and were permanently crippled by the disease, including her friends Lona Bowman and Genevieve Howell, both pianists.

Drug use was another serious problem at that time among musicians, particularly in jazz. Drugs destroyed many lives and careers. It was well-documented among men jazz musicians—Charlie Parker, Fats Navarro, Chet Baker, Sonny Rollins, Miles Davis, John Coltrane, Stan Getz—but it was also an issue among women in jazz, such as Billie Holiday. Heroin and marijuana were the drugs of choice for the "beat" generation.

Musical styles continued to evolve. By the late 1950s, "bop" was declining and "free" jazz was in vogue. By this time, however, many women musicians of Peggy's generation were no longer performing. Dixieland jazz also continued to decline steadily. The "crooners" were popular, including Nat King Cole, Frank Sinatra, Perry Como, and Dinah Shore, and the music of George Gershwin continued to be appreciated.

PEGGY GILBERT: ON THE UNEQUAL PLAYING FIELD[374]

Peace and tranquility never moved nations or caused contracts to be signed.—and in the life of a female musician, "[p]eace" had nothing to do with it. The piece you play may not be the piece you get (or gave) for the privilege of doing so. I sit here with my insatiable memories of good times and bad times in the wonderful 30s, 40s, and 50s, when a girl musician could play theaters from coast to coast and back again,

> *plus nightclubs, movies, etc. The girl who desires to make the music part of show biz her profession today really has to be prepared for many surprises. Women's Lib and equal rights and a few other human rights have come upon the scene. Somehow, women musicians have always been classed thusly—not by her ability to technically pour out her soul through a musical instrument, but rather how she fills out a gown, whether her entire appearance is gorgeous enough to keep the patrons interested in her musicianship, rather than her short wardrobe. And last, but not least, will she go to bed with the agent or club owner or producer or even, in some situations, the auditor who writes the checks?*
>
> *So the ultimate answer is, if you don't cooperate with the "funsy" department you must look like Zsa Zsa Gabor, have a figure resembling Ann Margaret, a strikingly beautiful smile, wardrobe by the top designers, at the same time execute passages on your chosen instrument beyond all understanding or comprehension, not equal to any of the top, top recording artists in the industry, but far better. For example, one of the finest musicians in the jazz field throughout the years was bald, wore glasses, and had a pot that indicated he was eating well, indeed. He received raves throughout the entire continent because of his performance and teaching, but do you for one moment believe that this could happen to a female of like proportions? She wouldn't even get past the Secretary in the office.*

While she worked at the union, Local 47 insisted that Peggy seek approval for every performing job she wanted to take outside of her office duties. They "allowed" her to play saxophone on the Ada Leonard television show, as long as she did not miss daytime, office hours to do it.

Ada Leonard

As television developed, changes in public tastes and social priorities followed. According to Peggy,

> I had decided I was too old to be playing jazz. It was pretty ridiculous. I was standing up there and maybe being made fun of. I thought I'll never wind up this way, you know. So, I won't have my own group anymore, but if anyone calls me, I'll play. So I was working at the Musicians Union days.
>
> Ina Ray [Hutton] was over at the Paramount TV doing her thing. They had asked me to come over there and work with them and I had already taken the job at the union, so I couldn't. Then Ada Leonard came into town and she wanted me to come and work with her and said I wouldn't have to do any of the daytime things if I just do the show. . . . So I asked the

> union if I could, and they said yes, and I joined her group and we were on KTTV television show for a year. And she is another fine, fine lady, very fine conductor. She's a wonderful person to work for. I can't say enough good things about her.[375]

KTTV, Channel 11 in Los Angeles, signed on the air on January 1, 1949; it was co-owned by the *Los Angeles Times* and CBS, the original Los Angeles affiliate of the CBS television network. In 1951, CBS sold its interest to the *Los Angeles Times*, which continued to own the station until 1963. Ada Leonard's show aired from 1952 to 1954. The theme song was "Sophisticated Lady." Peggy thinks that Ada's arranger for the TV show was "Woody," who also rehearsed the band.

When Peggy went before Local 47's board to seek permission to play Ada Leonard's TV show, they made "a big exception" in her case and allowed her to do it. She remembers that Ada had a great sense of rhythm and a sense of the right tempos. The show rehearsed at night and was broadcast live once a week. She remembers that, once when she was playing vibes, the head came off of the mallet and struck the bald head of a gentleman sitting in the audience. According to Peggy, Ada was elegant, but never pretentious. She was "real down to earth" and loved to fish and do ordinary things. Ada's mother made all of her costumes and traveled with Ada's band, as the wardrobe mistress. Peggy recalls that her first husband was her manager, when she worked alone as a "single."

"Autographed" postcard used to promote bandleader, singer, and actress Ada Leonard.

Ada Leonard was born on July 22, 1915, in Lawton, Oklahoma. She played both piano and cello, and sang. Her mother played piano, saxophone, violin, and had studied ballet; her father was an actor. Ada began performing at age three, along with her three siblings. When asked if she experienced discrimination as a female musician, Ada answered, "Yes, men refused to let me conduct them."[376]

In her early years, Ada was a vaudeville stripper. She had

gorgeous hazel eyes and a fabulous figure; she wore her long hair rolled up in a knot, pinned high on her head. She would remove her long gloves and her top to reveal a sequined bustier, but never anything more.[377] It was always tastefully done; she left the stage with the audience on their feet, demanding more, which of course, she never delivered.

Ada appeared in *Music for Madame* in 1937 (R.K.O.), as "Miss Goodwin," the bride. She also appeared as an uncredited actress in *Stage Door* (R.K.O., 1937), starring Katharine Hepburn. In addition, she was in the mystery *Forty Naughty Girls* (R.K.O., 1937) as "Lil," showgirl; in the comedy, *Meet the Missus* (R.K.O., 1937) as "Princess Zarina," stripper; and in *Behind the Headlines* (1937) [uncredited].

Ada's first all-girl band was called the "All-American Girls"; their agent was Al Borde and their first gig was in December 1940, at the State and Lake in Chicago. By November 1941, the sixteen-piece band became Unit 9 of the USO, which had been activated before the United States had entered World War II. They did two shows a day, six or seven days a week.[378]

Ada Leonard appears as herself in *My Dream Is Yours* (Warner Bros., 1949), starring Jack Carson and Doris Day;[379] and in *Connee Boswell and Ada Leonard* (Universal, 1952). Connee Boswell (1907–1976) was a singer, songwriter, composer, arranger, and actress, who had been paralyzed by polio at the age of three. With her sisters, Vet and Martha, The Boswell Sisters appeared in films, theater, radio, and recordings. Anita Aros played violin in this short, produced by Will Cowan (1911–1994).

An article about Ada Leonard in *The Overture* (April 1951) has the headline, "Search for Girls." At that time, she was on KTTV (Channel 11) every Thursday night from 8 to 9 p.m. The article states, "The 'Ada Leonard' show has the unique distinction of being sponsored 24 hours after it was previewed at the Earl Carroll Theater by the Western-Holly Stove Co., not only for its entertainment value, but because it spells C-L-A-S-S." The show was recorded at the Century Theater on La Cienega Boulevard before a live audience of five hundred.

In the 1940s, Ada's band included Jo Ella Wright, piano; Mildred Springer, bass and vocals; Helen Ireland, second alto and clarinet; Maxine Bleming,[380] drums; Evelyn Pennak, baritone sax; Evelyn Campbell, tenor; Marge Stafford, alto; Jackie Walters, alto; Peggy Gilbert, tenor and vibes; Fern Spaulding, trombone; as well as trumpeters Jane Sager,[381] Mary Demond,[382] Dorothy Lilly, Anita Sparkman, and Francis Rossiter.[383]

Peggy has identified the following musicians in a photograph of Ada Leonard's band from KTTV: Helen Kay, trumpet; Alice Oakason, drummer;

Eva Meyers, baritone sax; Virginia Darnell, tenor sax; Jackie Walters, alto sax; Peggy Gilbert, first alto and clarinet; Evelyn Pennak, baritone sax; Mildred Springer, bass and vocals; Lois Cronen, trombone.

Others who played with Ada's band include: Norma Carson, trumpet; Roz Cron,[384] saxophone, clarinet; Helen Day [Shuster], alto saxophone; Jenny Dudek, saxophones; Dolores Gomez, trumpet; Corky Hale, harp; Eunice "Johnny" Johnson, bass; Rita Kelly, piano; Betty Kidwell (Meriedeth), alto sax; Ethel Kirkpatrick Drehouse, instrument unknown; Fagle Liebman, drums and vocals; Betty Rosner,[385] saxophone; Fran Shirley, trumpet; Pat Stullkin, alto saxophone; Bernice Lobdell,[386] trumpet; and Norma Teagarden Friedlander, piano.[387]

Ada Leonard *(far right)* with the saxophone section from her KTTV television show *(left to right):* Peggy Gilbert, tenor; Evie Campbell, alto; Marge Stafford, alto; Helen Ireland, tenor; and Evelyn Pennak, baritone.

On a short musical film performance of Ada Leonard's band, Peggy can be seen and heard taking a solo on the tune, "Back Home in Indiana."[388] Ada Leonard married her second husband, Dr. Harold Bernstein, in 1956 and left the music business. They met while both were patients in a hospital.

In 1992, Peggy Gilbert, Kay Boley, and Evelyn Pennak organized a reunion of Ada's musicians at Peggy and Kay's home in Studio City.[389] When Ada had breast cancer, Peggy took her for her treatment sessions and was there for her to the end. She died of a heart attack on November 29, 1997, in Santa Monica. Peggy wrote the following obituary for her dear friend, published in *The Overture* (February 1998):

In Memoriam, Ada Leonard

> The "Sophisticated Lady" leader of her all-girl orchestra played an important role in the era of big bands during the 40s and 50s. She was the driving force in calling attention to the musical ability of the musicians in her band using the finest arrangers available at that time to bring out their individual talents.
>
> Ada Leonard was an exciting and beautiful leader who sang in a creative and delightful manner. Her sense of rhythm and freshness of style was unequaled. She was undeniably the "sophisticated lady."
>
> I was a member of her orchestra on her KTTV television show. The band was outstanding musically and she always featured many of us in the spotlight, performing "bits" and jazz solos. The year was 1952. Television was black and white and live—no tapes available.
>
> Ada Leonard was an extremely successful performer in theaters and night clubs long before she decided to lead a band. She was encouraged by her manager to give it a whirl. Her natural awareness of the audience and her instinct for choosing the finest musicians in order to receive a phenomenal performance led to another career. Her theme song was "Sophisticated Lady"[390] and her appearance in front of her band and personality plus was just that. Ada played theaters, ballrooms and night clubs and was performing on USO during World War II. She came to California, made a movie at RKO with her orchestra followed by a contract for her own weekly show on KTTV. At the same time she was booking "special appearances" and playing hotels and ballrooms. All musicians were members of Local 47 and I am indeed proud to have worked with her. She gave her utmost every time she picked up the baton and her style was working closely in collaboration with her musicians. We loved Ada Leonard, as a leader and as a friend. Her loss was a tremendous shock to everyone who knew her.
>
> Ada, your beauty and talent will continue to live in the history of your profession and in the hearts of many.

In June 1963, Peggy and Kay bought the house in Studio City, in which they lived for more than four decades. They remodeled it to create a large room for band rehearsals, equipped with a grand piano and Peggy's vibraphone. Their home was open to dozens of friends and family members and they entertained generously, particularly on Thanksgiving, Christmas, and Easter, taking in musicians who did not have families with whom to spend their holidays.[391] They also owned a house at Big Bear, where they went fishing and entertained.

Over the years, Peggy and Kay owned dogs, which they adored. Peggy sent a picture of her Maltese terrier, a gift from trumpeter Marnie Hall, to the *Los Angeles Times*, which published it, saying the dog, "Little Sister," was "a ringer for Mr. Whiskers."[392]

Peggy also took up oil painting in the 1960s and exhibited in the annual Local 47 Musicians' Art Show. For many years, Peggy produced the art show. In one photograph, she is pictured with Ada Leonard, in front of a couple of her paintings.[393]

For the film *The Second Time Around* (1961), starring Debbie Reynolds as "Lucretia Rogers," Peggy organized a group of women musicians to appear in it. A production of Twentieth Century Fox, it was directed by Vincent Sherman and produced by Jack Cummings. The score is by Gerald Fried with a title song by Henry Mancini. Debbie Reynolds plays a young widow who moves from New York City to an Arizona town with her two children in 1912. A comedy/Western, she is appointed sheriff, and courted by Andy Griffith and Steve Forrest. The women musicians, dressed in early twentieth-century "Victorian" garb, march while playing their instruments, in a parade in support of Reynold's character to be elected as sheriff. Peggy remembers that Debbie Reynolds "hung out" with the women musicians and jammed with them on a French horn, a photograph of which was published in *The Overture*.[394] The other women musicians in this scene are: Jessie Bailey, trombone; Marnie Wells, trumpet; Mabel Hicks, mellophone; Dody Jeshke, drums; and Peggy, clarinet. The caption states that Debbie Reynolds "plays a mean 'Peck Horn.'"[395]

By the late 1950s, television had become the primary source of entertainment and information for Americans. It had a major impact on American cultural life with shows like *The Honeymooners*, *Lassie*, *Father Knows Best*, *The Adventures of Ozzie and Harriet*, *The Ed Sullivan Show*, and the daytime soap opera, *Guiding Light*. As a result of Americans spending more time in front of the TV than going out to dance or listen to music, there were even fewer jobs for musicians, both men and women.

This was a challenging time for the musicians union, as well, with many internal squabbles and outside enemies. The March 1956 issue of *The Overture* carried an article, "From the President's Desk—John te Groen, Illegal Attempt to Remove Me from Office. The Membership Has A Right to Know the Facts." Peggy was then secretary to John Tranchitella, who was vice president during this period.[396]

In 1957, Peggy served on the Night Club Committee for the union, chaired by Marl Young. She appears in a group photo under the headline, "Auditions a 'First' at Local." Another headline states, "Musicians Available for Employment Audition for Prospective Employers." Peggy is quoted as saying, in her usual upbeat, enthusiastic way, "Considering the fact that only one session has been held, the response was remarkable according to both the musicians participating and the representatives of purchasers of music."[397]

Many musicians left the AFM in 1958 and founded the Musicians Guild of America, which won the rights to negotiate major contracts with the Hollywood studios. Petrillo resigned and MGA members returned to the AFM in 1961. During this crisis, Peggy was secretary to the president of Local 47. West coast AFM members had a wildcat strike against the motion picture and television production companies, including 303 contracted musicians who demanded wage increases. New film productions and TV series went to Mexico and Italy, to shoot and record. Finally, the new contract guaranteed thirty-nine weeks of work at higher salaries, but eliminated payments to the Music Performance Trust Fund (MPTF). However, there would be five percent musicians' residuals from TV sales.

At the end of 1958 there was another walkout of AFM, against the recording business. It resulted in a new five-year contract, increase in wages from 30 to 47 percent. There were no longer payments to the MPTF, but a pension was established. Peggy's work at the union put her right in the middle of these dramas. By the end of the 1950s, the Hollywood studio system had collapsed. More films were made by independent studios and fewer people were "on contract."

In the 1950s, African Americans still struggled for equal rights and the end of segregation. Segregation was ruled illegal in the United States with the 1954 landmark Supreme Court decision in Brown v. Board of Education, which determined that separate is not equal. This was a major turning point in race relations in the United States; the decision set into motion sweeping changes in society. When Rosa Parks refused to give up her seat on an Atlanta bus in 1955, it fueled demonstrations and protests against segregation throughout the country. The Civil Rights Act of 1957 allowed federal intervention where blacks were denied the right to vote. One of Peggy's close friends at that time was African American pianist and recording artist Nellie Lutcher. Nellie was a key figure in building unity among black and white musicians in Los Angeles following the 1953 merger of Local 47 with Local 767, the black musicians' chapter.

Nellie Lutcher

Born in 1915 in Lake Charles, Louisiana, pianist and vocalist Nellie Lutcher started her professional career with her father's band. Her brother was also a musician, saxophonist Joe Woodman Lutcher. At age fourteen, Nellie accompanied the famous blues singer Ma Rainey. She moved to Los Angeles in 1947, and became known for her distinctive vocal phrasing and pronunciation. In her thirties, as the mother of three, she needed to support her family. She tells this story:

> My first record, an original, 'Hurry On Down' was a hit, fortunately. My second record release was an original, 'He's Real Gone Guy,' and luckily it was a hit. My third record was 'Fine Brown Frame,' which I did not write, but I rearranged, and it was a tremendous hit in 1948. In 1947, I was heard on a benefit show at Hollywood High School for the March of Dimes over KFWM Radio (at that time a music station), was heard by Dave Dexter, a Capital Records record producer who had heard me before. He contacted me for an interview and a contract resulted from this.[398]

Peggy Gilbert and Nellie Lutcher in Peggy's Studio City home.

With a piano style that combined jazz, boogie woogie, and blues, Nellie's songs appeared on pop, jazz, and "R&B" charts. By 1948, she was in demand in jazz rooms and supper clubs across North America. In 1952, her life story was made into a television special.

Nellie started to work for Local 47 in 1953, and became a close colleague and friend of Peggy's. She retired from performing in 1957, but continued to work for Local 47, playing a key role in the merger of Local 47 with Local 767.[399] She died in 2007.

Rock 'n' Roll

When Elvis Presley appeared on *The Ed Sullivan Show* in 1956, musicians of Peggy's generation knew that a new era in music had arrived, and that the swing and big band era was over. Many women who had played with Peggy over the years were very unhappy about rock and roll, with its prominent bass and percussion parts, use of the electric guitar, and amplification of the other instruments, suggestive lyrics, and its jerky and rough vocal style. They felt attacked from both sides: offended not only by rock and roll, but also by the abstract and harsh dissonance of *avant-garde* jazz.

The Soviets sent their satellite Sputnik into orbit in 1957, thereby launching the space age. American school children were subjected to "duck-and-cover drills," as the threat loomed of possible atomic attack from the Soviets and the Cold War continued to escalate. In 1958, the United States creates NASA to join the race for space. In response to the Soviets' launch of a man into orbit around the earth in 1961, President John F. Kennedy announced that Americans would walk on the moon. Space exploration thus became another area of competition between the United States and the Soviet Union.

Peggy was a guest on the TV show, Ralph Edwards's *This Is Your Life*, in an episode about Thelma White, which aired May 29, 1957. The show, which originally aired on NBC from 1952 to 1961, had begun in 1948 as a radio program. Host Ralph Edwards would ambush a celebrity or guest and present him or her with surprise narrative biography, complete with the appearances of family members, colleagues, friends, and other reunions. Initially, the show was aired live. Peggy was asked to describe their USO tour in Alaska. Also on the program was theater organist Gaylord Carter, whom Peggy had known for many decades in Los Angeles. Peggy recalls that Ralph Edwards was so impressed with her drawings of the Alaska tour that he made copies to give to the other participants on that broadcast.[400]

Peggy recalls attending Duke Ellington's birthday party:

> There were at least eight different homes where blacks would have pianos in their homes or organs. The party migrated from one home to another with Duke Ellington and all the musicians from all over the country. I was fortunate to be invited with my girls and we attended it. It was just fantastic. Musicians were jamming in every one of those houses. And you'd go from one to the other and take your instruments and jam with different groups. That was his sixtieth birthday.[401]

The Sixties

Fidel Castro became the dictator of Cuba in 1959, setting the stage for the "Cuban Missile Crisis" in 1962. The Soviet Union had installed nuclear missiles in Cuba. President Kennedy decided to create a quarantine to prevent Soviet ships from delivering more missiles to Cuba and he demanded that the missiles be removed. After a few very tense days, the weapons were removed. However, because the security and safety of Americans on U.S. soil had been undermined, many felt anxiety and trepidation about the country's future.

In 1963, Betty Friedan (1921–2006) published her provocative book, *The Feminine Mystique*, which launched the second wave of feminism. Advocating equal opportunities for women in music, Peggy had always refused second-hand citizenship in her personal life. She was accustomed to being in charge, making decisions, and getting things accomplished, without having to defer to a man.

By the time Peggy met Kay Boley, Peggy had had numerous boyfriends, both short-term and long-term, and had been engaged to a man who died before they could marry. She had married a man, only to discover that the marriage could not work for several reasons. She readily admits that one of her reasons for marriage when she was thirty-seven was the thought that it would be her last chance to have a baby of her own. However, by the end of World War II, Peggy was past childbearing age and had to give up her dream of ever having a child.

For Peggy's generation, it was not a question of "coming out." It was a question of making a relationship work and surviving together. Peggy and Kay would never forget the Great Depression and how easy it was to lose everything through a few missteps. As Peggy says about Kay, "She's been through all of this with me."[402] Focusing on how to manage as two "single" women in an age when the nuclear family was idolized, they thrived.

Peggy and Kay developed a partnership that met their personal and domestic needs. Both of them worked to pay for their dreams: home ownership and a secure retirement. Society easily accepts two older women sharing a home; it was practical and neither was a burden on their respective families. There was no presumption or discussion of a lesbian lifestyle; no one asked and no one would tell. Peggy and Kay have always been surrounded by friends and family, with traditional and alternative living arrangements; their relationship to each other was not a big concern for others. In their respective families, they are each called "Aunt."

Many women musicians of Peggy's generation had women partners or "dated" other women musicians. But Peggy believes that such relationships have had no more of an impact on women in the music business than heterosexual relationships. Certainly, some women and men have "slept their way to the top" of their profession, or married their way into positions of power.[403]

However, in Peggy and Kay's partnership, each contributes what their talents allowed. Kay always ran the household and cooked; Peggy used her business skills to make a good living. Kay's outside jobs were in more traditional "female" jobs, such as in a beauty shop or as hostess in a restaurant.

Later in her life, she did extensive volunteer work at Providence Saint Joseph Medical Center in Burbank. They were not inventing a new way of living, although they registered their domestic partnership, when that opportunity became available in California. Not supporters of gay marriage, nevertheless they believe that their partnership should provide equal benefits and the same protections enjoyed by married couples.

When President John F. Kennedy was assassinated in 1963, the nation was shocked. His successor, Lyndon B. Johnson, initiated a number of social reforms, called "The Great Society." The struggle for equal rights for black Americans continued, with Martin Luther King, Jr., articulating the shared hopes in his "I Have a Dream. . . " speech. The 1965 Los Angeles riots left the city trembling and weak-kneed; it was hard to believe that such a thing could happen in California. That same year, the United States sent troops to Vietnam, escalating the war there, as part of the country's effort to stop the spread of communism around the world. This launched a formidable antiwar movement, with demonstrations throughout the country protesting American involvement in the war and the military draft beginning in 1966.

As the jobs for musicians declined, Peggy concentrated her efforts at Local 47 on helping younger musicians. For many years, she was in charge of orientation sessions for new members; she also served on the Trial Board and on the Board of Directors.

Trumpeter Tony Horowitz provides the following portrait of Peggy at that time:

> Upon joining the musician's union in Los Angeles, Local 47, in 1963, at the age of seventeen, and still in high school, one of the first "adult" members I encountered was a wonderful one-stop shop of friendship, history of our business, and encouragement, in the body of then fiery female tenor sax playing dynamo, Peggy Gilbert. Her sparkling eyes, ready smile, and voice that could charm the horns off of a raging bull, were the window dressing of a lady who would become a true friend of mine for the next forty-plus years. Armed with her encouragement, "Go to it, kid!" and her unabashed enthusiasm that accompanies most young artists, I set out to fulfill my dreams and ambitions.[404]

Political turmoil continued throughout the United States. The assassination in 1968 of Martin Luther King, Jr., led to race riots in more than a hundred cities, coast to coast. That same year, Robert F. Kennedy was assassinated in Los Angeles at the Ambassador Hotel. Lyndon B. Johnson decided not to run for a second term as president and Richard Nixon was elected. This was also the year marking the invention of the video cassette recorder, a device that would revolutionize delivery of films and television programs. The next year, Neil Armstrong became the first man to walk on the moon.

Peggy's job at the union provided constant contact with younger musicians, who came to Hollywood to seek fame and fortune; to them, she was "hip." She was also extremely generous in giving new union members useful tips for successful careers. By all accounts, she was positive and encouraging. She went out of her way particularly to help women musicians. Many women musicians were told, "When you go to Hollywood, get it touch with Peggy Gilbert at Local 47. She'll help you get work." Her counterpart for women in symphonic music in Los Angeles was Ruth Haroldson, then conductor of the Los Angeles Women's Symphony.

Peggy continued to work for Local 47 throughout the 1960s. Beginning in 1959, she was executive secretary to President John V. Tranchitella. Although the union continued its policy of discouraging her from performing while holding this position, she occasionally did TV shows and motion picture calls.

On July 29, 1967, Peggy Gilbert was feted at Dublin's Food 'n' Fun Restaurant, with sixty "gals" from the "Girls Big Band Era"; an event organized by Billie Cutler and Jackie Walters. Billie described the occasion in *The Overture* as a "surprise tribute to one of the most loved and respected leaders of 'show biz'—Peggy Gilbert."[405]

> It was a day of true recollection and memory as the assembled "greats" relived the days when Radio was supreme and TV just a dream. All—and some still active in the business, gave testimony to Peg's great faith in the girl musicians whom she hired and helped through the dazzling days of great bands and glittering lights. There was laughter and tears mingled with emotional joy as the glasses were raised and the voices blended in her theme song, "Peg O' My Heart."
>
> Congratulatory flowers, letters and telegrams arrived from all parts of the United States, including Hawaii. For many, who had not seen each other or talked together for 25 to 30 years, the reunion proved to be a "lady-stag" gabfest. Hilarity was at its peak.[406]

The following year, on March 11, saw the death of Peggy's mother, Edith Knechtges, who had lived in a convalescent home during the last years of her life. She had survived her husband John by forty years.[407]

CHAPTER X
The Dixie Belles: "And Away We Go!"

Peggy retired from Local 47 on January 17, 1970, her sixty-fifth birthday. She would have preferred to continue working, but had reached the mandatory retirement age. She was also beginning to have a heart problem, which required medical attention. At the time of her retirement, Peggy was secretary to President Tranchitella. The union newspaper declared, "So Long to Peggy," with a photograph of Peggy holding a painting given to her as a parting gift. She is quoted in the caption as saying that she'll "rest a couple of months before going on to other things, probably in the entertainment management field."[408] Retirement was a difficult adjustment for her, after having worked continuously since her teenage years.

From 1972 to 1984, Peggy served on the Trial Board of Local 47, hearing disputes between union members and employers. In 1985, she was elected to serve as a Trustee of the Union and continued in this capacity until 1989.[409] Serena Williams says,

> I saw Peggy working on the Board. She wouldn't say much. She would listen. She wasn't appreciated as much as she should have been on the Board. It was the good-ole-boy school. She should have had a good pension, but she didn't. They said she wasn't in that category. She worked here for 22 years [on the staff] and they left her with a small monthly pension and that is unconscionable.[410]

Her pension was based on twenty-two years of continuous service, but did not include the time she had worked part-time in the 1940s. With such a small pension, it was clear that Peggy needed to work after retirement. Fortunately, she had done well in real estate and had an income from social security.

Peggy missed performing in front of live audiences, so she started The Dixie Belles in the early 1970s. She pinpoints 1974 as the date, but Marnie Wells and others remember performances as early as 1971. Their first gig was a benefit for an ailing musician who needed help with medical bills.

According to Peggy, "Most of the girls have raised their families. They had been playing all the time. All professional musicians. I worked with them off and on through the years. And finally, I said, 'Let's get together and see what happens.' So I invited them all over to my home one night for a jam session and we had so much fun, we said, 'Let's do it!' And we did." The jam sessions took place at Peggy's house and at the home of Jerrie Thill, perhaps over a period of a year before the band performed publicly. Peggy invited an agent to hear the band, who told her without hesitation that he could start booking the band immediately. Peggy came up with the name The Dixie Belles, remembering the great success of The Victory Belles in the 1940s. The group was a hit and started to perform regularly. As with every band Peggy led, she took care of decisions regarding repertoire, costumes, and contracts.

Peggy Gilbert and The Dixie Belles, 1970s *(front row, left to right):* "band boy" Bill Wells, Naomi Preble, Natalie Robin, Marnie Wells; *(back row, left to right):* Jerrie Thill, Georgia Shilling, Peggy Gilbert, and Feather Johnston.

When contacted by Peggy to play in The Dixie Belles, Marnie Wells was working in linens at Butler's department store in North Hollywood, her two children grown up. Drummer Jerrie Thill was a receptionist in a medical office. The original band also included trombone player Naomi Preble, whom Peggy had known since the 1920s.[411] Feather Johnston played bass. Later, Karen Donley[412] played bass with The Dixie Belles before Pearl Powers joined the group. At one point, Bonnie Janofsky played drums, although she was much too young to be a permanent member. Occasionally there were other "subs."

Peggy has always believed that:

> Women who are dedicated musicians in the jazz field as well as the classical field, or whatever field, I think women who are in music, who are really dedicated to the idea of being a musician will never, ever give up. And I hope they don't, because why shouldn't they be allowed to play all their lives as well as the men can? Just because they are women, when they reach a certain age, doesn't make them have to give up and hang their instrument on the wall.[413]

Howard Lucraft wrote an article for the *Los Angeles Times* (December 18, 1974), which included a review of the first concert performance of Peggy Gilbert and The Dixie Belles. "Other jazz was provided by tenorist Peggy Gilbert and Her Dixie Belles—six ladies attired in natty, colorful outfits with straw hats."[414] The performance was a part of Southern California Hot Jazz Society Silver Jubilee concert, which last six-and-a-half hours and involved fourteen bands, including more than a hundred musicians. The musicians donated their fees to musicians' union Local 47.

In 1975, Peggy put together a girls' band that appeared in *Long Last Love* (1975), starring Burt Reynolds and Cybill Shepherd. They "played" at a club dance. Peggy wears a gray wig and plays a clarinet. She started to promote The Dixie Belles for film and television appearances and was very successful at it.

A Women-in-Music Column for *The Overture*

How frustrating it must have been for Peggy in the late 1970s and early '80s to hear and read about all-girl bands and orchestras spawned by the women's liberation movement, then in full swing! This new generation of all-girl bands was promoted as if such a thing had never happened before: the solution to the problem of discrimination against women instrumentalists.

Yet the big band histories by Leo Walker[415] and others never even mentioned women instrumentalists.

Peggy's column in *The Overture* gave her a platform to voice her frustrations and to promote the professional women in music. In her first column, published in February 1979, she writes:

> Surprised? So was I when our Editor Marl Young suggested writing a column especially designed to let you know what is happening in the world of female musicians. To say that this is an extremely pleasant assignment for me is putting it mildly. I am delighted!
>
> "Are You Ready for a Live All Girl Band?" This is the headline I read in the *Valley Times* on February 6. I could hardly believe my eyes and eagerly scanned the review written by Bernard Beck (Bless his heart).
>
> First of all, it has been the assumption of the general public, and many booking agents as well, that "all-girl" bands went out with high button shoes. Be that as it may, the fact is that there has been and will always be successful female musicians in all fields of our business. The review captioned per above quote, was a beautifully-written article about a seven-piece orchestra called "New Miss Alice Stone Ladies Society Orchestra," and after reading about this instrumental group of talented entertainers and musicians, I knew the time was returning for all femme musicians to literally 'break out' again. . . . In each girl musician there is a bit of a rebel. I know, because I was one of the biggest rebels in my day—imposing upon the press to get equal billing for outstanding female musicians as compared to well-known and much publicized 'sidemen' in the big band era. So it is today—and let's take a new view of the entire field of women in music. You will be amazed to know who has been there, who is still there and who is coming into the scene today.[416]

Peggy also used her column to encourage musicians:

> Just as a last thought. The bias against women musicians, especially jazz oriented, is still much stronger than it should be in this day and age. Women musicians must actually learn to support each other and encourage one another to step out and be heard . . . a little confidence never hurt anyone, male or female. Without it, our sense of freedom in performance is lacking. Indeed we have more and better jazz stars in our midst today than ever before. Listen to one another and encourage your fellow femme musicians to let it all out![417]

This was not a new message for Peggy; this was her lifetime message for musicians, women and men. It was a natural extension of her advocacy work to write the column and promote women musicians. In total, she wrote sixty columns, the last one in January 1984. She also wrote many obituaries for her friends. In the last column she wrote, "The first thing learned as a professional entertainer is when to get off the stage."[418]

Peggy took on big band historians[419] Leo Walker and George Simon, as well as music critics, such as Leonard Feather. Her invaluable perspective represented the opinions of at least three generations of American women musicians:

> During my years at Local 47 as a playing musician and later as a secretary, it was my good fortune to have met and become personally acquainted with many of the brilliant, talented and dedicated femme musicians in the competitive fields of TV, Symphony, Opera, Motion Pictures and Recording. Our Local can truthfully boast to the world that we have within our ranks some of the most exciting and prominent women successfully performing in these areas.
>
> Competition in the past has been, to put it mildly . . . "fierce," . . . but as more and more extremely competent gals continue to invade this particular segment of our business, we find the old fantasy "Let's allow a few women in the orchestra to make it look good," is fast disappearing. Today, we are not only holding down first chairs in all sections, but performing as Contractors and Managers—and doing a great job![420]

In another column Peggy wrote,

> The joys of writing this column are many and I am truly grateful that in so doing I can bring attention to the gloriously talented and successful women in music today. It is inspiring to every young girl who intends making music her profession. It has been rewarding for me to know that discrimination is fast disappearing and the "powers that be" are realizing that a musician is a musician! Women in music no longer need to feel the hopelessness of "weaving a rope of sand" because the opportunities are here and they are surmountable.[421]

Peggy was baffled by the fact that few Los Angeles women musicians were documented in the jazz histories being published in the 1970s, '80s, and '90s, although they were heard internationally due to Los Angeles's status as the media capital of the world, especially in film. As Peggy would always say, "We were there!"

As a senior member of Local 47, Peggy served as a mentor to the younger generations. After being on the road with Louis Bellson, Jimmy Wakely, Ray Charles, Louis Prima, Lou Rawls and others, trumpet player Tony Horowitz returned to Los Angeles to work in the studios. In 1978, he started writing a monthly column for *The Overture* and was invited to serve on the Trial Board for the local:

> Peggy was a long time member of this august body of arbiters. I, of course, was a bit daunted by the company in which I was thrown. . . . Peggy handed me a copy of the Bylaws, and Constitution of the local and said, "Go to it, kid." I took her advice and studied it like a monk. After a while of our

> weekly meetings, hearing cases, weighing evidence, and decision making, I felt like I fit in with the others. One afternoon meeting that stands out in my mind was when we were hearing a rebuttal by a bandleader with whom I had dealt in the past. He was what we referred to as a "cheater." He would routinely underpay his musicians, and then threaten not to rehire them if they reported him to the union. As he went on and on in his manure-filled diatribe, I was becoming more and more incensed at his audacity.
>
> Keeping with decorum, I said nothing at this point, but tapped out in Morse code with my pen on the desk, S-H-I-T, which elicited no response from anyone but Peggy, who let out a yelp of laughter, which she attempted to cover by feigning a cough. Yes, unbeknownst to me, Peg understood Morse Code. This seemingly minor incident led us to more interactions at lunch breaks, as well as after the board ended its sessions.[422]

Peggy and Tony became good friends and together wrote songs for a musical she hoped to have produced, called *Chick Tap*. She had pitched it to Walt Disney, who liked it and promised to do it, but then he died a few weeks after their meeting. Peggy wrote the lyrics and Tony wrote some of the songs. Tony wrote a couple of songs for Peggy, performed regularly by The Dixie Belles, including "Peggy's Place," recorded on the compact disc and used in the documentary film, *Peggy Gilbert & Her All-Girl Band.*

CHICK TAP

A song with words and music by
Peggy Gilbert and Anthony Horowitz

Chick Tap, Chick Tap
All the kids love chick tap
You never saw a chicken with such feet
Got a heart of gold the world can't beat
Chick Tap, Chick tap.
All the Kids Love Chick Tap.

He's not a super hero.
He can't fly.
Just a dancin' chick, my oh my
Chick Tap, Chick Tap.[423]

Peggy Gilbert's Advocacy for Women Musicians

Not only did Peggy offer herself as a source of information and as a role model, but she often told women the secrets of success in the music business. In her July 1982 column, she wrote:

> Seldom, if ever, do I speak of 'rules' and the 'Union' in this column, but I feel it is necessary to make an observation at this time concerning femmes.
>
> I have fought for many years to have women musicians accepted as 'musicians' along with men. If this is true, please remember that it works both ways—we are NOT entitled to special concessions because we are women, and we must abide by the same rules within our Union as every other dues paying member. If you have a problem, before doing anything, call the Union and discuss it with your Business Rep—You will find it is much easier to work things out to everyone's advantage before the 'fall' than after everything has gone wrong. The Union belongs to every one of its dues paying members, and it is here for you to use. SO PLEASE DO![424]

She also used her *Overture* column to scold male music critics for their thoughtless and insulting comments about women jazz musicians. In 1980, she wrote about famous jazz critic Leonard Feather[425]:

> Leonard Feather, whom we all know and respect highly as a top jazz critic, must have been double parked to have had to resort to those old clichés in his review of Ruth Kissane's "Quintess" group when they played at Snooky's a few weeks ago. To me, it seems utterly archaic to compare female and male musician. . . . A musician is a musician. . . . Besides, have you ever heard the remark, "He plays as well as a girl"? I must admit, Leonard Feather has been a staunch supporter of many girl jazz musicians, and the fact that he went to hear them is gratifying. . . . But, I am convinced the only way an all-girl group can get a judgment of musicianship is either to blindfold the reviewer or work behind a screen! All of the musicians in that combo are fine, and I liked what I heard, which is superbly played jazz in good taste, without permeating the ozone with unrelated gems of dissonant sounds. Wow them in Kansas City [a reference to the Kansas City Women's Jazz Festival]—I know you will.[426]

In the 1970s, symphony orchestras like the New York Philharmonic began auditioning musicians behind a screen. Manager Nat Webster advised women to wear masculine shoes and stomp across the stage, to deceive the judges, in order to make it through the first round solely on merit. Proof that this behind-the-screen auditioning worked can be seen in the dramatic increase in the number of women and minorities hired in the 1980s.

The Eighties

Percussionist Judy Chilnick met Peggy in 1980, during the Musicians' Union Strike, where Peggy carried a sign on the picket line. Judy moved from

Connecticut to Los Angeles in the late 1970s and served with Peggy on the Board of Trustees of Local 47. Peggy was her mentor. Judy once remarked that she had thought her generation was a trailblazing one for women in music, but as she learned from Peggy about the struggle in the 1920s, '30s, and '40s—when women had to play, dance, and dress—Judy began to understand that Peggy's generation paved the way for women later in the twentieth century. Peggy has helped many musicians understand upon whose shoulders they stand professionally in Los Angeles and throughout the United States.

According to Judy, "As far as Peggy and the musicians' union, she was a champion from day one. Nothing was never in the contract. All of her musicians were well taken care of, got their pension, health and welfare and worked as union musicians."

Peggy continued to advocate union membership for all musicians. In 1988, she wrote:

> "I believe that musicians need their union more than any other members of the entertainment business. Others have agents. We have only the union. Many musicians don't realize what the union does for them. But I do. It is our mother, father, lawyer, accountant, booking agent. The union provides us with advice, practice studios, and helps us get work. It sets scales and does all negotiating for recordings for everybody including symphony players. Without the union we'd be working for practically nothing."[427]

In 1980, Peggy chaired a fundraising concert called the "Jazz Blowout," which raised more than $3,000 for the Musicians Strike Fund. Held at the auditorium of Local 47, it featured many well-known Los Angeles musicians and bands.[428]

Along with violist Lou Kievman, Peggy continued to work as a volunteer on Local 47's Congress of Strings. Developed from an idea of composer Roy Harris, dozens of young artists have received a boost from the project. The first Congress of Strings winner was violinist Ronald Goldman, in 1959. AFM sponsors a school open to string players between the ages of sixteen and twenty-three, taught by great string players and professional conductors. They are coached during this summer session.

A letter from Max Herman to Peggy dated March 3, 1983 states:

> I have just returned from Cincinnati, Ohio, where I was part of the A.F.M. Committee planning a celebration for the 25th Anniversary of the Congress of Strings.
>
> This is the most successful program that the A.F.M. has ever undertaken, with scholarship winners now performing as renowned soloists and members of many of our outstanding symphony orchestras.
>
> Local 47 has done more than any other local to make this program world

> renown, and YOU, ABOVE ANYONE, deserve the most praise, since you have been co-chairman for every audition since this program started!

By 1984, the 26th consecutive year, more than 150 students were sent from Local 47 to the Congress of String's annual event.

Throughout the late 1970s, '80s, and '90s, Peggy was active in the Pacific Pioneer Broadcasters. Founded in 1966, the purpose of the organization was to renew old friendships from earlier days and to pay tribute to great entertainers, writers, producers, directors, and others who have made important contributions to the history of radio and television.[429] Peggy attended their monthly luncheons at the Sportsman's Lodge in Sherman Oaks, where she met many others with long histories in the radio and entertainment business.

The Not-Ready-For-Retirement Band

The Dixie Belles began the decade on New Year's Day on the "Candy Man" float in the Pasadena Rose Parade. The float of the Baker, Confectionery and Tobacco Workers' Union was in the shape of a brightly colored tugboat, full of tasty treats. The Dixie Belles (Peggy, Marnie, Jerrie, Natalie, plus Feather Johnston and Ruth Kissane) played Dixieland jazz, as the float went down the parade route. Later that month, they performed at the American Legion Convention in Las Vegas, on a show organized by Bob Hope. There were two orchestras, one on each end of the large ballroom. For this event, Peggy hired extra musicians to play with The Dixie Belles.[430]

Performances with The Dixie Belles kept Peggy busy. They performed all over Southern California. They were regulars at several street fairs and festivals: they played the annual Los Angeles Street Scene Festival from 1978 until 1983, and appeared often at the Sunset Junction Street Fair in East Hollywood and the Santa Monica Art Fair.

The Dixie Belles frequently appeared at fundraising events, including benefits for The Women's Center, Planned Parenthood, and the National Organization for Women. They also played memorial services for other jazz musicians. In May 1981, Peggy's band played for the Bi-Centennial railroad celebration organized by Amtrak at Union Station in Los Angeles. This became an annual gig for The Dixie Belles. They were also regular guests for The Valley Dixieland Jazz Club, a nonprofit organization dedicated to the preservation of Dixieland Jazz.

On July 12, 1981, when The Dixie Belles performed at the Ambassador Auditorium in Pasadena, Local 47 Secretary Marl Young presented Peggy with a "Live Music Award" in recognition of her years of varied service to the local—as secretary to President Tranchitella, Trio Board member, cochairman of the Congress of Strings, coordinator of the Strike Benefit Concert held in Local 47's auditorium.[431] This concert was presented by the Ambassador Foundation and the Music Performance Trust Funds of the Recording Companies of America, in cooperation with Local 47. Mike Silverman's Hot Frogs Jumping Jazz Band was also on the program.

The Dixie Belles also played for Local 47's Dixieland Jamboree on August 2, 1981, again with the Hot Frogs Jumping Jazz Band, as well as the Resurrection Brass Band, Jake Porter's Jazz Band, and Andy Florio's Band Featuring "Zackie Cooper" [Jackie Walters], among others.

Peggy Gilbert and The Dixie Belles, 1980s *(left to right):* Marnie Wells, Natalie Robin, Pearl Powers, Peggy Gilbert, Georgia Shilling, and Jerrie Thill.

September 18, 1981, is the date of the band's appearance on *The Tonight Show Starring Johnny Carson*. Another guest on the show that night was actor Robert Blake.[432] In the band was Feather Johnston on bass and Naomi Preble on trombone, along with Natalie Robin, Marnie Wells, Georgia Shilling, and

Jerrie Thill. They played "Back Home in Indiana" and "If You Don't See Your Mama Every Night, You Can't See Your Mama at All." By choosing those pieces, Peggy was intentionally tweaking Johnny's nose, because his divorce had been announced in the press that day. Between tunes Peggy bantered with Johnny in an interview.

In November, they performed at a benefit, sponsored by Toyota, for the National Multiple Sclerosis Society. As master of ceremonies, Bob Hope referred to The Dixie Belles as "my groupies."[433] The program was entitled, "Vaudeville: A Contemporary Look at the Past." Also that month, they performed for the State of California Department of Transportation at the inauguration of the "Overnight Train" and at the Jazz Forum's 1981 Fall Festival of Jazz. In December, they performed at the Second Annual San Diego Holiday Bowl Dixieland Jazz Festival and at the Christmas Party for the County of Los Angeles Board of Supervisors.

Of their appearance in his city, *San Diego Union* music critic Bob Laurence wrote:

> The Belles, a group of ladies of advanced years togged out in candy-stripe blazers and straw boaters, were, in the words of saxophonist Peggy Gilbert, 'not too bad for a bunch of old gals.' Trumpeter Marny *(sic)* Wells played in a graceful, fluid style, and clarinetist Natalie Robin provided a lovely opening for "Just a Closer Walk with Thee."[434]

Jo Ann Baldinger began her 1981 article in the *Los Angeles Times* with: "Whatever it is that little old ladies are supposed to do, Peggy Gilbert, 76, isn't doing it."[435] This article was a boost for The Dixie Belles, coming a few weeks after their appearance on Johnny Carson's show.

In 1982, they played for the City of Los Angeles Street Scene Festival; Ambassador Auditorium and the City of Beverly Hills "Affaire in the Gardens." The next year, their engagements included the Eighteenth Annual Older Americans Recognition Day of the County of Los Angeles Department of Senior Citizens Affairs and a commercial for Coca-Cola.

Sometime in the early 1980s, writer Larry Gelbart (creator of *M.A.S.H.*) met Peggy Gilbert and started to work on a project about women jazz musicians in the 1930s, called "Jazz Babies." He met with Peggy many times to discuss the history of women jazz musicians and she generously shared many stories with him. For a while, he and film director Herbert Ross had a development deal for a film project, but it folded when the studio was sold. Marilyn Beck's column in the *Los Angeles Times* reported that "Gelbart was writing the script for [producer] Norman Jewison's 'Jazz Babies.'" Larry Gelbart's script is now in Special Collections of the UCLA Library.

PEGGY GILBERT: THE INJUSTICE OF IT ALL[436]

Many outstanding male horn players and jazzmen in the great days of vaudeville, ballrooms and night clubs, were no better and indeed not as good as some of the gals I met along the way and who have never had the opportunity to become nationally known through records—because nobody, and I mean absolutely nobody—would give them a chance. Why? Because they were girls.

The fact is that, regardless of how great a girl trumpet, trombone, sax, clarinet, drums, etc., played, first of all, she was female and had 99 strikes against her, because she wasn't born male. Her success was limited and not only because she was a femme but, in addition, if she failed to look like what most booking agents thought a girl musician should look like while she was blowing a horn—let's say for instance, if a trumpet player, being a gal, blew her cheeks out like Dizzy Gillespie—she could play like Gabriel, but she didn't get the job. Can you in your wildest imagination see a fat, buxom gal down in the spotlight blowing her cheeks out like Dizzy and wiping her brow like "Louis"? If you have been around in the days of the all-girl bands, I'll make a bet that you never saw a gal in the spotlite who looked like that. And yet, there may have been a few who got by, who were sitting in the back row of the orchestra but actually carried the entire section, because of her musical ability. But the gal who claimed the "cads" in the papers or had the publicity in interviews, was always the prettiest girl in the band.

And while we are on the subject, most of the leaders of all-girl bands were not really musicians, but were first glamour girls who waved a baton through the air, knowing not where the beat is, but where the meat is. She always depended almost entirely upon one of the girls in the band to actually give the down beat and cut offs, while she charmed the audience by wearing low cut gowns or in one instance wore a gown with solid sequined fish tails which she managed to sexily maneuver, while singing "Three Little Fishes on the Bottom of the Sea." The band played on and on, but the applause was thunderous and long for the contortions engaged by this particular girl bandleader, who had the audience literally in her frenzied fish tails. Maybe there were a few girl musicians sitting out in front during some shows who actually noticed what the band was doing and how well the musicians technically controlled their instruments, but I'll guarantee you, girl bands were never known for their musical ability, except by other female musicians, who gave credit to those who performed outstandingly on their respective instruments.

I may as well put it down for the record, here and now that many of the greatest and best were the gay girls. There were many reasons for this. First of all, the number one compliment ever passed on to a girl musician by a man, or for that matter, many women, too, was that "You really play well. You play just like a man!" I have heard lots of men say that I could have said, "You play just like a girl" and that would have been the most degrading and insulting remark I could have made. I only wish I could count the number of times the remark, "She's very good. She plays like a man," has been made. So, if you are a girl musician, who wants to be good, you have to play like a man—so if that is the case, then go all the way and act like one and maybe cut your hair short, wear men's shorts and men's slacks, men's shoes and develop a few male gestures, so there can be no doubt about it, "You play like a man." It not only gets you places on your horn, but helps you to go through the band with a feeling of superiority, because you can give the feminine members a reason for being there outside of decorating the bandstand while you carry the load.

"The Belles Are on Their Way"

Few bands offer the breadth of experience encompassed in the biographies of the individual members of The Dixie Belles.

Marian "Marnie" M. Elzea Wells was born in Lime Springs, Iowa, in 1915, and grew up in Minnesota. Beginning trumpet at the age of ten, she wanted to be a symphonic musician: "I used to play triple tongue solos by Herbert L. Clarke, including 'Carnival of Venice' by Arban. When I grew up and came to the realization that there were no women musicians in the symphonies [at that time], I turned to Jazz."[437] Also playing piano and bass, she performed with such groups as The Pepperettes, 1932–33; The Rosebuds, 1933–34; Al Miller Band, 1934–35; Nick Bolla Orchestra, 1935–37; Ina Ray Hutton, 1937–40; Rita Rio, 1939–40; Count Berni Vici, 1940–41; Sally Banning Orchestra, 1940–41; Peggy Gilbert Big Band and Peggy Gilbert's Jacks and Jills, 1941–47; and the Swingin' Mothers, 1960–61. Marnie appeared in the film *The Second Time Around* (1961), and played with The Dixie Belles from their inception (1971–86).[438] After marrying Wilfred Thomas Wells in 1947, she did not perform for thirteen years, while raising her children. Later in life, her husband served as "band boy" for The Dixie Belles in the 1970s and '80s. Marnie died in 2005.

Clarinetist, saxophonist, and oboist Natalie Robin (1919–1998)[439] moved to Los Angeles at age five from New York City. Her father was a furrier; her mother played piano; her sisters were also musicians: Lois Robbins (Isaacs) played trombone and bass with Count Berni Vici and Charlotte Robbins Reed was a trumpeter with Count Berni Vici and with Thelma White. Natalie started working professionally at age fifteen; her first tour was with "Blondes on Parade," which was stranded in Mexico and her parents had to send money to get her home. She joined Local 47 in 1940. Before becoming a founding member of The Dixie Belles, she played with Helen Morgan, Faith Bacon, Marie Wilson; Hollywood Ingenues, 1938–39; Ina Ray Hutton, 1939; Rita Rio's band, with whom her solo version of "Bolero" was a specialty number, 1939–41; Sally Banning, 1942–1943; Jimmie Medina-Barclay Allen, 1946–1948; Kay O'Grady, 1950; Jimmie Knepper, in 1954; Scott Man Brothers, 1960; Buddy Harper, 1978; and Bob Portugal, 1968–84, four nights a week for fifteen-and-a-half years in one club. Natalie married three times, including two trumpet players. Of discrimination because she was a woman, Natalie said: "Jealousy mostly. It's a dog-eat-dog business and they resented a woman taking their job."[440] She stopped playing clarinet only a week before she died.

Trombonist Naomi "Pee Wee" Lawson Preble (1904–1995) was born in Reynolds, Indiana. She joined Local 47 in 1927 and played with Peggy Gilbert's band at Club New Yorker; Phil Spitalny's band; and Ina Ray Hutton. She married trombonist Charlie Preble (1904–1978), who played with Woody Herman's band, and was a cousin to John Philip Sousa.

Pearl Powers—bassist, drummer, and vocalist—was born in Seattle in 1917 and grew up in Manitoba, Canada. She came to Los Angeles in the late 1930s and joined Local 42 in 1942 as a drummer. As a student of Herman Reinshagen, who retired as principal bassist of the New York Philharmonic to head the University of Southern California's bass department, she devoted herself to the string bass. Before joining The Dixie Belles, she performed with the Wild Ones at the Portofino Club in Redondo Beach; Ted Bacon's Golden Strings in the late 1940s; Four Guys and the Doll; Johnny David and the Catalinians in the Casino Ballroom at Catalina; and at Myron's Ballroom in Los Angeles. She also played in San Francisco, Tahoe, Las Vegas, and Reno. Of Icelandic heritage, she took an interest in her ancestors and traveled to Iceland several times. With her husband James Powers, she had three children. She died in 2005.[441]

Born in Dubuque, Iowa, in 1917, Jerrie Thill began playing the saxophone at age twelve, but stopped after being "kicked in the mouth at a club"[442] and took up the drums. She started her professional career at age eighteen, as leader of an all-girl swing band that played on the Pantages and Gus Sun Times vaudeville circuits.[443] Jerrie came to Los Angeles in the mid 1940s, and has been living in Studio City since 1963. She worked at Douglas Aircraft, and in gangster Mickey Cohen's club and at the Flamingo Night Club in Hollywood, 1945–52. In addition to The Dixie Belles, she played with the Hollywood Sweethearts; Danny Ferguson Society Orchestra, 1953–54; Ada Leonard's All-Girl Orchestra; and in the mid-1950s, The Biltmore Girls. She

Peggy Gilbert and The Dixie Belles

Peggy Gilbert, leader, saxophones, vibes, vocals

Marion "Marnie" M. Elzea Wells, trumpet

Natalie Robin, clarinet, saxophone, oboe

Georgia Cotner Shilling, piano

Pearl Powers, bass

Jerrie Thill, drums

Naomi "Pee Wee" Preble, trombone

Feather Johnston, bass

Karen Donley, bass

has survived two bouts with cancer, first at age thirty-eight and again at age eighty-one. Since 1985, Jerrie has played Sunday Jazz Brunch at El Cid's, 4212 Sunset Boulevard in Silverlake—originally built a century ago as the sound stage for D. W. Griffith's film *Birth of a Nation* (Epoch Producing Corp., 1915)—with trumpeter/flugelhornist Stacy Rowles and pianist Marty Harris.[444]

Georgia Cotner Shilling was born in Iowa in 1916, but raised in South Dakota. At the age of fifteen, she began playing piano professionally with an all-male dance band in Phoenix, Arizona, that was featured on radio station KTAR. She worked her way through college, training to be a music teacher, by playing in dance bands. Georgia came to Los Angeles in 1946, got married, and stopped playing for about ten years. She owned her own nightclub, where she played cocktail piano. The Dixie Belles is the only all-female band with whom Georgia has ever played. She continues to play weekly at Casey's Tavern in the San Fernando Valley, a gig she's had for twenty-five years.

The members of The Dixie Belles were interviewed as a group at the Tribute to the Pioneer Women Musicians in Los Angeles in 1986:[445]

> *Natalie Robin*: I knew Marnie back in 1938 with Rita Rio and that was a big band that played all over the country with Helen Morgan, Faith Bacon, Marie Wilson,[446] and Toby Wing. We did a lot of things together.
>
> *Marnie Wells:* Ada Leonard was with us.
>
> *Georgia Shilling*: I just met these ladies about 11 years ago. Peggy got a band together to play for a benefit for a musician and we all started playing together, never dreaming that we'd last ten or eleven years, but that's what happened.
>
> *Marnie:* I wanted to play in the school band, so that's why I took the trumpet up.
>
> *Natalie:* The clarinet. Benny Goodman. He was happening at the Palomar here.
>
> *Georgia:* I started real early. When I was about five I could play anything I heard. Then I took about seven years of classical and I finally ended up being a music teacher.
>
> *Jerrie Thill:* I play drums. I fell into them accidentally. Yeah, I started out on sax when I was a kid.
>
> *Pearl Powers:* I play the string bass. I always loved the sound of the bass and Benny Goodman, I must also admit inspired me to be a musician. It's pretty self-evident, isn't it? It is so enthusiastic and wonderful and we just have a lot of fun and make a lot of people happy.
>
> *Georgia:* This is the first time I've ever played with women. I always played with men's bands. And you have more in common with women, you know.

I was playing with the fellows in high school and college and I always felt kind of . . . you know, I was the only woman and I think, especially at that time, they looked down on girl musicians. This really has been great.

Marnie: Oh, I love playing with the girls. Peggy. I've worked with her in other groups. We've known each other for years and years since, well, in the forties.

Natalie: Well, we're all products of pre-women's lib. What can I say? But anyway, these girls are easy to get along with and they are a lot of fun to work with and they are all real good musicians and that makes life a ball.

REPERTOIRE LIST FOR PEGGY GILBERT AND THE DIXIE BELLES

A hand-written list (in Peggy's writing) of tunes performed by Peggy Gilbert and The Dixie Belles gives the following repertoire:

"[Put on Your] Old Gray Bonnet" (1909). Words by Stanley Murphy. Music by Percy Wenrich. Key of F. Vocal (by Peggy).

"Exactly Like You" (1930). Words by Dorothy Fields. Music by Jimmy McHugh. Key of C. Vocal by Jerrie (Thill).

"Out of Nowhere" (1931). Words by Edward Heyman. Music by Johnny Green. Key of G. Vocal (by Peggy).

"[Back] Home in Indiana" (1917). Words by Ballard MacDonald. Music by James Hanley. Key of F.

"On the Sunny Side [of the Street]" (1930). Words by Dorothy Fields. Music by Jimmy McHugh. Key of C. Vocal by Jerrie [Thill].

"[It's the] Talk of the Town" (1933). Words by Marty Symes and Al J. Neiburg. Music by Jerry Livingstone. Key of F. Peggy, Intro.

"The Darktown Strutters' Ball" (1917). Words and music by Shelton Brooks. Key of C.

"Charmaine" (1926). Words and music by Erno Rapee and Lew Pollack.

"Diane" (1927). Words and music by Erno Rapee and Lew Pollack.

"The Waltz You Saved for Me" (1930). Words by Gus Kahn. Music by Wayne King, Emil Flindt.

"For You" (1930). Words and music by Al Dubin and Joe Burke. Key of F; Key of E-flat. Vocal (by Peggy).

"Bugle Call Rag" (1916). Music by J. Hubert (Eubie) Blake, Carey Morgan. Intro in the Key of C; repeat in B-flat.

"Marie" (1928). Words and music by Irving Berlin. Key of B-flat. Vocal by Jerrie Thill.

"Tea for Two." Key of A-flat.

"Alexander's Ragtime Band" (1911). Words and music by Irving Berlin.

"Lulu's Back in Town" (1935). Words by Al Dubin. Music by Harry Warren. Key of F.

"The Birth of the Blues" (1926). Words by B. G. DeSylva, Lew Brown. Music by Ray Henderson. Jerrie voc. [Key of] C vocal; B-flat play.

"Sweet Georgia Brown" (1925). Words and music by Kenneth Case, Maceo Pinkard. [Key of] A-flat.

"I'm Gonna Sit Right Down and Write Myself a Letter" (1935). Words by Joe Young. Music by Fred E. Ahlert. [Key of] C orig.

Waltz [unknown].

"When My Sugar Walks Down the Street All the Birdies Go Tweet-Tweet-Tweet." (1924). Words and music by Irving Mills. [Key of] F.

"Ma! He's Making Eyes at Me" (1921). Words by Sidney Clare. Music by Con Conrad.

"Goody Goody" (1936). Words and music by Johnny Mercer, Matt Malneck. [Key of] C.

"When the Saints Go Marching In" (1896). Words by Katharine E. Purvis. Music by James M. Black. Key of F.

"Walkin' My Baby Back Home" (1930). Words and music by Roy Turk, Fred E. Ahlert, Harry Richman. Key of E-flat.

"Sweet Sue" (1928). Words by Will J. Harris. Music by Victor Young. Key of G.

"Don't Take Your Love" (1941). Words and music by Henry Nemo. Key of F.

"Honeysuckle Rose" (1929). Words by Andry Razaf. Music by Thomas "Fats" Waller. Key of F.

"At Sundown" (1927). Words and music by Walter Donaldson. [Key of] F.

"You Gotta See Your Mamma Ev'ry Night" (1923). Words and music by Billy Rose.

"B-flat Blues"

"Ol' Rockin' Chair" (1930). Words and music by Hoagy Carmichael.

"New Orleans." Key of F.

"Ain't She Sweet" (1927). Words and music by Jack Yellen and Milton Ager. flat Voc.

"It All Depends on You" (1926). Words and music by B. G. DeSylva, Lew Brown, Ray Henderson. Key of C.

On the reverse side, Peggy had written the following introduction for the band:

Welcome to the forties. Today we would like to jog your memories a bit—and for those who are a little bit younger, a short course of the War years. It was the time of Pearl Harbor, Gasoline Rationing, and Sugar Snaps—But we had Radio! President Roosevelt's "Fireside Chats" and "Call for Philip Morris-Who Dunit's," "Mr. District Attorney," "Sam Spade," "Dragnet," and the "Whistler." "I'd Walk a Mile for a Camel"—Then Drama shows—1st nighter and Big Town Among Many—Preferred by Millions . . . Old Golds . . . Family and Comedy Shows, Corlis Archer, Ozzie and Harriet, The Aldrich Family, Lum and Abner, "Fibber Magee and Molly," "Life of Riley," Bob Burns, Grace Allen and George Burns, Jack Benny, "Bob Hope and Duffy's Tavern" . . . a long time popular soap opera "One Man's Family" and "Lucky Strikes."

A change in office, President Truman and General MacArthur. Last, but not least, Kate Smith's "God Bless America." So . . . on with the show and the nostalgic years. . . . Let us begin with the Big Band Era.

Peggy always took pride in serving as emcee for her band. Her act was completely self-sufficient; she was in charge and everyone knew it. She was fun, yet dignified, always entertaining. Even though every detail was carefully prepared, she could improvise her way through any circumstance.

On August 19, 1982, The Dixie Belles recorded an episode of the television show, *Madame's Place*, a half-hour comedy series for Paramount television. In one scene, Peggy shows up to audition for "Madame," a notoriously ugly puppet, created by Wayland Flowers. Peggy plays the clarinet badly, but by a fluke the band is hired to perform anyway. Then she plays "Bill Bailey Won't You Please Come Home," and is a big hit. Dressed as "an old woman" in an antiquated outfit and hat that she would never wear in real life, Peggy reveals her solid talents as a comedic actress. This show was broadcast on September 23, 1982.[447]

Peggy Gilbert and The Dixie Belles[448] appeared on a number of television program, including an episode of *The Golden Girls* aired October 22, 1988. The Dixie Belles appear momentarily at the end of the show on *ABC's Funniest Home Videos,* which aired May 12, 1991. Peggy appeared on *You Bet Your Life*, which aired January 22, 1993. Peggy often wrote in the publicity materials for The Dixie Belles that, "Without a doubt, this group has received more television coverage every time they appear in public places than any group."

Peggy enjoyed the audience's first shock of seeing the band on stage—these lady musicians "of a certain age." She could see it on their faces, "Oh, no, a bunch of old ladies! How awful can this be?" Peggy made sure that the first number was upbeat and hot. She wanted to knock their socks off from the first note and the band always did. As soon as the band started to play, the audience would applaud and cheer: "Wow!" "What a band!" "Nothing old about 'em, but the tunes they play!"

Peggy's banter was flirtatious and filled with quips about old age and the aging process. She would egg the audience on: "Get out of that rocker, get up and let's dance. You're not dead yet!" Young and old alike loved the band.

Although The Dixie Belles continued to perform, they began to deal with health problems. Trombonist Naomi Preble had a stroke and died a few years later in a nursing home. Peggy could not find a senior female trombone player to replace Naomi, so they continued without one.

Peggy had to have a second heart surgery and sent The Dixie Belles out on jobs without her. In fact, Peggy and Kay spent much of their time in the late 1980s and '90s helping friends and family facing serious illnesses. They often picked up prescriptions and groceries and drove from home to home to assist people. They took people to their doctor's appointments; they visited friends and musicians in nursing homes and acted as advocates for their care. Kay became an expert on Medicare benefits and helped everyone take full advantage of what was available to them. In the 1980s, Kay suffered from depression, caused by grief over all her friends and family members who had died. In the late 1990s Peggy had a bout with colon cancer, but recovered fully from her surgery. Despite the problems, they did what they could and Peggy continued to perform.

Peggy's brother, Orval Knechtges Gilbert, lived in a nursing home during his last years. He died on February 2, 1988, at the age of eighty-seven.

Inter-Guild Women's Committee

In an attempt to address the lack of women in prominent management positions in the entertainment industry, the Inter-Guild Women's Committee was established. Serena Williams, representative for Local 47 of the AFM, wrote in *The Overture*: "The main reason for this group is to encourage females in all professions to aim for positions heretofore not available to the female sex. Great strides are being made and opportunities are opening up for those who are interested. Attend the meetings and meet interesting people."[449]

Along with AFM, there were representatives from AFTRA, SAG, SEG, AEA, DGA, and WGA in attendance, including Rhoda Williams, actress and member of AFTRA's women's Committee and vice president, Los Angeles Chapter of the Coalition of Labor Union Women; Rebecca Goldstein, co-chair of the Inter-Guild Women's Caucus and member of the Writers Guild of America Women's Committee.[450] They met at Local 47 on November 7, 1983, where Ann Patterson[451] and Maiden Voyage performed; at the next meeting, on January 16, 1984, Peggy Gilbert and The Dixie Belles entertained.

In September 1983, *The Overture* published a list of members of the "Women's Committee" of Local 47. It included Louise Baranger, Judy Chilnick, Roz Cron, Peggy Gilbert, Bonnie Janofsky, Debbie Jones, Nellie Lutcher, Niki Magee, Lydia Mather, Ann Patterson, Dorye Roettger, Roz Trotter, and Serena Kay Williams.[452] Among the many issues to consider were the fact that Local 47 was still sending letters to its membership addressed, "Dear Brother." Sexual harassment on gigs was an issue, as it is today. Having lived with discrimination and harassment during her entire career in Hollywood, Peggy was keen to see changes in the working conditions for women in the industry.

The Recording: *Peggy Gilbert and The Dixie Belles: Dixieland Jazz*

The Dixie Belles recorded their only album in 1986 for the Cambria Master Recording label. Recorded in a single two-hour session, it was originally released on LP, but was rereleased in 2006 on compact disc. Lance Bowling was executive producer; Jeannie Pool, producer; and Steve Barker, recording engineer. Peggy was delighted to have an opportunity to record The Dixie Belles, because she did not have a professional recording of her big band from the 1930s and '40s.

The recording was dedicated to Naomi "Pee Wee" Preble, trombonist for The Dixie Belle, who had a stroke the year before the recording session. Although Peggy hesitated to make the recording without a trombonist, she had not found anyone to replace Naomi, and so decided to dedicate the album to her.

It was recorded in Studio A of Pacifica Radio Station, KPFK, Los Angeles, in November 1985, with Peggy Gilbert, saxophone; Natalie Robin, clarinet; Marnie Wells, trumpet; Jerrie Thill, drums; Georgia Shilling, piano; and Pearl Powers, bass. Peggy sang on "Peggy's Place" and "Struttin' with some Barbeque." Although "When You're Smiling" was also recorded, it was not released on the original LP.[453] The session was only two hours long: the band played all the tunes twice, straight through, ate lunch, and left. Each take was slightly different. For a small label, the sales were good. Peggy often sold the LPs and cassettes at Dixie Belle performances.

CONTENTS OF LP:
PEGGY GILBERT AND THE DIXIE BELLES: DIXIELAND JAZZ

1. "Alexander's Ragtime Band"—Irving Berlin (3:50)
2. "Boogie ala Georgia"—Georgia Shilling (2:05)
3. "Sweet Georgia Brown"—Bernie, Pinkard, Casey (4:01)
4. "A Closer Walk With Thee"—Traditional (3:49)
5. "When The Saints Come Marching In"—Traditional (3:45)
6. "Jada"—Bob Carleton (4:12)
7. "Georgia on My Mind"—Hoagy Carmichael (5:16)
8. "Struttin' with Some Barbecue"—Lil Armstrong; Vocal: Peggy Gilbert, Lyric: Peggy Gilbert (5:16)
9. "Back Home in Indiana"—James Hanley (3:49)

All arrangements by Peggy Gilbert. All selections ASCAP.[454]

Luncheon to Honor the Pioneer Women of Los Angeles

On March 8, 1986, Jeannie Pool produced a luncheon and concert in "Tribute to the Pioneer Women Musicians of Los Angeles," held at the Ambassador Hotel in Los Angeles. It was a project of the International Institute for the Study of Women in Music at California State University Northridge Department of Music, codirected by Beverly Grigsby. The idea of the luncheon developed out of a research project funded by the California Council for the Humanities entitled, "The Story of the All-Women Orchestras of California," which documented the history of all-female ensembles in the state. In conversations with Peggy Gilbert, it became clear that there should be a reunion of women musicians. Peggy provided names of many of the jazz musicians to be honored at the event.

The program honored 106 women musicians active in Los Angeles in the 1920s, '30s, and '40s (see Appendix D). It featured performances of Peggy

Gilbert and The Dixie Belles, as well as Ann Patterson's Maiden Voyage, a seventeen-piece big jazz band. The event was the subject of an eleven-minute feature on the *McNeil-Lehrer NewsHour*, heard coast-to-coast on PBS, and in Los Angeles on KCET. The event was also covered on Cable News Network (CNN). In addition, there was coverage by veteran TV journalist Ruth Ashton Taylor at KCBS.[455] The event was broadcast live on KPFK Radio in Los Angeles, hosted by broadcasters Fred Hyatt and Ruthie Buell.[456] Music broadcaster and guitarist John Schneider was the event's emcee.

Here is a partial transcript of that broadcast:

> *Fred Hyatt:* This is Fred Hyatt live from the Tribute to Honor the Pioneer Women Musicians of Los Angeles and we are broadcasting from the Ambassador Hotel Ballroom. When I walked in here this afternoon, I got something I was really unprepared for and that was a tremendous rush of nostalgia, a tremendous rush of sentiment and I really had to fight back the tears. Every band you can think of, every instrumental soloist you can think of, with the rarest of exceptions, has been a male. True? But how many of the women instrumentalists come to mind? You know of some of the all-women, so-called all-girl, orchestras over the years. Ada Leonard, Ina Ray Hutton. There was a man named Phil Spitalny who had an all-girl orchestra for many years out of the Midwest. But how many, in terms of the excellence of the individual women instrumentalists, how many names come to mind? I can tell you that this ballroom [is filled] with qualified, capable, wondrous women musicians from times past and, as you are about to hear, times present, as well.
>
> *John Schneider:* First, I'd like to introduce Peggy Gilbert, saxophonist, big bandleader, active in Los Angeles since 1928. A one-woman network for women musicians in this city.

Peggy was greeted with enthusiastic applause. She said:

> Thank you very much. . . . Sit down everybody. I'm so happy to be here today and see all these smiling faces and a notice on the program that it says "Opening Statements, Welcoming Speech." How can I say welcome? This is one of the greatest things that has ever happened. I've never seen so many excellent, fine musicians together in one group in all my life. There just aren't any words to really explain it or to say it because emotions are running high today. I know that because mine are. My head is wet and I am about to shed my jackets and everything else, but this is . . . really. All right, if you want to take me back to the days we played for strippers, I'll go there, too. Ta-da! Anyway, I guess in my own small way, I'd like to say thank you for coming today and taking a part in this wonderful, wonderful celebration of Pioneer Women Musicians. I mean, this is the first time that this has ever happened, and I hope it won't be the last.

Ann Patterson's Maiden Voyage, an all-women's big band, performed at the luncheon, as the highlight of the event, with brass player Betty O'Hara[457] as featured soloist on "God Bless the Child." Ann Patterson, an accomplished, classically trained oboist, as well as jazz saxophonist and flute player, is active as a studio player and has appeared with many jazz bands. Since its founding in 1980, Maiden Voyage has appeared at the Playboy, Monterey, Concord, Tucson Primavera, and Jazz on the Rocks (Sedona) Jazz Festivals; at the Hollywood Bowl, as guests of the Los Angeles Philharmonic Orchestra; and on NBC's *The Tonight Show with Jay Leno*. The band toured Japan three times and has performed twice at the Kennedy Center's Mary Lou Williams Women in Jazz Festival. In recent years, Ann Patterson has become involved in jazz education and has taught at several universities.

The Dixie Belles played the opening reception for the event. As the honored guests, friends, and family arrived, they heard The Dixie Belles playing in the lobby. Peggy shouted out greetings to the special guests. Each "pioneer" received a red carnation corsage. After everyone was seated, John Schneider welcomed the guests. Sister Nancy Fierro delivered grace. Peggy presented Jeannie Pool with an award from Local 47, in appreciation for organizing the event. Ruthie Buell performed "I'm Not Getting Older, I'm Getting Better Baby," accompanying herself on guitar. During the luncheon, an all-girl classical wind trio performed, including Alice McGonigal, flute; Jenice Rosen, bassoon; Louise MacGillivray, horn.

John Schneider read a list of the honored guests, and each received a Certificate of Honor. Those unable to attend received their certificates in the mail. It was good that the event took place when it did—many of the women honored there died during the next decade. Only a few were still living twenty years later![458]

Late 1980s and 1990s

In 1986, veteran Los Angeles television personality Ruth Ashton Taylor asked Peggy, "Do you ever think of retiring?" Peggy answered, "Many times. I do. I've retired I don't know how many times. Then I get out the horn and away I go. It's crazy. You can't stop!"

In 1989, Peggy Gilbert and The Dixie Belles appeared in the internationally distributed *People Weekly* magazine. The article, with a photograph by Mark Sennet, comments on the fact that many audiences react to the band with "stunned surprise," because of the age of the players and the high quality of their performance, playing all the tunes from memory. By 1989, the band was averaging 150 jobs per year. Marnie Wells was quoted as saying, "I'll be okay as long as I have my teeth."[459]

Throughout her eighties and nineties, still an age-defying maverick, Peggy appeared in commercials for Coca-Cola, Kentucky Fried Chicken, HoneyBaked Ham, Suzuki Auto, Albertson's supermarkets, and Lucky Stores, among others. In 1997 or '98, Peggy is featured in a hilarious commercial for Ultimate Electronics, where she puts a compact disc into a toaster and causes a fire. Often she would show up for a casting call to be told they wanted an old woman and she was "too young."

On January 27, 1990, Peggy Gilbert and The Dixie Belles were featured on *ABC-TV World News Saturday*, with Jed Duval reporting. Peggy and The Dixie Belles appeared on the local Los Angeles television program, *The Home Show*, on October 29, 1990. Peggy was an extra in *Wings*, aired October 4, 1994. In an episode of *Dharma & Greg*, she plays Henry Mancini's "Baby Elephant Walk"[460] on a small upright piano, for a scene with seniors dancing in a retirement home, first aired on February 24, 1999.

The band also appeared on *Ellen* (starring Ellen DeGeneres). In this episode, aired on March 13, 1996, Ellen dons a Dixie Belles band member outfit and plays a triangle with the band. The Dixie Belles also recorded the last episode of *Life with Lucy*, called "World's Greatest Grandma," that was never aired. The Aaron Spelling sitcom, designed as Lucille Ball's "comeback," was canceled before this could be broadcast. The Dixie Belles perform at Lucy's granddaughter's school in a talent show.

Peggy is an extra in a *Lois & Clark: The New Adventures of Superman* episode aired on November 13, 1994. She is playing a slot machine in a casino and takes the winnings that "Lois" has left behind. Peggy was also in a Lucky Stores commercial that was taped on January 22, 1999, and broadcast many times that year.

On February 26, 1993, Peggy, Jerrie, Georgia, and Marnie appeared as "cheerleaders" in an episode of the television show, *Married ... with Children*. The episode, which aired March 14, is entitled, "Go for the Old." The character "Al" is mistaken for being sixty-five, so he takes revenge by using a senior citizen discount card and competing in senior athletic games. The "cheerleader" choir sings "The Star-Spangled Banner."

The Dixie Belles appeared on *Simon & Simon* on CBS, during the last ten minutes of the hour-long show.

During the last years of The Dixie Belles, Peggy drove her station wagon loaded full of equipment; she would pick up the girls who were no longer driving and take them to the gig. She eventually had to hire a driver[461] for the band. Finally, the logistics became so difficult that she had to stop booking the band, because the fees could not cover a driver as well as the rental of pianos and sound equipment.

Clarinetist Natalie Robin's death on March 30, 1998, marks the end of The Dixie Belles. Natalie played right up to the end, despite her oxygen tank. She took the oxygen tube out of her mouth and put in the clarinet, without hesitation. When they played the recording of "A Closer Walk with Thee" at her funeral, there were no dry eyes.

Peggy had just celebrated her ninety-third birthday and was being treated for colon cancer, from which she made a full recovery. The newsletter of the Pacific Pioneer Broadcasters states,

> Peggy Gilbert, Diamond Circle member recovering from the Big "C," is back in the field again and is working with her agent TGI on some new commercials, plus booking some future engagements with her group "The Dixie Belles" and "The Dixie Belles and Beaus." The 93-year-old Gilbert currently is completing a book she started many years ago. Should be interesting considering Peggy's history in the entertainment business which started in the 20s and encompasses theater, dance, radio, television, music and movies.[462]

Was Peggy considering adding men to The Dixie Belles? Perhaps, but she did not do it. She had been determined to keep performing, as long as possible:

> I never wanted to give up music. I thought about it often. I thought, someday, when I can't play anymore. I thought about it when I was thirty years old. In those days, they hired girls that were young and as good looking as possible and they didn't want you to play if your cheeks stuck out and didn't look as good as possible. They always wanted different musicians, but I always had a job. When I was on a job, I contacted other people to come and hear us. That's the way it was. I had to work. I couldn't do anything else. I didn't have a rich family to support me.
>
> There are many things I can't do now. I finally had to give up playing because we had to carry our horns, carry the speakers, carry the piano. Jazz has changed tremendously. You weren't just a player; all the hotels used to have pianos. Now if you want a good piano in a hotel for your act, you have to rent it. You have to pay the movers. Today very few hotels have bands.[463]

The Belles stopped performing after nearly twenty-four years. Some of the members continued to play Sunday brunch at El Cid's, but did not bill themselves as The Dixie Belles. Peggy also started to write her memoirs, but life intervened and she only managed to complete an introduction and part of the first chapter.[464]

CHAPTER XI
Celebrating the Nineties and Beyond

Peggy Fredericks, who had worked with Peggy Gilbert at Local 47, had been secretary to President Bernie Fleischer. She retired in 1988 and wrote a letter to Peggy Gilbert that expresses the feelings of many:

> Peggy Gilbert—a person I have always been proud to call my friend. She is not only a friend to musicians but to all who have known her—as a person who has been taking care of sick friends and doing all that she can for others all her life. Local 47 has always been proud of 'our Peg' who has worked tirelessly through Congress of Strings programs, her duties as a member of the Trial Board, Board of Directors, and helping establish office procedures (in fact she was the one, along with Phyllis Sherwood Welsch, who started the first Directory Office) and was in charge of the Music Performance Trust Funds at Local 47 for many years. From Georgia Street to Vine Street her praises have been sung (and rightfully so) because she doesn't have the word 'no' in her vocabulary when someone asks her to do something for them. Now and then we meet someone who makes life more worthwhile, who makes our journey brighter by the sunshine of a smile, who seems to understand us in a way few people do, and I met someone just like that on the day that I met you. I am sorry I could not be with you tonight Peg, but my heart and love are with you—a worthy, talented and dedicated person to the music industry—and my friend. Continued good health, happiness, and prosperity to you, Peg. Love Peg (The big one that is).[465]

Peggy Gilbert was a loving and supportive friend to all. Peggy was asked to tell the secret of living to one hundred years of age and she said:

> Well, the first thing that you have to think of as important is your health, so you can help others. The most important thing in this life is that you are here for a reason; and the reason you are here is to help other people who are not as fortunate as you are. All along the way that's what music did, that's

> what I was taught when I was growing up, to help other people. I think if you can get up every day and do one thing for someone else, that's your life. That's what you are here for.

That is how Peggy Gilbert lived her life. Judy Chilnick made the following observation about Peggy's home life:

> It is the most wonderful home and the circle of people she has always surrounded herself with was always evident when there was a get-together. She led by example and she and Kay always had a beautiful home. Musicians and non-musicians and people who have been in their lives forty and fifty years. Through it all and through what everyone goes through in their relationship, Peggy and Kay have always hung in and are a wonderful example for all of us.[466]

In 2005, Local 47 Vice President and saxophonist Vincent J. Trombetta told a story about Peggy that reveals her seriousness as a saxophonist, well into her nineties:

> I was playing an engagement about ten or eleven years ago and I knew that Peggy was there and that she is a big fan of saxophone players. She was intently listening to our quartet. At one point, once the job was over and I'm packing up my instruments, Peggy walks over to me and says, "I really like the sound you are getting. What's the mouthpiece you are using?" I say, "It's an Otto Link metal mouthpiece, resurfaced by Phil Barone in New York, a friend of mine." She says, "Well, how much does a mouthpiece like that cost?" "This mouthpiece probably runs in the $400 to $500 range." She walked away and I thought to myself, how interesting, to be in your nineties and to be asking what equipment someone is using because you want to purchase a new mouthpiece. It just put her on a different level for me. Not only is she wonderful as a person, but also as a musician. Most people in their fifties and sixties are not thinking about what new equipment they are going to use. And here she was in her nineties, researching new equipment. It showed not only a lot of character, but also the depth of her love for music and the art form that she tried to share with others over so many years.[467]

Peggy finally sold her beloved tenor saxophone when she was in her late nineties.

Peggy Gilbert's One Hundredth Birthday Party

On January 17, 2005, AFM Local 47 gave Peggy a one hundredth birthday party[468] in the same auditorium that she had helped to build back in 1949. Nearly 150 people attended, including family, friends, and neighbors. Los Angeles Councilwoman Wendy Gruell presented Peggy with a certificate from the City of Los Angeles; Ruth Ashton Taylor presented a proclamation from the California Legislature. The room was festively decorated with red and white balloons and red-and-white-checkered tablecloths. Red inflatable saxophones were used as centerpieces. There was a beautiful cake with a picture of Peggy playing her saxophone. One friend sent a hundred roses. Another arranged for her to be picked up in a limousine, served champagne, and taken to the party.

At the party, Peggy sang "It Had to Be You," accompanied by pianist Jack Hyatt. Her voice was clear and tuneful. When she blew out the birthday candles on her cake, she was asked, "For what did you wish?" She answered, "I wished that I would be 102. No older than that. 102."

Union Vice President Vince Trombetta talked about Peggy Gilbert and Lyle "Spud" Murphy, who had died in 2005:

> These are legendary figures, not only as musicians but as labor leaders. Her hard work, her trials and tribulations and all the issues she had to deal with, being a lady in the music business, is the reason this business still exists. I can't emphasize more that these people [like Peggy and Spud] planted the seed, and we're just the fruit on the vine. I think all of us are affected by their presence, whether they come in [to the union office] every day or once a month.[469]

Peggy was not one to nag younger people about the way things used to be done, but often reminded them of the basic principles at work in earlier times. She had a special knack for urging people to do the right thing. She was also very supportive, known to call staff members of Local 47 and congratulate them on their work, even when she did not know them personally. She read the minutes of board meetings and often called members to discuss certain issues. Even at age 102, her comments and suggestions were wise and welcomed.

Local 47 President Hal Espinosa praised Peggy:

> You are the epitome of a Local 47 member. You have accomplished more as a musician than we ever will in our lifetime. You have done everything in live performance field there is to do. You've been on television. You've been in movies. You've done everything!
>
> *Peggy:* And commercials.
>
> *Hal:* And commercials. Peggy, you make us all proud.

The audience applauded enthusiastically. Local 47 presented her with a special Musicians' Union jacket, embroidered, "Member since 1929."

Serena Williams told this story:

> Peggy had had a problem with her heart and she was back home, and my daughter Shelley and I went to visit her. Kay had her sitting there, all

propped up with pillows, with her hair done just so, and Peggy had makeup on, and she looked like a little Dresden doll. The phone rings and Kay answers the phone. And Peggy says, "Who is it?" Kay says, "You don't want to talk to them. They want to hire The Dixie Belles." Peggy says, "Let me talk."

So she gets the phone, and says, "Hello. So you want to hire The Dixie Belles? What was that date? Oh, just a minute, let me look at the book. . . Oh, I'm so sorry. We're already booked. In fact, we're booked for the next three months. Would you call me then and I will see if we can put something together then?"

Peggy Gilbert on her one hundredth birthday, January 17, 2005. Photo by Elliott Barker.

So when we have orientation for the new [union] members here, I tell this story and tell them, "Now, just remember. Don't tell them you're sick. Tell them you're booked."

Awards and Honors

Peggy has received many awards and honors in her long life.

On July 12, 1981, at the Dixie Belles' concert at Ambassador Auditorium in Pasadena, Local 47 presented Peggy with a "Live Music Award in recognition of her years of varied service to the local, including Secretary to President Tranchitella, Trial Board member, co-chairman of the Congress of Strings Auditions, coordinator of the Strike Benefit Concert held at Local 48 Auditorium."

Also in 1981, she received the Mayor's Certificate of Appreciation, signed by Mayor Tom Bradley:

> As Mayor of the City of Los Angeles, I am pleased to recognize the outstanding activities of Peggy Gilbert in support of the 1981 Los Angeles Street Scene Festival, Who is awarded this Mayor's Certificate of Appreciation for outstanding efforts and accomplishments which have been of great benefit to our community and particularly to the City of Los Angeles. Your community spirit and interest have helped make our City a better place in which to live, and have greatly assisted me in conducting the affairs of this City."

She received a similar one from the Mayor for her "longstanding commitment to the betterment of the visual and performing arts and for your support toward making the Los Angeles Street Scene Festival a showcase for performing artists.

On June 2, 1982, Peggy received the Bronze Halo Award of Special Merit from the Southern California Motion Picture Council, signed by Jean Daran, president; Bonnie Stewart, recording secretary; and Motion Picture/TV Preview Chairman Bee Boywer; "for her outstanding contribution to the Music, Motion Picture and Television Industry."

Peggy was particularly pleased to be honored by the Pacific Pioneer Broadcasters on September 10, 1982, with their Diamond Circle Award, presented at the Sportsman's Lodge luncheon, because this was recognition from other pioneers in the broadcasting field. The award states: "Congratulations Peggy Gilbert for many distinguished years in radio and television, Pacific Pioneer Broadcasters, Diamond Circle, September 10, 1982." There is a photograph from that occasion with Peggy and George Liberace.[470]

Also in 1982, she received the "Hollywood Appreciation Society Golden Mask Award."

Among her awards was a certificate signed by Bette Davis, president of the Hollywood Canteen: "Peggy Gilbert, In Appreciation of Your Loyal Services to The Hollywood Canteen."[471]

In September 1983, Peggy received a Southern California Motion Picture Council Award "for special merit in the field of music."[472]

Peggy Gilbert was named a "Friend of the Arts" member of Sigma Alpha Iota, International Music Fraternity, at their Province Day held at California State University, San Diego, on March 7, 1987. It was presented by bass player Marilyn Mayland,[473] a longtime friend of Peggy's.

Local 47 presented Peggy with the Life Member of the Year Award on January 9, 1989.[474] The award states, "Peggy Gilbert, Life Member of the Year, A unique musician and the ultimate in dedication, hard work, and commitment to her union colleagues. Given this day by the Officers and Board Members with profound respect and admiration for an exemplary life and with deep affection for an exceptional human being." It was signed by President Bernie Fleischer, Vice President Vince Di Bari, Secretary Serena Kay Williams, and Treasurer Bill Douglas.

There was yet another award from Local 47 in 1989: "Musicians' Union Local 47 Expresses its appreciation to and bestows the honor of Life Member of the Year 1989 on Peggy Gilbert." This award was signed by President Bill Peterson, Vice President Richard Q. Totusek, Secretary Serena Kay Williams, and Treasurer Chase E. Craig.

Peggy Gilbert received a Commendation from the County of Los Angeles, "In recognition of dedicated service to the affairs of the community and for the civic pride demonstrated by numerous contributions for the benefit of all the citizens of Los Angeles County. It is signed by Michael D. Antonovich, Chairman of the Board, Supervisor Fifth District.

In 1990, The Dixie Belles received "The Commitment to Feminism Award, In recognition of their substantial contribution to the pioneering spirit in lessons of feminism, as beacons and guideposts to help us find our needs and strength, and our own path to growth and maturity. Thank you for being another reason why 'Sunset Junction Does it Best!'" presented by the City of Los Angeles Street Fair, 1990.

For Peggy's ninety-eighth birthday, AFM Local 47 gave her an award, "Professional Musicians Local 47 Expresses its appreciation to Peggy Gilbert on the Occasion of her 98th birthday and for her love and devotion, since 1929 to Local 47 and its members." It was signed by President Hal Espinosa, Vice President David Schubach, and Secretary Serena Kay Williams.

Peggy Gilbert received the Lil Hardin Armstrong Award for Pioneering Jazz Women at the 29th Annual Conference of the International Association of Jazz Educators. It was presented on January 11, 2002, at the reception of the Women's Caucus, hosted by the Ford Research Institute for Women in Jazz at the American Jazz Museum. Trumpeter Jane Sager was also honored at this event.[475]

For Peggy's one hundredth birthday, she received a California Legislature Assembly Resolution, signed by Honorable Dario J. Frommer, Assembly Majority Leader. This was presented by her longtime friend Ruth Ashton Taylor.

Not to be outdone, the City of Los Angeles issued a similar proclamation for Peggy's one hundredth birthday. It was presented by Wendy Greuel, Councilmember 2nd District.

PROCLAMATION

City of Los Angeles
State of California
Resolution
Peggy Gilbert
one hundredth birthday
January 17, 2005

WHEREAS, Peggy Gilbert was born in 1905 in Sioux City, Iowa, into a musical family and began performing in public at age 9; and

WHEREAS, active in the Los Angeles music scene since 1928, tenor saxophonist Peggy Gilbert is a leading advocate for women musicians; and

WHEREAS, in the 1920s, 30s, 40s, and 50s, she performed with a number of all-women orchestras, including many which she organized and led; and

WHEREAS, she performed coast-to-coast on the vaudeville circuit and even did a U.S.O. tour of Alaska during World War II; and

WHEREAS, she contracted women musicians for many films including the famous beer garden scene in *The Great Waltz*; and

WHEREAS, for more than 75 years, she has served as a one-woman support network for women instrumentalists in the jazz field; and

WHEREAS, in the 1950s and 60s, she worked for Local 47 of the Musicians' Union, and in 1970 began writing a column in the Union paper, *The Overture*, on women in music, and

WHEREAS, in 1974, she formed the senior citizen women's band, The Dixie Belles, when she was 69. The Dixie Belles appeared on a number of television shows including *The Tonight Show Starring Johnny Carson, The Golden Girls, Madam's Place, Simon and Simon, The Home Show, Father Murphy,* and *L.A.'s PM Magazine*; she performed in concert, at jazz festivals, in community and senior centers throughout the Southland; and

WHEREAS, Peggy Gilbert, while in her late 80s and early 90s, appeared in television commercials for such companies as Coca-Cola, Kentucky Fried Chicken, Honey-Baked Hams, among others;

NOW THEREFORE, BE IT RESOLVED, that the Major and City Council of the City of Los Angeles by adoption of this resolution wish PEGGY GILBERT a very happy one hundredth birthday.

RESOLUTION BY

Wendy Greuel, Councilmember 2nd District

James K. Hahn, MAYOR

Seconded By

Tom La Bonge, Councilmember 4th District

Attest: Frank I. Martinez, City Clerk

I HEREBY CERTIFY that the foregoing resolution was adopted by the Council of the City of Los Angeles at its meeting held January 12, 2005.

The Dominant Club of Los Angeles gave Peggy a Certificate of Life Membership: "This is to certify that Peggy Gilbert was elected in loving gratitude by the members of The Dominant Club, and is hereby granted all the honors and privileges pertaining thereto. Arlene Thomas, President, 2006–2007." The award was given on February 9, 2007; because Peggy was not able to appear to receive it, it was delivered to her home.

Years 101 and 102

After Peggy's one hundredth birthday, she became increasingly frail and found it difficult to leave her home. Although she attended few events, she and Kay had a steady stream of visitors, both from the local area and from out of town. Kay's health continued to deteriorate and Peggy worked diligently to arrange the necessary care for her, including home nursing and housekeepers. Kay was hospitalized numerous times for breast and lung cancer, as well as leukemia. In the fall of 2006, Kay had hip replacement surgery and circulation problems. Throughout these difficult times, Peggy and Kay persevered and taught those around them to never give up: there is always hope; tomorrow would be a better day. Peggy's loyalty to Kay and her commitment to secure the best care, were inspirational.

On Peggy's 102nd birthday, with Kay in the hospital, Peggy did not want a party. A few close friends came by, including Lily Tomlin, who brought a bottle of pink champagne and crystal glasses in a shoe box. Everyone toasted Peggy, who then said, "I'd like another glass of champagne, but you know, I'm not supposed to drink with my heart medication." Lily leapt off the couch, grabbed Peggy's champagne glass and downed the last of the bubbly. "You can't drink this! We need you here!" It was a hysterically funny moment, full of joy with a beloved friend. "Can you imagine?" Peggy said. "102 years old. Imagine that!" Witnessing her long and extraordinary life, we all dare to imagine a century for ourselves.

Epilogue

Well, we were not quite finished, but we ran out of time. Peggy Gilbert's ashes were buried on Ash Wednesday, February 21, 2007, at Forest Lawn Cemetery in the Hollywood Hills, with a clear view of many of the movie and TV studios—NBC, Disney, Warner Bros., and Universal. We tried. Two days before she died, I was by her side at the hospital, reading to her from this manuscript, checking names, dates, and places. We talked about the 1930s. She smiled as she told me how she hired a limousine and a driver to chauffeur the big band from gig to gig, sometimes five or six a day. Some girls did not drive or have cars; besides, they were too tired to drive and also perform. She told me, "It was practical. It made them feel special . . . but they *were* special. We did it right!" How I wish I had had more time with her, to hear the rest of those stories.

A few days earlier, Peggy had asked me to help her get Kay out of a rehabilitation center. She said, "If I go and leave Kay there, she will never forgive me." I said, "Go? Where are you going?" She said, "I can't last much longer, you know. I'm going to die soon." The day after Kay came home, Peggy tripped over her walker and fell, fracturing her hip. She underwent hip surgery and was overwhelmed by the anesthesia. Her heart failed. Peggy died in my arms on Monday morning, February 12, 2007, at Providence Saint Joseph Providence Medical Center in Burbank, California. She could rest assured that I would make certain that her story would be heard—and not just her story, but the story of an entire generation of women musicians.[476]

I knew, during the last two years, that she was anxious that I finish the book and the documentary. On her one hundredth birthday, as she blew out the candles on her cake, she made a wish. I asked her what she wished for and she said, "I wished that I would be 102. No older than that. 102."

A rough cut of the documentary was premiered in May 2006 in Miami, Florida, at the International Congress of the International Alliance for Women in Music. The reviews started to come in, along with invitations for more screenings. Although Peggy was unable to attend, she enjoyed the phone calls and notes she received from people who had seen the documentary. Several times during the last few months, she reminded me that she "couldn't possibly stay much longer." Even though she was tired and preoccupied with arranging for Kay's medical care, she patiently answered my questions and handed over more materials. I'm sure she stayed as long as she did to make sure that her biography was completed. Thank you, Peggy, for that.

In the days that followed, her obituary appeared in the *Los Angeles Times*,[477] *The New York Times*, *Entertainment Weekly*, *Time* magazine and, through the wire services, in newspapers across the country, from *The Boston Globe* and Cleveland *Plain Dealer* to the *San Francisco Chronicle* and the *Mercury News*. Peggy Gilbert's story appeared on blogs and Internet sites; she was mentioned on radio, including a BBC radio segment.[478] The Peggy Gilbert Collection is now housed in Special Collections at California State University, Northridge.

Dozens of strangers sent me e-mails describing how inspired they were to hear about her long life and her determined struggle to be a jazz musician. Peggy would have been proud.

Good-bye, "Peg O' My Heart." Sweet dreams.

—Jeannie Pool

P.S. Kay Boley died on April 1, 2007, and was buried next to Peggy Gilbert at Forest Lawn, Hollywood Hills.

APPENDIX A
"Tuning in on Femme Musicians"

From February 1979 through January 1984, Peggy Gilbert wrote a regular column for *The Overture*, the monthly publication of Local 47 of the musicians' union. These columns served to promote and document the activities of women musicians in the Los Angeles area during this period. They were an important form of Peggy Gilbert's advocacy of women musicians at the time, and are now an invaluable record of the work of these women.

Here follows a summary of the contents, in chronological order.

February 1979. Peggy Gilbert's first column on women in music.

March 1979. Mentions many women musicians, including Mary Kaye Trio, Betty Hall Jones, Naomi Preble, Roz Cron, among others.

May 1979. Mentions Toshiko Akiyoshi, Virginia Bartold, and Stash Records' recording of women jazz musicians.

June 1979. Mentions Barbara Simons, Ann Reiling, Doris Pressler, and Juanita Connors.

July 1979. Mentions Joanne Grauer, Kay Carlson, and Ruth Anderson.

August 1979. Mentions Ina Ray Hutton, Edna Lewis, Elaine Mitchell, Janofsky-Cron Big Band, and Leslie Baker.

September 1979. Mentions Joyce Collins, Evie Campbell, Sara Paeff Robinson, and Phyllis Brownell.

October 1979. Mentions Fern Buckner, Jackie Lustgarten, Marge Jasper, and Vern Swingle.

November 1979. Mentions Nan Schwartz, composer; Muriel Donnellan, arranger; Dorye Roettger, manager; Jana Jae, artist; and Harriett Gibson, pianist.

December 1979. Mentions the Di Tullio family (Louise, Stella, Virginia); Geraldine Rotella; Eunice Wennermark Price; Debra Price; Rosita Malla; Linda Malla; Carmen Dragon (daughter of Carmen Dragon); Eleanor Slatkin; Stella Castellucci; Rosemary and Terri Davis; Nan Schwartz; and Grace Pappalardo.

January 1980. Happy new year greeting.

February 1980. Mentions Ruth Kissane and a new group "Quintess," which is participating in Kansas City Women's Jazz Festival in March, including Ruth, leader, trumpet, flugelhorn; Marilyn Donadt, percussion; Carrie Barton, bass; Janet Jones, piano; and Kay Blanchard, tenor saxophone, clarinet. Also mentions Kellie Greene, Nina Russell, Joanne Grauer, and Diane Chassman.

March 1980. Takes Leonard Feather to task for sexist review of Ruth Kissane "Quintess" group's performance at Snooky's. Mentions Geraldine Whitworth, vibes, alto, tenor, baritone; Marilyn Mayland, bass, banjo, mandolin; Marie Ford O'Sullivan, violin; Kathleen McArtor, drums; Clora Bryant, trumpet; and Carol Kaye, bass.

April 1980. Mentions Rita Rio all-girl band; Janofsky-Patterson Band; Radie Britain, composer; Evie King, singer-pianist; Lois Robbins (Isaacs), trombone; Annis Elliott, piano; and Dody Jeshke, percussion. Complains that not one women's band was included at the Fourth Annual Big Band Reunion in March 1980.

May 1980. Mentions motion picture, *The Competition*, included seventeen women musicians as sideliners, including Constance Pressman, Cynthia Kovak, Lusic Bruch, Bonnie Ann Schwartz, Rima Rudina, Lillian Akersborg, Bertha Ann Betty, violins; Karen Donley, bass; Janice Simmons, Hedy De Rimanoczy, Ruth Drouet, violas; Alice Ober, Kristin Krieger, Mary Lee Tyson, and Mary Gari, celli; Karen Lynch, oboe; and Peggy Gilbert, flute. Also mentions Leo Arnaud; Harriet Davidson, singer-pianist; Katy Cruise, saxophone, clarinet; mentions good review by Leonard Feather of Janofsky-Patterson band, Maiden Voyage.

June 1980. Mentions Karen Donley, bass; Betty Reilly, guitar, vocals; Billie Cutler, trumpet, entertainer; and Nellie Lutcher, piano, vocals. Peggy thanks the musicians who wrote to her in response to Leo Walker's article in *The Overture*: "I shall continue to try to get acknowledgement for these fine musicians as long as I am able to speak or write."

July 1980. Mentions that The Dixie Belles played in a park in Montebello for the 4th of July. Mentions Janice D. Dineen, Ruth Kissane, Veda Hol, Teto Heffington, Kristin Kreiger, Ann Patterson, and E. Marcy Dicterow (Vaj).

August 1980. Mentions Vi Redd, Bonnie Janofsky, Ann Patterson's Maiden Voyage, and Audrey Hall Petroff.

September 1980. Mentions Anita De Fabris; Betty O'Hara, valve trombone, vocals, composer, arranger; Juanita Connors, leader, drums; Bee [Turpin] Butler, organ, piano; and Jill Fraser.

October 1980. Mentions picketing with members of Local 47; Jill Fraser, electronic synthesizer, scoring; and Judy Wood, bass, violin, vocals.

November 1980. Mentions Ginger Smock Shipp,[479] violin; Mary Kaye; Lanny Morgan, alto saxophone; and Carol Anderson, piano.

December 1980. Mentions Ginger Smock, violin; Libbie Jo Snyder, flute; Dorye Roettger; First International Congress on Women in Music; Betty Reilly.

January 1981. Mentions Ginger Smock; the strike; Libbie Jo Snyder, flute, and her new group The Classy Jazzy Ensemble; and Betty Reilly, guitar.

February 1981. Some general observations about music; mentions Sally Banning, leader of all-girl group in the 1940s; and that the strike is over.

March 1981. Mentions the December 1951 issue of *The Overture,* with a centerfold devoted to women in music; February 1947 issue with a cover on women in music and numerous articles; Joanne Grauer; Ann Patterson and Maiden Voyage.

April 1981. Reprints "The Grand Piano," a poem by Doris Austin; mentions the Leventritt Foundation; Ida Levin; and Alberta Hurst, cello.

May 1981. Mentions the 1981 Congress of Strings, Beverly Carmen, Doriot Anthony, and Gladys Lyon.

June 1981. Mentions Stephanie Pelz Bennett, harp; Ann Patterson and Maiden Voyage; Vi Redd; Fern Spaulding Jaros; Jerrie Stanley Shaw, saxophone; Estelle Dilthey Hambaugh, drums; Shirley Thomas Brush, trumpet; Virginia Creitz; and Gisele MacKenzie.

July 1981. Mentions Rose Parenti, piano, accordion.

August 1981. Mentions problems facing all musicians; Bonnie Janofsky, drums; and women in symphonies.

September 1981. Mentions the Equal Rights Amendment; Ann Patterson and Maiden Voyage; L.A. Street Scene Festival; and Clora Bryant.

October 1981. Mentions The Dixie Belles' appearance on *The Tonight Show with Johnny Carson*; Harriet Gibson, piano, vocals; Betty Hall Jones, piano, vocals, hats; Kellie Greene, piano; Karen Lynch, oboe; and equal pay for equal work.

November 1981. Mentions Virginia Bartold, violin, viola, and The Prometheus Quartet; Louise Di Tullio; Eubie Blackwell, viola; Philip Kahgan,[480] music contractor.

December 1981. Mentions Kellie Greene, piano; Virginia Darnell; Edna Lewis; and The Dixie Belles.

February 1982. Mentions Alive! (women's jazz band); Deedee Ball; Nellie Lutcher, piano, vocals; Jean Strickland, flute; and Fern Buckner, violin.

March 1982. Mentions Louise Baranger; Judy Chilnick, percussion; Betty Hall Jones; Joanne Grauer, piano; and Women's Jazz All-Star Combo.

April 1982. Mentions Nellie Lutcher, piano, vocals; Tony Horowitz; and that The Dixie Belles warmed up the audience at NBC for the TV show, *The Shape of Things*. Peggy was in New Orleans when she wrote this column.

May 1982. Mentions New Orleans; Joanne Grauer, piano; and June Derry Weston, piano.

June 1982. Mentions Cay Due Eckmier, piano; Pamela Ann Re, cello, vocals; Joyce Collins, Wini Beatty, piano, vocals; Bonnie Janofsky, drums; Rosanne Hill; and Dorye Roettger.

July 1982. Mentions Sally Placksin, author; Nina Goldin, keyboards; Winni Beatty.

August, 1982. Mentions Libbie Jo Snyder; Rosalind Cron, saxophone, clarinet; Valda Hammick, bass; Lacey Jones, guitar, vocals; Laura Lee Lukas, piano; Kellie Greene, piano.

September 1982. Mentions Terri Paul, bass; Serena Williams, bass; Joyce Collins, piano; Francesca Bori, cello; and Eunice Wennermark Price. Last article before the Local 47 elections.

December 1982. Mentions Linda Twine, conductor; Ann Reiling, organ; Nan Schwartz, composer; Marion Gange, guitar; Ann Patterson's Maiden Voyage; and Marilyn Mayland's International Strings.

January 1983. Wishes everyone a happy new year and discusses the election at Local 47.

February 1983. Mentions Audrey Barnett, guitar; Dorothy Ray, accordion; Elisabeth Waldo, violin, composer; and Eunice Wennermark Price.

March 1983. Mentions Congress on Strings; Ginger Smock Shipp, violin; Harriet Davidson, piano, vocals; Deedee Ball, piano, vocals; Nancy Geerlings; Luella Smith; Joyce Collins, piano; and Billie Cutler, trumpet.

April 1983. Mentions Sally Placksin, author; Inter-Guild Women's Caucus; and Joyce Collins, piano.

May 1983. Mentions her article from 1938 in *Downbeat*; Leonard Feather; Betty O'Hara; Maiden Voyage; Temi Nahman, booking agent; and Evelyn Pennak.

June 1983. Mentions Kellie Greene, piano; Doris Pressler, trumpet; Sally Placksin, author; and proposes a Women's Jazz Festival in Los Angeles.

July 1983. Mentions Gloria Chappell and the Congress of Strings.

September 1983. Mentions Miriam Cutler, composer; Stella Castellucci, harp; and Courtney Sappington, guitar.

October 1983. Mentions Betty Jones; Neva Ames, piano; Genevieve Howell, piano; Marie Coker, bass; and Mildred Chase, piano, author.

November 1983. Mentions death of George Liberace, who often hired women instrumentalists.

December 1983. Mentions Joanne Grauer, piano; Katy Cruise, clarinet, sax; Georgia Shilling, piano; Natalie Robin, clarinet; and Laura Lee Lukas, piano.

January 1984. This was Peggy's last column, "Au Revoir." She writes, "The first thing learned as a professional entertainer is when to get off the stage."

"Tuning in on Femme Musicians"

Clora Bryant, trumpet

Judy Chilnick, percussion, Local 47 trustee. Photo from *Overture* archive.

Bonnie Janofsky, drums, composer, Local 47 trustee. Photo from *Overture* archive.

Kathleen "Mac" McArtor, drums

Betty O'Hara, brass

Ann Patterson, saxophone, bandleader, Maiden Voyage. Photo by Carl Studna. Courtesy Ann Patterson.

Jane Sager, trumpet

E. Ginger Smock Shipp, violin, studio musician

Serena Kay Williams, bass, vocals, Local 47 Secretary/Treasurer. Photo from *Overture* archive.

APPENDIX B
Filmography[481]

Peggy acted as the union contractor for these engagements and often appeared in the films, as well.

1931 *Politics* (MGM), directed by Charles Reisner; starring Maria Dressler.

1932 *The Wet Parade* (MGM), directed by Victor Fleming.

1932 *That's My Boy* (Columbia), directed by Roy William Neill; starring Jimmy Durante.

1937 *Melody for Two* (Warner Bros.)

1938 *The Great Waltz* (MGM).

1938 *Rhythm of the Saddle* (Republic), starring Gene Autry.

1938 *Reckless Living* (Universal), directed by Frank McDonald; starring Robert Wilcox, Nan Grey, and Jimmy Savo.

1938 *Start Cheering* (Columbia), directed by Albert S. Rogell; starring Jimmy Durante. Peggy played saxophone and clarinet; Kathleen McArtor is on drums.

1940 *Lillian Russell* (Twentieth Century Fox), directed by Irving Cummings; starring Alice Faye, Don Ameche, and Henry Fonda.

1943 *Salute for Three* (Paramount), with Dona Drake (a.k.a. Rita Rio) and her Girl Band.

1946 Soundie with Thelma White and Her All-Girl Orchestra, performing "Hollywood Boogie."

1949 *Sirens of Atlantis* (United Artists), starring Maria Montez.

1961 *How The West Was Won* (MGM), directed by John Ford.

1961 *The Second Time Around* (Twentieth Century Fox), with Debbie Reynolds. Peggy was in an all-girl marching band.[482]

1975 *At Long Last Love* (Twentieth Century Fox).

1979 *The In-Laws* (Warner Bros.), directed by Arthur Hiller; starring Peter Falk, Alan Arkin, and Richard Libertini. Peggy plays in a band conducted by Carmen Dragon.

1980 *The Competition* (Twentieth Century Fox), starring Richard Dreyfuss. Peggy (on flute) was one among many musician-extras.

1985 *Wellness after Sixty* (Spectrum Films), documentary film. Peggy Gilbert and The Dixie Belles. Currently owned by Discovery Education.

2006 *Peggy Gilbert & Her All-Girl Band*, directed by Jeannie Pool.

Peggy Gilbert, at home, in her nineties.

APPENDIX C
Television Appearances

1950s	Ada Leonard's TV show on KTTV in Los Angeles. Peggy played in the band for an entire year on this weekly show.
May 21, 1957	*This Is Your Life*, hosted by Ralph Edwards (NBC). Episode honoring Thelma White.
September 18, 1981	*The Tonight Show Starring Johnny Carson* (NBC). Peggy Gilbert and The Dixie Belles perform; Peggy is interviewed by Johnny Carson.
1981–82	*Father Murphy* (NBC/TPI Entertainment Partners)
April 6, 1982	*Shape of Things* (NBC).[483] The Dixie Belles recorded March 28, April 3 and 14; the show was canceled on April 16, due to bad reviews.
September 23, 1982	*Madame's Place* (Paramount). Show #004, Act 2, Scene J. Features Peggy Gilbert and The Dixie Belles.
April 9, 1983	*PM Magazine* (CBS). The show broadcast a Los Angeles performance by The Dixie Belles for the Boy Scouts; also on June 30, 1983: "Six grandmothers who comprise the jazz band known as the Dixiebells [sic]."

Peggy Gilbert and Johnny Carson sharing a laugh on *The Tonight Show starring Johnny Carson.* Courtesy Carson Productions Group.

Peggy Gilbert and The Dixie Belles performing on *The Tonight Show* *(left to right)*: Georgia Shilling, Peggy Gilbert, Feather Johnston, Natalie Robin, Jerrie Thill, Marnie Wells, Pee Wee Preble. Courtesy Carson Productions Group.

December 15, 1983	*Simon & Simon* (CBS). The Dixie Belles appear as the band on a cruise ship that is hijacked. Filmed on the Queen Mary in Long Beach.
September 3, 1984	KCBS News clip of The Dixie Belles performing at a Ronald Reagan for President Rally and George Deukmejian for Governor Rally.
March 8, 1986	*McNeil-Lehrer NewsHour* (PBS). Eleven-minute segment on Luncheon to Honor the Pioneer Women Musicians of Los Angeles.
November 1986	*Life With Lucy* (ABC), Episode #13, Episode "World's Greatest Grandma," filmed but not aired. The Dixie Belles perform at Lucille Ball's granddaughter's school in a talent show.
October 22, 1988	*The Golden Girls* (NBC). Peggy plays "Esther" in Episode #42, "The Days and Nights of Sophia Petrillo."
1989	*News Australia*, Channel 9.
July 20, 1989	*CNN News*. Report of The Dixie Belles performing at St. Vincent's Hospital in Los Angeles.
January 27, 1990	*ABC-TV World News Saturday*, feature on Peggy Gilbert and The Dixie Belles, with Jed Duval reporting.
October 29, 1990	*The Home Show* (ABC), feature on Peggy Gilbert and The Dixie Belles.
March 14, 1993	*Married ... with Children* (Fox). Episode #150, "Go for the Old." Peggy Gilbert, Jerrie Thill, Georgia Shilling, and Marnie Wells appear as "cheerleaders," and sing "The Star-Spangled Banner."
November 13, 1994	*Lois & Clark: The New Adventures of Superman* (ABC). Peggy plays a slot machine and takes the winnings that "Lois" has left behind.
October 4, 1994	*Wings* (NBC). Peggy appears as an extra.
March 13, 1996	*Ellen* (CBS). Peggy Gilbert and The Dixie Belles. Ellen dons a Dixie Belles costume and plays triangle with the band.

February 24, 1999	*Dharma & Greg* (ABC). Peggy plays piano for a scene with seniors dancing at a retirement home.
date unknown	*Trapper John, M.D.* (CBS). The Dixie Belles appear without Peggy.
date unknown	*America's Funniest Home Videos* (ABC)

In her nineties, Peggy Gilbert continued to appear in commercials. This was her promotional headshot.

APPENDIX D
Pioneer Women Musicians of Los Angeles

Jeanne E. Aiken, Los Angeles, CA. Violinist, players' representative of the Los Angeles Philharmonic

Luruth Anderson, San Clemente, CA. Violin, assistant conductor, Los Angeles Women's Symphony

Anita Aros (Tuttle), Pacific Palisades, CA. Violin, with *The Spade Cooley Show*

Micki "O" Bailey, Federal Way, WA. Played with Sweethearts of Rhythm and with Helen Gissin

Deedee (Glee) Ball, Costa Mesa, CA. Piano, played with Ina Ray Hutton's band, toured with Hormel Show; also bandleader

Sally Banning (Porter), Inyokern, CA. Bandleader, organ, saxophone

Audrey Barnett, La Cañada Flintridge, CA. Guitar, producer, played with Ada Leonard, Peggy Gilbert, and George Liberace

Dixie Blackstone (Eger), Los Angeles, CA. Piano, vocalist, entertainer

Margaret H. Brady, Huntington Beach, CA. Violin, Long Beach Women's Symphony, conductor

Radie Britain, Hollywood, CA. Composer of symphonic music

Clora Bryant, Los Angeles, CA. Jazz trumpet, with Prairie View's All Girl Band, with the Sweethearts of Rhythm, to mention a few

Evie Campbell, Los Angeles, CA. Saxophone, played with Ada Leonard and Ina Ray Hutton

Stella Castellucci, Santa Monica, CA. Harp, symphonic player, studio musician

Geneva Merle Chappele (Guerrero), Los Angeles, CA. Drums

Mildred Portney Chase, Hollywood. Pianist, writer

Maria Coker (Dickerson), Los Angeles, CA. Bass, jazz, played USO tours, among other jobs

Lorenza Jordan Cole, Altadena, CA. Pianist, educator

Joyce Collins, Studio City, CA. Piano, bandleader; one of the first women to serve on the Board of Local 47, AF of M

Dorothy Compinsky, Santa Monica, CA. Violin, Los Angeles Women's Symphony, Brodetsky Ensemble

Zackie Walters Cooper, Los Angeles, CA. Saxophone

Katherine "Katy" Cruise, Ventura, CA. Saxophone, clarinet, played with Boots and Her Buddies, Nellie Jay and Her Jay Birds, and Peggy Gilbert

Mary Demond, Pebble Beach, CA. Trumpet, played with Ada Leonard

Rose Diamond, Los Angeles, CA. Piano, President of Women's Club of Musicians Union

Karen Donley, Studio City, CA. Bass, played with Peggy Gilbert's band and The Dixie Belles and Ina Ray Hutton.

Marion Downs, Los Angeles, CA. Singer of spirituals and promoter of Black American music

Eunice Johnson Duroe, Los Angeles, CA. Trombone, played with Ada Leonard's band

Marie Ford (O'Sullivan), Burbank, CA. Violin, played in *The Great Waltz*, with Peggy Gilbert's band

Peggy Gilbert, Studio City, CA. Saxophone, bandleader, vocalist, arranger, clarinet, vibes, violin, has had many all-girl bands, leader of The Dixie Belles

Kellie Greene, Studio City, CA. Piano, French horn, flute and arranger, has her own band, plays jazz and classical

Virginia Gregg, Los Angeles, CA. Bass, with the Singing Strings on radio, actress

Helen Gissin, Santa Monica, CA. Drummer, vocalist, bandleader

Audrey Hall (Petroff), Tacoma, WA. Saxophone, clarinet, and violin

Estelle Dilthey Hambaugh, Rancho Palos Verdes, CA. Drummer, Babe Egan and Her Hollywood Redheads

Helen Lorraine Hammond, Lakewood, CA. Trumpet, worked with Ada Leonard's band

Chris Hollis, Los Angeles, CA. Pianist, vocalist, played with Louis Jordan, played with Helen Gissin's band

June Robin Howard, Tujunga, CA. Violin, symphonic player

Luella Howard, Los Angeles, CA. Flute

Genevieve B. Howell, North Hollywood, CA. Piano, played with Peggy Gilbert

Wen-Ying Hsu, Pasadena, CA. Composer of symphonic music

Davida Jackson, Beverly Hills, CA. Organ, studio work

Fern Spaulding Jaros, Sun City, CA. Trombone and French horn, featured with Babe Egan's band, with symphonies

Dody Jeshke, Palm Desert, CA. Drums

Feather Johnston, North Hollywood, CA. Bass and reeds, played with Peggy Gilbert and with Freddie Schaeffer and Joy Caylor

Alberta Jones. Cello, played with Los Angeles Women's Philharmonic

Francis Kass, Miami, FL. Trumpet, played with Ada Leonard

Sally Brown (Flint) Kempster, Los Angeles, CA. Trumpet, played with Peggy Gilbert's band, also with Boots and Her Buddies

Ruth Kirkpatrick, Laguna Hills, CA. Violin, Long Beach's Women's Symphony concertmaster, symphonies

Ann Leaf, Los Angeles, CA. Theater organist and studio player

Ada Leonard, Los Angeles, CA. Vocalist, bandleader

Thelma L. Lewis, Compton, CA. Played with Sweethearts of Rhythm

Bernice Lobdell, Hermosa Beach, CA. Trumpet, played with Ada Leonard, with Ina Ray Hutton's band, with Count Berni Vici and with Rita Rio

Nellie Lutcher, Los Angeles, CA. Piano, vocalist, songwriter, bandleader

Barbara Neece MacNair,[485] Canoga Park, CA. Piano, played with Ada Leonard's band

Elva Dilthey MacNair, North Hollywood, CA. Saxophone and violin, played with Babe Egan and Her Hollywood Redheads

Lois Cronen Magee, Sepulveda, CA. Trombone and vibraharp, played with Ina Ray Hutton, Ada Leonard

Virginia Majewski, Los Angeles, CA. Viola, played with The American Quartet

Marilyn Mayland, Newport Beach, CA. Bass, played with Los Angeles Women's Philharmonic, has her own group

Mildred Myers, Laguna Hills, CA. Played with Phil Spitalny's All-Girls Orchestra

Bridget O'Flynn,[486] Forest Hills, NY. Drums

Alice Oakason (Dexter), Los Angeles, CA. Drums, played with Fanchon and Marco, in Peggy Gilbert's band, studio musician

Rose [Haber] Parenti, Ventura, CA. Piano, played with Fanchon and Marco, with Peggy Gilbert's band

June Smith Parra, Los Angeles, CA. Cello, studio work, teacher

Harriet Payne, Laguna Hills, CA. Viola, composer, conductor, Glendale Symphony, Long Beach Symphony, studio work

Evelyn Pennak, Woodland Hills, CA. Saxophone, toured Europe with American Legion Band, played in Ada Leonard's band

Pearl Powers, Santa Ana, CA. Bass, with The Dixie Belles, played with The Wild Ones, Four Guys and the Doll

Naomi Preble, North Hollywood, CA. Trombone, with Peggy Gilbert's band, with The Dixie Belles

Doris E. Pressler, Las Vegas, NV. Trumpet, with the Bricktops, played with Peggy Gilbert's band, with Senior Citizen Orchestra in Las Vegas

Eunice Wennermark Price,North Hollywood, CA. Violin, studio work[487]

Bessie Van Wagner Quinzel, Long Beach, CA. Clarinet, Long Beach Women's Symphony, has her own big band, symphony player

Dorothy Ray, La Cañada Flintridge, CA. Accordion, saxophone and producer

Charlotte (Robbins) Reed, West Hollywood, CA. Trumpet, played with Count Berni Vici and Thelma White

Naomi Reynolds, Los Angeles, CA. Piano and organ, radio broadcaster

Lois Robbins [Isaacs], Beverly Hills, CA. Trombone and bass, with Count Berni Vici's band

Natalie Robin, Los Angeles, CA. Clarinet, oboe, and saxophone, one of The Dixie Belles, played with Rita Rio and Ina Ray Hutton

Betty "Roz" Rosner, North Hollywood, CA. Saxophone, clarinet, played with Sweethearts of Rhythm and Ada Leonard's band

Frances Rossiter, Los Angeles, CA. Trumpet

Florence Russell, Laguna Hills, CA. Publisher of *Pacific Coast Musician*

Jane Sager, Los Angeles, CA. Trumpet, played with Ona Munson, Ada Leonard, Ina Ray Hutton

Eudice Shapiro, Studio City, CA. Violin, with The American Quartet, taught at USC, played at the Evenings on the Roof concerts

Mary Crawford Shattuck, Costa Mesa, CA. Violin, Los Angeles Women's Symphony concertmaster, plays with International Strings

Georgia Cotner Shilling, Van Nuys, CA. Piano, one of The Dixie Belles

E. Ginger Smock Shipp, Las Vegas, NV. Violin, featured on *The Spade Cooley Show,* studio player

Constance Shirley, Hollywood, CA. Composer

Ethel (Jenkins) Siegfried (Mrs. Frank L.), Whittier, CA. Bass, Los Angeles Women's Symphony

Lucille B. Silverstone, Glendale, CA. Piano, played at the Brown Derby Restaurant

Barbara Simons, Los Angeles, CA. Violin and viola, symphony player

Mildred Springer, Fresno, CA. Bass, played with Ada Leonard

Geraldine Stanley (Shaw), Fullerton, CA. Saxophone

Verna Arvey Still, Los Angeles, CA. Piano, lyricist

Ann Mason Stockton, Los Angeles, CA. Harp, studio player

Florence L. Strnad, Fontana, CA. Bassoon, Los Angeles Women's Symphony

Pat Stullkin, Los Angeles, CA. Saxophone, played with Sweethearts of Rhythm

Norma Teagarden (Friedlander), San Francisco, CA. Piano

Jerrie Thill, Studio City, CA. Drums, vocalist, with The Dixie Belles, played with Ada Leonard

Bee Turpin (Butler), Indianapolis, IN. Piano, played with the Ona Munson show and with Peggy Gilbert

Elisabeth Waldo, Northridge, CA. Violin, composer, promoter of music of the Americas

Elinor Remick Warren, Los Angeles, CA. Composer

Gayle Warren, Orange, CA. Piano

Marian "Marnie" [Elzea] Wells, Van Nuys, CA. Trumpet, bass, with The Dixie Belles, played with Ina Ray Hutton, Rita Rio, and Count Berni Vici

Wilma Wescott (Bobby Tremain), Hollywood, CA. Tuba, entertainer

June Derry Weston, Thousand Palms, CA. Piano, did USO shows in Alaska with Thelma White

Olive Williams, Whittier, CA. Clarinet, Los Angeles Women's Symphony

Violet Wilson, Los Angeles, CA. Bass, played with Terry McLaughlin and Sarah Vaughan

Judy [June] Winsor, Big Bear City, CA. Piano, played at Brown Derby Restaurant

The following women were invited, but did not attend:

Virginia Alten, Della Anderson, Dorothy J. Ashby, Jane Avelar, Jessie Bailey, Bebe Barron, Frieda Belinfante, Fanny Benjamin, Marion Carter, Suzi Chandler, Rose Diamond, Dorothy Donegan, Annis Elliott, June Everett, Thelma Beach Hanau, Julia M. Hazen, Danielle Josephson, Pescha Kagan, Annette Kaufman, Pearl Kaufman, Margaretha Lohmann, Sybil Maxwell, Elaine Mitchell, Elise Baxter Moennig, Norma Petersen, Phyllis Plambeck, Perri Lee Poston, Margaret Ranker, Vi Redd, Dorothy Remsen, and Joella [Jo Ella] Wright.

APPENDIX E : DOCUMENTARY
Peggy Gilbert & Her All-Girl Band

As a performer on saxophones, clarinet, violin, and vibes, as well as a singer, arranger, and contractor for women musicians, Peggy Gilbert has been a one-woman support network and staunch advocate for women since the 1920s. A professional tenor saxophonist for more than eighty years, she has been an inspiration for several generations of musicians. In January 2007, Peggy Gilbert celebrated her 102nd birthday, displaying a vivacity that belied her age. Perhaps she has lived so long so that she can tell the stories of the remarkable women musicians of her generation. These women broke down the barriers before them, enabling female instrumentalists both to be taken seriously as musicians and to develop professional careers.

Her last ensemble, Peggy Gilbert and The Dixie Belles, played hot Dixieland jazz on national television, at jazz festivals, and in concerts from 1974 to 1994. Appearances on *The Tonight Show Starring Johnny Carson, The Golden Girls, Ellen, Simon & Simon*, and other sitcoms made them famous coast-to-coast, even as octogenarians. Peggy herself continued to do television commercials well into her nineties.

This documentary tells Peggy Gilbert's story with more than seven hundred photographs of women musicians and all-girl bands. The film also includes rare film clips and stills from movies (beginning in 1931) in which Peggy's band appeared, plus invaluable radio air-check tapes and recordings from the 1930s and '40s.

Directed, written, and produced by Jeannie Pool, a music historian and composer, the production was made possible with funding from The Silva Watson Moonwalk Foundation and private donors, in association with North

Wind Quintet of Los Angeles. Lily Tomlin is the narrator; Glenn Winters is editor. The film features performances of The Dixie Belles and includes an original score composed by Jeannie Pool. It had its premiere screening in May of 2006 in Miami, Florida.

Peggy was able to see the finished film and to observe the enthusiasm that it generated.[488]

Peggy Gilbert, at age 101, holding the poster for the documentary, *Peggy Gilbert & Her All-Girl Band.* Photo by Beverly Simmons.

Notes

Introduction and Acknowledgments

[1] For more about this event, see Chapter X.

[2] Cambria Master Recordings released the compact disc (CD-1024) version in September 2006. See www.cambriamus.com

[3] Jeannie Pool, "Peggy Gilbert, Saxophonist and Bandleader, Turns 90," *ILWC Journal* [now *Journal of the International Alliance for Women in Music*] (February 1995): 4–5.

[4] Peggy Gilbert, letter (February 9, 1982) to Gene M. Gressley, at the University of Wyoming, Division of Rare Books and Special Collections, in response to his request that she donate her papers to the University of Wyoming. Peggy was a fine writer in her own right.

[5] Jeannie Pool, director, writer, producer, *Peggy Gilbert & Her All-Girl Band*, 2006.

[6] For more than forty years, Peggy collected photographs, letters, articles, and other biographical materials about the women with whom she had performed. She identified women musicians in many group photographs, including stills from Hollywood films. As a result, her collection was one of the leading resources for women in jazz, particularly in Southern California.

Chapter I: The Early Years

[7] Peggy took her mother's maiden name, Gilbert, when she moved to Hollywood and found that people had trouble spelling and pronouncing Knechtges. Her brother Orval followed suit, although he did not legally change his name.

[8] A business card lists J. D. Knechtges as the Manager of the Hawkeye Concert Orchestra, 306 West 7th Street, Sioux City, Iowa. "Music Furnished for All Occasions. Ask for Prices."

[9] She was born January 31, 1880. Her father, Judson Gilbert, was a tinsmith, who died at a young age. His brother owned land in San Bernardino, California, which Peggy later inherited.

[10] Her name may have been spelled Madalina, but her tombstone simply says, "Mother." Her daughter's name was Magdalene (1876–1903). In the 1880 U.S. Census, the family gave their country of origin as Prussia, the historic state originating in Brandenburg. The last

capital of Prussia was Berlin. The name comes from a Baltic people related to Lithuanians and Latvians, conquered by the Teutonic knights and eventually "Germanized." When asked about this, Peggy said they were Germans, not Prussians, but her cousin Betty Lundberg says she has a Prussian vase among her family heirlooms.

[11] The first three children were born in Wisconsin; the others in Charles City, Iowa. Anthony's name is given as Anton in the 1880 census.

[12] Peggy's grandfather, Paulus, was born in 1827 in Mayen, Germany, and was blind for the last 30 years of his life. He died in 1913, shortly after his wife's death in 1912. Peggy does not recall meeting them in Charles City, but remembers that her father often went alone to see them.

[13] Peggy Gilbert, "Drummer Boy," unpublished manuscript, fictionalized story about her brother Orval, 4 pp., incomplete (c.1988).

[14] An avid conservationist, Roosevelt established bird sanctuaries, national parks, and monuments. He was a "Rough Rider" (1st U.S. Volunteer Calvary Regiment, so called by the American press) in the Spanish-American War and a cowboy in the Dakota Territory.

[15] Videotaped interview (August 6, 2005).

[16] Ibid. This was a Price-Teeple Cabinet grand piano with a red mahogany finish, manufactured in Chicago.

[17] Iowa was nicknamed the "Hawkeye State" by Iowa governor James G. Edwars.

[18] Videotaped interview (August 6, 2005).

[19] Gilbert, "Drummer Boy."

[20] Phone interview (July 5, 2006).

[21] Oral history interview (1985), Studio City, California.

[22] See Lauder's autobiography, *Roamin' in the Gloamin'* (Philadelphia & London: J. B. Lippincott Company, 1928). There is no specific mention of his Midwest tour, c.1912.

[23] Videotaped interview (August 6, 2005). On a photograph of the group, Peggy has written "1913" and that she was eight years old.

[24] Her mother's maiden name was Taft. Grandma Gilbert is buried in Inglewood Cemetery, next to Darlene Knechtges (her granddaughter, Peggy's niece) and Edith Gilbert Knechtges (her daughter). Grandma Gilbert had two sisters, Ella Cutting and Sara Culver, who both married railroad engineers and lived in Los Angeles in the 1920s.

[25] Gilbert, "Drummer Boy."

[26] Even at 102 years old, Peggy was working on her own and Kay's tax returns. Legislation should certainly be enacted that no federal tax return be required after one's one hundredth birthday!

[27] Gilbert, "Drummer Boy." Intended as a fictionalized story about her brother, these passages reveal much about Peggy's life and attitudes. She supported Orval's children, as well as her mother and grandmother, and was head of the household and breadwinner for many years. Although sharing a home in Los Angeles with their mother and grandmother, Orval lived for himself, while Peggy lived to take care of everyone else.

[28] Peggy learned Morse code from her Uncle Bert and her mother.

[29] Eventually Uncle Bert and Aunt Lett moved to Los Angeles and lived with Peggy, Peggy's mother, Peggy's brother, and Peggy's partner, Kay Boley, in a big house on South Ardmore, near Venice Boulevard.

[30] Videotaped interview (August 6, 2005).

[31] For more information and photographs on Sioux City history, visit www.siouxcity-history.org.

[32] See Marjorie Spruill Wheeler, *One Woman One Vote: Rediscovering the Woman Suffrage Movement* (Troutdale, Oregon: New Sage Press, 1995), an anthology companion to the PBS "American Experience" documentary; also Aileen S. Kraditor, *The Ideas of the Woman Suffrage Movement, 1890–1920* (New York: W. W. Norton & Company, 1981).

[33] Paul Whiteman and his Orchestra recorded "Whispering," by J. Schonberger, R. Coburn, V. Rose, on a Victor recording #18690, 1920.

[34] www.siouxcityhistory.org. This building is now on the National Register of Historic Sites. The school was closed in 1972. Recently, it has been renovated into apartments. For other sources on the history of the public schools there, see: B. Paul Chicoine and Scott Sorensen, *Sioux City: A Pictorial History* (Norfolk/Virginia Beach: Donning Company, 1982); *History of the Counties of Woodbury and Plymouth Iowa* (Chicago: A Warner and Co., 1890); and *The Public Schools of Sioux City, Iowa* (Sioux City: n.p., 1955).

[35] The Art Institute of Chicago, established in 1866. Peggy drew throughout her life. Her paintings were exhibited at Local 47 art shows in the 1960s and '70s. Drawings from her Alaska trip in the 1940s are shown in the film, *Peggy Gilbert & Her All-Girl Band.*

[36] Videotaped interview (August 6, 2005). A liberal arts institution, Morningside College was founded in 1894 by the Methodist Episcopal Church and is now affiliated with the United Methodist Church.

[37] Although the Sioux City Orpheum Theater, well-known today, was not built until 1927, the Orpheum Circuit performed earlier in the decade in another theater. According to a special souvenir program to celebrate the opening of the Orpheum Circuit's new Orpheum Theater in Omaha (October 10, 1927): "The Orpheum Circuit obtained the present Orpheum Theater, Sioux City, its third vaudeville house in Iowa, on March 11, 1918. Prior thereto Orpheum Circuit vaudeville were given in [rented theaters in] Sioux City for several years. Both vaudeville and feature photoplays make up its programs, playing continuously from 1 to 11 p.m. daily. The theater situation in Iowa is unique. In this great corn and hog country, the farms and countryside yield the greater prosperity, rather than the manufacturers of cities. Consequently, such a thriving center as Sioux City finds many patrons in localities for miles around the city, and Orpheum vaudeville is as well known and appreciated in the Iowa farm-home as it is in the residence of the city dweller."

[38] Throughout her life, Peggy was thrilled by live music performance and was unfailingly elated when she stepped on stage.

[39] Phone interview (July 5, 2006).

[40] Circuit refers to a preset travel itinerary for troupes of performers.

[41] On the history of vaudeville, see Douglas Gilbert, *American Vaudeville: Its Life and Times* (New York: Dover Publications, 1962); and Anthony Slide, *The Encyclopedia of Vaudeville* (Westport, CT: Greenwood Press, 1994).

[42] Gilbert, "Drummer Boy."

[43] Ibid.

[44] Darlene Maryland was born in 1923; John Darwin in 1925; June in 1928.

[45] Cecilia Rasmussen, "At 101, 'All-Girl' Bandleader Can Toot Own Horn," *Los Angeles Times*, (August 27, 2006), California Section: 1–2.

[46] Oral history interview (1985). The American Federation of Musicians was founded in 1896 as the trade union for professional musicians.

[47] For more about the Nighthawks, see Bob Harrington and Rex Downing, "Tales of Coon-Sanders," *The Mississippi Rag* (April 1991): 10–14; and Joe Popper's "America's Band," *The Kansas City Star Magazine* (July 9, 1984): 8–27. See also Chuck Haddix, "The Coon-Sanders Original Nighthawk Orchestra: Radio Aces" at "Club Kaycee: Kansas City Jazz History" on the web site of the University of Missouri, Kansas City at www.umkc.edu/orgs/kcjazz/.

[48] This text, written on a steno pad in 1998, was found after Peggy died. Peggy had told the newsletter of the Pacific Pioneer Broadcasters (*Who's What/What's Where*) that she was writing a book about her life as a musician.

Chapter II: The Melody Girls

[49] In the 1930s, other all-girl bands included Dixie Rhythm Girls, from St. Louis, Missouri (active 1935–45); The Harlem Playgirls (all black); Ina Ray Hutton and her Melodears; International Sweethearts of Rhythm (mixed race), led by Anna Mae Winburn; and Phil Spitalny and His All-Girl Orchestra. In the 1940s, there were Ada Leonard's All-American Girls; Prairie View Co-Eds (all black); and Virgil Whyte's All Girl Band (later called Virgil Whyte's Musicgals), among others. See pages 67–69 for a list of all-girl bands.

[50] Actor and director James Cruze (1884–1942), born Jens Vera Cruz Bosen, a.k.a. James Bosen.

[51] French Line's cruise ship, launched in 1927, known for its lavish interior design.

[52] Letter from Dorothy "Dot" Sauter to Peggy Gilbert (probably from the late 1970s).

[53] Cellist and bassist Dot Sauter (1903–1979) was born in Chicago, joined Local 47 in 1925, and died in Los Angeles. In addition to playing in Babe Egan's band, she also played with Peggy Gilbert on KMPC, in Peggy's big band, and with Ted Bacon's Golden Strings. A lovely photograph of the Golden Strings is published in Jimmie de Michele, ed. and pub., *Musicians Advertising Graphic*, Issue A, Volume I (1940), 39.

[54] Edith "Eadie" Griffith also performed in a two-piano act in Hollywood nightclubs.

[55] Geraldine "Jerrie" Stanley (Shaw) (1909–1993) was born in Cardington, Ohio. Later, she played in Peggy's big band.

[56] Interview (1986) for documentary, *All Women's Orchestras*, produced by Jeannie Pool.

[57] Videotaped interview (August 6, 2005).

[58] Peggy's scrapbooks contain many fan letters received by The Melody Girls.

[59] Videotaped interview (August 6, 2005).

[60] Jo Ann Baldinger, "The Dixie Belles—Peggy Gilbert's Not-Ready-For-Retirement Band," *Los Angeles Times* (November 8, 1981), Calendar, 4.

[61] Viola E. Nordstrom (1904–1992).

[62] In 1983, it was added to the National Register of Historic Places, Building #8300044. The address is 410 Pierce Street.

[63] The technology was called "wire telephony."

[64] KSCJ was the radio station of the *Sioux City Journal* newspaper. Visit www.kscj.com for more information.

[65] The members of the Melody Girls changed several times during the years.

[66] Also known as Sally Brown Flint Kempster.

[67] Dakota City is part of the Sioux City metropolitan area.

[68] Sally Brown performed with The Melody Girls; Boots and Her Buddies, and with Peggy's bands at the Las Vegas Meadows Casino and in Hawaii. In 1934, she married Alvin Flint, whom she had met while on tour with the band; Peggy was a witness at their wedding. In 1942, Sally and Alvin were taken as Japanese Army prisoners and spent three years in internment camps in the Philippines. Sally was able to secure extra food for herself and her husband—and thereby survive—by playing trumpet each evening for the prison guards. They were finally liberated by an American Army task force that struck behind enemy lines; this rescue effort was documented in many sources about World War II in the South Pacific. This information is from an interview with Sally Brown's brother, Harry Brown (Burbank, California, October 6, 2006); many thanks to Sally's family for sharing her scrapbook and their memories of her.

[69] There were three Orpheum Theaters in Sioux City; the one currently in use is the third, built in 1927.

[70] The Sioux City Orpheum Theater boasted 2,650 seats and a Wurlitzer pipe organ. It was designed by the nationally known Chicago firm, Rapp & Rapp. It was renovated and reopened in 2001 as the home of the Sioux City Symphony. For more information, visit www.orpheumlive.com.

[71] Fern Spaulding (Jaros) was born in 1908 in Loveland, Ohio. She played trombone, mellophone, baritone, tuba, French horn, and sang. Among the groups with whom she performed were The Gypsy Wayfarers, 1925–26; Gibson's Navigators, 1926–27; Babe Egan and Her Hollywood Redheads, 1927–30; Mary and Her Platinum Blondes, 1931–32; Chicago Women's Symphony, 1941–48; Victory Belles; Ada Leonard and Her All-Girl Orchestra, 1949–53. Her sister Blanche played accordion and several other instruments, also with Mary and Her Platinum Blondes. Fern married, had three children, and lived in Cicero, Illinois; she moved to Los Angeles in 1948. Currently living in Texas, she has been active in symphonic music well into her nineties.

[72] Peggy is quoted as saying that seeing the Gibson (sic) Navigators at the Orpheum in Sioux City inspired her to start her own girls' band (see Sally Placksin, *American Women in Jazz: 1900 to the Present, Their Words, Lives, and Music* ([n.p.]: Wideview Books, 1982), 82–83). However, in interviews in 2006, Peggy said that she met the Navigators while her band was playing at the Martin Hotel.

[73] This clipping was provided by Fern Spaulding. It probably dates from 1925–27, when Fern played with Gibson's Navigators. This source is important, despite its lack of date or publication name, because it confirms Gibson's first name, as well as names of the other musicians.

[74] Fern Spaulding Jaros's letter to author (July 22, 2006) provided information about the players' instruments.

[75] The correct spelling is Crystal.

[76] This clipping, from Fern Spaulding, also has no date or newspaper name. It mentions the film, *Bitter Apples*, which was released in 1927 by Warner Bros.

[77] Peggy and trumpeter Sarah Brown.

[78] He was buried at Floyd Cemetery in Sioux City.

[79] Mail in May 1928 was addressed to Peggy at 519 Isabella Street, Sioux City, Iowa.

[80] Letter (May 12, 1928), on letterhead of the Eppley Hotels Company.

[81] Peggy recalls that they rented a house on Hallmark Street in West Los Angeles. When she was on tour with "Jazz Temple Idea," the family lived on Vermont Avenue in a duplex. While she toured with "Busy Bee Idea," they bought a house on Ardmore.

[82] Consumption is another name for tuberculosis. She was buried on July 16, 1928, in Floyd Cemetery, Sioux City, near her father-in-law, John D. Knechtges.

[83] Her name was June Anders; she had one child, a son, who lives in New Jersey. He has two daughters, Peggy's great-grandnieces, one of whom is a fifth-grade teacher and the other a flight attendant.

[84] Oral history interview (1985).

[85] This includes the Los Angeles Women's Symphony, conducted by Henry Schoenefeld in the 1920s. In 1922, the orchestra had sixty-five players. Arthur Alexander was named conductor in 1929; Domenico Cianfoni in 1935; James Guthrie in 1937; Vernon Robinson in 1939. Later in 1939, Ruth Haroldson became conductor, remaining with the orchestra until 1961, when it folded.

[86] Oral history interview (1985).

[87] *Los Angeles County Culture and the Community* (Los Angeles: Los Angeles Civic Bureau of Music and Art, 1927). This pamphlet is in Honnold Library, Claremont Graduate University Library.

[88] See "Irene Franklin" in *Who's Who in Comedy* by Ronald L. Smith (New York: Facts on File, 1992), 167–68. She appeared in numerous films in the 1930s. A ten-minute Vitaphone short from 1929, entitled *Irene Franklin, The American Comedienne*, was directed by Murray Roth.

[89] She may be the same Juanita Connors who appeared in the movie *Sweet Adeline* (Warner Bros., 1934). In her column, "Tuning in on Femme Musicians" (June 1979), Peggy wrote: "Juanita Connors (drums) is living in San Diego. Juanita had the best known all girl band when I arrived in L.A. and she played ballrooms, theaters and night clubs."

[90] Baldinger.

[91] See Barry Kernfeld, *The Story of Fake Books: Bootlegging Songs to Musicians* (Lanham, MD: The Scarecrow Press, Inc., 2006).

[92] Edna Lewis played alto and tenor saxophone, and clarinet for more than six decades. She performed with Peggy's band on casuals, and with Meta Moore's band; joined Local 47 in 1932. During the 1970s, she was featured annually at the Sacramento Jazz Festival and with the Monterey Bay Hot Jazz Society.

[93] Gilbert, "Tuning in on Femme Musicians," *The Overture* (September 1980).

[94] See Jeannie Pool, "The Story of the All-Women's Orchestras in California" (Northridge, CA: CSUN International Institute for the Study of Women in Music, 1985), detailing many female instrumental ensembles in California.

Chapter III: On Tour with Fanchon and Marco

[95] Gilbert, "Tuning in on Femme Musicians," *The Overture* (April 1980).

[96] She was sometimes known as Mrs. Fanchon Simon.

[97] Little has been written about Fanchon and Marco, although their story and vast influence on the entertainment business merits detailed examination. Fanchon's daughter, Faye, is working on a biography.

[98] Loews Theaters was founded in 1904 by Marcus Loew in Cincinnati, Ohio.

[99] Many thanks to Sandra Holden, Marco's granddaughter and Fanchon's grand-niece, who shared her extensive collection of Fanchon and Marco photographs—more than two thousand images—revealing Fanchon's signature look for the shows. Fanchon and Marco had offices in Los Angeles as late as 1956 and were listed as booking agents in Local 47's publication, *The Overture*. In 1940, their offices were at 5600 Sunset Boulevard in Hollywood; in November 1942, at 1584 West Washington Boulevard; in 1956, at 6838 Hollywood Boulevard.

[100] Arthur Ungar, "A Five Year Achievement," *Variety* XCVIII:3 (January 29, 1930).

[101] Ungar, ibid. In the 1940s, Harry Bourne worked as a costume designer for films for Monogram Pictures Corporation, a low-budget Hollywood film studio active from 1931 until 1953. Who knows what a "tab" organization is?

[102] Ungar.

[103] Fanchon even produced a movie in 1939, *Yankee Doodle Home*, for Columbia Pictures Corporation.

[104] See C. L. Bagley's obituary of Wiedoeft in *The Overture* (March 1940): 17.

[105] The saxophone craze was at its height when the city of Kansas City, Missouri, passed a saxophone curfew in 1926.

[106] Based on existing recordings of Wiedoeft performing, saxophonist Ted Hegvik made a CD in 1995 called, "The Legacy of Rudy Wiedoeft: Saxophone Nostalgia of the 20s" (Golden Crest 4183), which gives an accurate idea of how the saxophone sounded at that time. It includes Wiedoeft numbers, *Sax-O-Trix* (with Savino), *Valse Sonia* (with Frey), *Saxophobia*, *Sax-O-Plum*, *Saxema*, and *Sax-O-doddle*, along with two Wiedoeft transcriptions, *Melody* (by Dawes) and *Serenade* (by Drigo). Gertrude gave Wiedoeft's personal scrapbook to Hegvik in 1978.

[107] Oral history interview (1985).

[108] Ena Weckerling (1904–2002) was from Goodhue, MN. Jackie Barton played sax with Peggy on "Jazz Temple Idea," too.

[109] Written in Peggy's hand next to his picture in her scrapbook about the "Jazz Temple Idea" tour.

[110] Peggy used French reeds, although for a while she tried to make her own.

[111] Understanding vaudeville history is crucial to comprehending the contemporary entertainment, broadcasting, film, and recording businesses, all of which developed out of vaudeville. See D. Travis Stewart, *No Applause—Just Throw Money: the Book that Made Vaudeville Famous* (New York: Faber & Faber, 2005), and Arthur Frank Wertheim, *Vaudeville Wars: How the Keith-Albee and Orpheum Circuits Controlled The Big-Time and Its Performers* (New York: Palgrave MacMillan, 2006).

[112] Peggy's scrapbook of the "Saxophobia" tour has unfortunately been lost.

[113] The Fox Manchester was used as a "break-in" theater for Fanchon and Marco productions. Opened January 30, 1930, it has since been demolished.

[114] The Oakland Fox opened on October 27, 1928.

[115] Date confirmed as starting January 9, 1929, from clipping in *The Tacoma Times*, dated January 9, "Saxophone King Coming." The film ("sight-sound picture") being shown was *Romance of the Underworld.*

[116] Many thanks to Doug Caldwell, who helped recreate this possible itinerary for the Fanchon and Marco tour, confirming some of these dates. As author of a forthcoming biography of Rudy Wiedoeft, he has access to Wiedoeft's personal scrapbooks.

[117] Vol. 2, no. 48 (December 1, 1928).

[118] "Radha" is the name of Krishna's paramour in Hindu tradition; she is one of the cow-herding girls (gopis).

[119] *The Overture* (July 1942): 5.

[120] Conversation (July 22, 2006). In another interview, Peggy indicated that the job at El Mirador was her first in Southern California, before her contract with Fanchon and Marco. She probably could not have worked there before joining Local 47.

[121] Oral history interview (1985).

[122] Baldinger.

[123] Oral history interview (1985). On the back of a photo of the troupe at a mine in Butte, Montana, Peggy wrote that the tour was in 1930 and lasted twenty-seven weeks. Peggy is pictured arm-in-arm with the president of the copper mine.

[124] The Millar Family web site, created by Ben Millar, states that Gus Elmore was a stage name for "Uncle Lloyd Byron Millar." He was famous for his role as the Zulu warrior and also as "Cannibal King," wearing blackface, an "Afro" wig, and carrying a spear. Ben Millar has several pictures of "Gus Elmore," who married four times, to women also performing on vaudeville; he had one son. After vaudeville, "Uncle Lloyd" had difficulty supporting himself and his family.

[125] This refers to an early Fox sound film.

[126] Hazel Livingston, "Great Show, Circus at P.E. Yule Party," paper unknown, Oakland, California (c. December 13, 1929).

[127] Baldinger. Peggy kept a scrapbook labeled, "Property of Margaret Knechtges, 'Jazz Temple Idea,' 1929–1930," with newspaper clippings and memorabilia from that tour.

[128] The Zulu people, from Natal Province in South Africa, are known today for their beadwork and basketry. In the nineteenth century, however, they were famous warriors who fought against the British invasion. The last Zulu "uprising" was in 1906.

[129] Presumably, this is George E. Stoll (1905–1985), called "Georgie," who worked in Hollywood as a music director, conductor, and composer on many MGM musicals. He won an Oscar for *Anchors Aweigh* (1944). He started his career as a radio orchestra leader and touring violinist.

[130] This is probably a reference to the famous Russian dancer Anna Pavlova (1881–1931), whose dance company toured internationally.

[131] Arthur Ungar, "Loew's State ('Jazz Temple'-Unit)," *Variety* (October 30, 1929). The hand routine involved glow-in-the-dark fluorescent gloves.

[132] "Woody, Loew's State Los Angeles (reviewed Oct. 25)," *Inside Facts of Stage and Screen* [1929].

[133] O. K. Hoffman, "Fox-West Coast Long Beach" (reviewed Nov. 16), *Inside Facts of Stage and Screen* [1929].

[134] By Milton Ager and Jack Yellen from the show *Honky Tonk.*

[135] Abe Lyman (1876–1957), drummer, bandleader, and composer, began recording in 1923, the first such recordings in California. His California Ambassador Orchestra played at the Ambassador Hotel in the 1920s.

[136] "Girls Band Proves Decided Hit in Novelty Number at Fox Broadway: Stage Show Has Big Edge on Picture," *The Oregon Daily Journal* [Portland] (January 3, 1930).

[137] This theater, now called Copley Symphony Hall, is home to the San Diego Symphony. Designed by W. Templeton Johnson and William Day, it was restored in 1985.

[138] The review refers to Nora Shilling as "The little 'half-pint-of-blues' singer, already known to Seattle audiences; [and] Wally Jackson [as] nimble-footed dancer," in "Jazz Templars Winners at 5th," *The Seattle Star* (January 9, 1930).

[139] Peggy Gilbert's original program from opening night of the theater has been donated to the archive of the San Diego Symphony.

[140] This list is found in "Jazz Templars Winners at 5th," *Seattle Star* (January [n.d.], 1930). In all of the press clippings in Peggy's scrapbook from the tour, this is the only published list of band members' names. In the back of her scrapbook, Peggy cut out the individual girls' pictures, wrote their names and drew their instruments. She gives the names of the girls on "Jazz Temple Idea" as follows: Peggy Gilbert, leader, saxophone, clarinet, and vibes; Jackie Barton, saxophone and clarinet; Liana Galen, star singer; [unidentified], violinist; Alice Oakason, drums; Helen Kay [Kaplan], first trumpet; [unidentified], second trumpet; [unidentified], contortionist, actor, and wife; Rose Haber [Parenti], piano; Dorothy Greene, bass; Ena Weckerling, saxophone and clarinet.

[141] It is not clear when Peggy began to use her mother's maiden name, but this newspaper article, from January 1930, lists her as Knechtges.

[142] In the photograph that Peggy has, where some of the girls wrote their signatures above their picture, the name is given as Helen Kaplan. Later, there is a Helen Kay who plays trumpet with Peggy's big band in Hollywood. Are Helen Kaplan and Helen Kay the same trumpet player, or two different women?

[143] Pianist, organist, and accordionist Rose Haber Parenti (1911–1996) was born in St. Louis, moving to California and joining Local 47 in 1945. She toured, along with Peggy, on the Fanchon and Marco "Jazz Temple Idea" and "Busy Bee Idea" tours. In 1931, she married Fred L. Parenti. According to Peggy, she and Rose were often mistaken for sisters while touring with Fanchon and Marco.

[144] This itinerary is compiled from Peggy Gilbert's scrapbook of the "Jazz Temple Idea" tour, which includes newspaper clippings, theater advertisements, reviews, and Peggy's handwritten notes. The dates are for the opening of her show at that theater, not necessarily for the entire run date.

[145] Al Lyons appears as himself with the Al Lyons Band in an MGM short, *Hollywood Party* (1937), available on DVD through Warner Home Video.

[146] Milt Franklyn later became a composer for Warner Bros. cartoons.

[147] The newspaper ad gives his name as "Hermie."

[148] Bert Frohman (1900–1974) appeared in the Paramount Pictures film, *Back Door to Heaven* (1939).

[149] In 1925, Bradford's band broadcast live from the Palace Rose Room Bowl over KPO in San Francisco. He was a pianist and vocalist.

[150] Next to his name in her scrapbook, Peggy has written "Spanish."

[151] Barney Rapps (d. 1968) and His New Englanders Orchestra toured throughout the country in the 1930s and eventually settled in Cincinnati. Doris Day got her start with his band, as did the Clooney Sisters, including Rosemary. His band recorded for Victor, RCA, and Bluebird records.

[152] Among the songs Rube Wolf composed is "Do You Love Me?" (1927).

[153] Leon Brusiloff (1899–1973) was a well-known Washington, D.C., orchestra leader. Born near Kiev, he moved to the United States at age six. He attended the Peabody Conservatory of Music and, in 1917, became the youngest member of the Baltimore Symphony. After directing the Columbia Theater Orchestra in Washington, he became conductor for the Fox Theater in 1927. Joining the Marine Corps in 1932, he organized the 6th Marine Reserve Brigade Band. During World War II, he and his band saw action in Cape Gloucester, New Britain. Eventually he became a Colonel in the Marine Corps Reserves. His family donated his collection, including published music and ten boxes of personal and professional papers, to the Music Division of the Library of Congress. He donated his military music collection to the U.S. Marine Band.

[154] Peggy's scrapbook ends with this date, but there is evidence that "Jazz Temple Idea" may have continued.

[155] Enrico Leide was the first conductor of the Atlanta Symphony Orchestra, which began in 1923 as a group of musicians from the Howard and Metropolitan Theater Orchestras.

CHAPTER IV: The Depression, the Movies, and the Hawaiian Tour

[156] "One-nighter" or "one-night stand" is the term for a band or performers' engagement at a club or a theater for only one night.

[157] Since 1984, Peggy has always said that she did films in the 1930s, but only remembered the title of *The Great Waltz*. Other titles of films in which she appears are mentioned in newspaper clippings and in her personal scrapbooks. There may, in fact, be other films in which her band appeared, but sideliners generally did not receive screen credit for their appearances in films; and the online International Movie Data Base (www.IMDB.com) has few listings for sideliners.

[158] Peggy Gilbert says she appeared in several Marie Dressler films in the early thirties. Many of the dance numbers in these early movies seem to be inspired by, if not actually created by, Fanchon, because the look resembles that in photographs of Fanchon and Marco vaudeville productions. This requires more research. Peggy confirms that many of the Fanchon and Marco girls appeared in movies in the late 1920s and '30s. For more information, see Betty Lee, *Marie Dressler: The Unlikeliest Star* (Lexington: The University Press of Kentucky, 1997).

[159] See Marie Dressler, *The Life Story of an Ugly Duckling: An Autobiographical Fragment in Seven Parts* (New York: Robert McBride & Co., 1924).

[160] This newspaper clipping is from the band's 1933 appearances in Bakersfield, California.

[161] Oral history interview (1985).

[162] Ibid.

[163] Meta Moore (1902–1941) was a trumpeter and bandleader, who performed with Peggy Gilbert in theaters and ballrooms. She was featured in "Stars and Stripes" and "Washington Post March," as part of a 1928 memorial tribute to American bandleader and composer John Philip Sousa (1854–1932) at the Pom Pom in Hollywood (*Los Angeles Times* (November 4,

and October 12, 1928)). According to Peggy, Meta "was a very fine trumpet player, with a beautiful straight tone like Harry James." She moved to the Bay Area and "tragically killed herself over some guy."

[164] On the back of this photograph, Peggy wrote: "Trumpet & Ldr.—Meta Moore."

[165] Peggy looks like a brunette in this photograph.

[166] Mabel "Hixie" "Hix" Hicks (1907–1975) played trumpet, flugelhorn, and mellophone, and was also an arranger, composer, and copyist. She was born in Macon, Missouri, worked out of New York with all-girl bands in the late 1920s, and moved with her mother to Los Angeles in 1931 or '32. She counted Louis Armstrong and Bix Biederbecke among her friends. She played with Meta Moore's band, with Peggy's big band at Club New Yorker in the 1930s and '40s, and in ballrooms. She also appeared in the film *The Second Time Around* (1961). When she married her composition and arranging teacher, Raoul H. "Fergie" Ferguson, they moved to Escondido, CA. When Mabel died, Peggy wrote: "Mabel Hicks is a name respected among all musicians, and especially girl musicians from the Big Band era. Talk about talent—there it was . . . all wrapped up in one small girl, who could 'sound off' on both trumpet and mellophone to make the greatest of jazz musicians stand up and applaud. . . . She loved music and put everything she had into it. Those of us privileged to work beside her and with her during the late 30s, 40, and 50s, will never forget her." See Gilbert, "Tribute to Mabel Hicks," *The Overture* (September 1975). Correspondence found at Paramount Pictures, dated October 21, 1942, indicates that Mabel Hicks was also a songwriter. She had submitted a song, "Misguided Heart," with lyric by Waiora Rogers, to the studio's music director, Louis R. Lipstone, for consideration for a film.

[167] Peggy Russell was on the USO tour with Thelma White, discussed in Chapter VII.

[168] According to *The Overture* (May 1932): 18, Edna Lewis transferred to Local 47 that month. When musicians toured, their union membership remained with their original "home" local, so they did not transfer to Local 47 unless they had relocated and were working in Los Angeles. Local unions have jurisdiction over local areas of employment, but the international union has jurisdiction over recordings, films, and network broadcasting. Today, the international agreements contain pension, health, and welfare benefits.

[169] *The Overture* (November 1932): 15, published a change of address for Margaret Knechtges to 1216 Serrano.

[170] Gilbert, "Tuning in on Femme Musicians," *The Overture* (November 1981).

[171] Grace Kingsley, "Marx Brothers Stay Together . . . Vivian Duncan Prepares to Lead Girl Orchestra," *Los Angeles Times* (August 11, 1932).

[172] "Topsy and Eva 'Broke'; File Bankruptcy Plea," *Los Angeles Times* (December 8, 1931).

[173] "Vivian Duncan Denies Rumors of Separation," *Los Angeles Times* (September 22, 1932).

[174] "Vivian Duncan Wins Divorce: Woes Laid to Too Much Mother-in-Law," *Los Angeles Times* (November 11, 1932).

[175] Peggy remembers that they were the same girls who toured with her in the spring of 1932.

[176] The paper was published from 1931 to 1948. Before the *Hollywood Citizen-News,* there was the *Hollywood Daily Citizen,* published between 1921 and 1931.

[177] "Music Mostly in the Air: Regarding Southland Broadcasting Activities," edited by Bruno David Ussher, *Who's Who in Music and Dance in Southern California* (Hollywood: Bureau of Musical Research, 1933), 120–21.

[178] In two decades of researching Peggy's story, few radio air-check tapes of her band (KMPC and KNX) have been found, despite many references to her band being broadcast live over several stations in the 1930s and '40s. She married her sound engineer from KFI in the early 1940s, who likely made many air-check recordings of her bands, although they have not been located. Peggy is a member of the Pacific Pioneer Broadcasters and has been honored by them for her early work in radio.

[179] Oral history interview (1985).

[180] Ibid.

[181] Peggy gave a different account of this story in her interview with Sally Placksin: "I went back . . . thinking I was gonna get married to a boyfriend who was also a saxophone player. I thought I'd miss all that, so I went back there, and as soon as I got off the train, I looked at Sioux City and I said, 'Wow, boyfriend be damned! This is it! I can't stand it!' So I borrowed his horn and joined Boots and her Buddies." See Placksin, 83.

[182] Peggy's collection includes a flyer for the "Show of Shows, Warners, Big Stage Show featuring Boots and Her Buddies, Sensational All Girl Band, with Hally Kester, acrobatic dancer, Lulu Hyland, Piano and Accordion Helen Hard, Eccentric Dancer and the Famous Nelson Female Quartet, Plus on the Screen 'Suicide Fleet,' [1931] with Bill Boyd, Ginger Rogers, and Robert Armstrong. A picture that is in the class with 'Cimarron' 'Hell'e *[sic]* Angels: 'All Quiet.'"

[183] Kathleen "Mac" McArtor (1903–1985) was born in Bluefield, West Virginia, and grew up in Columbus, Ohio. She had a twin brother and two sisters, one of whom became a Catholic nun. She performed with Boots and Her Buddies; Peggy's big band, including the Meadows Hotel in Las Vegas and Hawaii tour; Peggy's band at Club New Yorker; and took over Peggy's band at The Rice Bowl in the 1940s. She transferred to Local 47 in 1935. When she died of pneumonia, Peggy was her beneficiary. These details of Mac's life are from Kay Boley (interviewed June 10, 2006). Many of the photographs of Boots and Her Buddies Band come from Mac's estate; they were given to Peggy Gilbert and are now part of the Peggy Gilbert Collection.

[184] Born in Virginia, Nebraska, Katherine "Katy" Lawson Cruise (1910–2001) was named after her Aunt Katherine, one of the first women to graduate from University of Chicago Medical School in the 1890s, who worked as pioneer doctor in the Colorado mines. Katy's father owned a lumber mill; her brother Tom was a professional violinist in Los Angeles in the 1920s. Possessing a very high I.Q., Katy earned a degree in accounting from the University of Nebraska at a young age. Thanks to Bruce Miner for this information about Katy Cruise, who, along with his mother, Ruth Miner, raised him (phone conversation, October 20, 2006). Katy performed on saxophone, clarinet, and vocals with Boots and Her Buddies, 1931–32; Nellie Jay and Her Jay Birds, 1927–28; Peggy's big band in Hawaii; Peggy's big band at Meadows Casino, Las Vegas; Peggy's band at Club New Yorker, ballrooms, and on KMPC, 1933–40. She also played with The Jazz Pirates in Texas, Oklahoma, Iowa, and Nebraska, 1927 (it is not known whether this is an all-girl band or a mixed band); and with The Four Star Girls, lead by Virginia Rush, 1941–42. She served in the Marine Corps Women's Reserve from 1943 to '45. (WMCR was established in February 1943, as part of the Marine Corp Reserves. See www.womenmarines.org for more information.) After WWII, she stopped playing music professionally and worked as assistant bookkeeper for Local 47, retiring at the age of sixty-two. In the 1950s, she managed a "31 Flavors Ice Cream" franchise in Los Angeles, with her sister Harriet Cruise Davidson, a successful radio performer, and Kathleen McArtor.

[185] Baldinger.

[186] The address was 3070 – 12th Place, Girard Terrace Apartments, Apt. 8, Los Angeles.

[187] Oral history interview (1985).

[188] It appeared from 1924 to 1934 as "Boots and Her Buddies," and from 1934 to 1968 as "Boots." When Martin stopped doing the comic strip, it was continued by Thomas B. Harris, then by Les Carroll. The Edgar E. Martin Collection is held at the University of Missouri Libraries. A compact disc of "Boots and His Buddies" (issued March 13, 1994, in France on the Classics Jazz label) includes the group's last three sessions together in 1937–38. That black "territory" band, led by Clifford "Boots" Douglas, was founded in San Antonio in 1932. There is another release from 1991 on JSP/Delta Music/Arvato Services.

[189] See www.toonopedia.com/boots.htm, written by Don Markstein.

[190] Written on letterhead of The Holt Hotel, 600 Eighth Street, Wichita Falls, Texas, built in 1910 and recently renovated as a project of the Wichita County Heritage Society.

[191] Thanks to Harry Brown for permission to quote from this letter.

[192] Conversation (September 24, 2006).

[193] Peggy shared these letters with the author. During the Depression, Sally Brown's family lost their title to the family farm and were not in a position to help her. Undoubtedly, it was a relief for them to receive this letter and know that Sally would be able to support herself in music. The other girls were likely in similar situations, in that going back home again was not an available option.

[194] Peggy's archives include rare photographs of her band taken inside the casino, including one in front of the gaming tables and the roulette wheel.

[195] Cornero later had a gambling ship, The Rex, outside the three-mile limit, and ten minutes by water taxi from the Santa Monica Pier. This operation was also shut down by California officials. In 1955, he was involved in construction of the Stardust Hotel in Las Vegas, but he died at a gambling table on July 31, 1955. See Alan Balboni, *Beyond the Mafia: Italian Americans and the Development of Las Vegas* (Las Vegas: University of Nevada Press, 1996).

[196] See Joe Stevens, *Hoover Dam: An American Adventure* (Norman: University of Oklahoma Press, 1988). Warner Bros. made a movie about the building of the dam, which depicts the engineering and construction challenges of this project.

[197] The Olympics were held in Los Angeles in the summer of 1932 (not 1933). No country had offered to host the Games six months before they were to begin, because the world was mired in depression. Eventually 37 countries participated, including some 1,300 athletes. The white suits can be seen in photos of the band at the Club New Yorker, taken in 1935.

[198] Oral history interview (1985).

[199] Baldinger.

[200] The Pantages Theater in Hollywood was named after the great impresario Alexander Pantages. It opened June 4, 1930, as part of the Fox Theater Chain. At the height of his career, in 1926, Pantages owned thirty theaters and had controlling shares in forty-two more.

[201] *That's My Boy* (Columbia Pictures, 1932), directed by Roy William Neill, starring Richard Cromwell; *Politics* (MGM, 1931), directed by Charles Reisner and starring Maria Dressler; *The Wet Parade* (MGM, 1932), directed by Victor Fleming. The "Buddies" were not with Peggy when her band appeared in these films.

[202] "Peggy Gilbert's Famous Coeds to Open Coconut Grove, Girls' Band to be Featured at Saturday Dance; Pretty Syncopators Are Billed to Play Many Kern Engagements," *The Bakersfield Californian* (September 21, 1933), 12.

[203] This is Bunny Hart from Boots and Her Buddies.

[204] Taft is in Kern County. Visalia, 190 miles north of Los Angeles, is the economic center of the Sequoia Valley.

[205] The novelty song "Goofus" was written in 1930 by Wayne King and William Harold, with a lyric by Gus Kahn.

[206] U.S. Television History, Various Articles, http://members.aol.com/jeff99500/tv9.html. For more information on the history of early television, see www.earlytelevision.org/museum_information.html. Located in Hilliard, Ohio, the Early Television Museum has a large collection of televisions from the 1920s and '30s.

[207] Many entertainers from Los Angeles toured the Hawaiian Islands with E. K. Fernandez's organization. Edwin Kane Fernandez died in 1970, but the company continues as a family-owned and -operated entertainment organization.

[208] During World War II, the ship was assigned to the U.S. Navy to transport troops, but it was returned to public service in 1948.

[209] Baldinger.

[210] Moloka'i is also the oldest site for leprosy (today called Hansen's disease) sufferers. The leper colony at Kalnupapa and the work of Roman Catholic missionary Father Damien (1840–1889) is known worldwide.

[211] "Stairway to the Stars," written in 1935 by Mitchell Parrish and Frank Signorelli, was revived in 1939. Perhaps Peggy means, "I'll Build a Stairway to Paradise," composed in 1922 by B. G. DeSylva and Ira and George Gershwin.

[212] Oral history interview (1985).

[213] Caryl Agnew (a.k.a. Helen Carroll, a.k.a. Helen Barbee, a.k.a. Caryl Agnew Browning) was born in 1903 and named Helen Wright. She began her career playing piano in her brother's band in the 1920s; and played with Peggy's band in Hawaii. She married a man in Hawaii whom she met on tour; she lived there throughout the 1930s and was at Pearl Harbor on December 7, 1941. Altogether, she married seven times and had one daughter, Betty Jean Wheaton (b. 1923). She wrote and self-published several songs, including: "Tell the World the Yanks Will Win!"; "The Freeway Song" (1964); "Lucky Los Angeles —The Gold in the Golden State" (1959); and some women's clubs songs (1964, 1965). She spent many years playing solo piano in lounges. As a soloist, she was known for her powerful left hand. Thanks to Larry Wright for this information about his aunt.

[214] Beryl Booker, piano; Elaine Leighton, drums; Bonnie Wetzel, bass.

[215] Peggy mentions this band: "Remember that fabulous blond violinist, Anita De Fabris? I met her and worked with her while we were playing Orpheum Theaters with D'Artega's All Girl Band out of N.Y.C. Following the completion of this tour, she stayed in Los Angeles and continued to work in the Motion Picture area of our business, for MGM, Paramount, etc." Anita was founder-president of Lend-A-Paw Operation Shelter, Inc., in Palm Springs, devoted to saving abandoned cats and dogs. See Gilbert, "Tuning in on Femme Musicians," *The Overture* (September 1980).

[216] This may be the first all-girl band to have been filmed *with* sound. Lee De Forest (1873–1961) *was* filmed *with* her band in 1924 in New York City. A clip is available on the DVD, *First Sound of Movies: The Story of the Original De Forest Phonfilm Sound Motion Pictures*, produced by Ray Pointer. Although the audio is of her band, it is not what they were performing at the moment; in other words, the sync has been "faked." Hopefully, someday the footage and sound

will be matched properly and made available to researchers. Some De Forest footage is available from the Library of Congress.

[217] The Hip Chicks were Marge Hyams, Mary Osborne, and L'Ana Webster.

[218] The band included Vi Burnside, saxophone; Flo Dryer, trumpet; Edna Smith, bass; Shirley Moore, piano; Pauline Brady, drums.

[219] Virgil Whyte's all-girl band (appearing under various names, including America's Musical Sweethearts and Whyte's Musicgals) was well known from 1944 until 1948. They hailed from Racine, Wisconsin. Many assume that Whyte's band was the inspiration for the comedy *Some Like It Hot* (United Artists, 1959), because Ben Hecht, who wrote the screenplay, was also from Racine. Women in Whyte's band included trombonists Trudy Gosieski Whyte and Alice Jacoby; and trumpeters Dorothy Reigart, Virginia Schumacher, and Jeannette Cramer. His sister, Alice Whyte, played drums.

CHAPTER V: Peggy Gilbert's Big Band & the Hollywood Nightclub Scene

[220] Baldinger.

[221] Conversation with author (October 14, 2006).

[222] Baldinger.

[223] According to another story she tells, Peggy's band played at the Figueroa Ballroom in 1945, and were forced out at the end of the war.

[224] Oral history interview (1985).

[225] Phone interview (July 7, 2005).

[226] Radio listings were found for the following dates in 1935: August 22; September 3, 7, 13, 14, 19, 20, and 27; October 2, 11, 16, and 17.

[227] "Campaign on Cruelty Aids Many; News of the Cafes," *Los Angeles Times* (February 15, 1935).

[228] "News of the Cafes," *Los Angeles Times* (March 22, 1935).

[229] In 1932, the female impersonator Jean Malin appeared at Club New Yorker. The club's reputation by 1935, under the new management, is unclear. See Lillian Faderman and Stuart Timmons, *Gay L.A.: A History of Sexual Outlaws, Power Politics, and Lipstick Lesbians* (New York: Basic Books, 2006), 42.

[230] These discs have not been located.

[231] Lona Bowman may have also played piano with Peggy's band at Club New Yorker in 1935.

[232] *Los Angeles Times* (September 28, 1935).

[233] The photograph of Peggy's band at Club New Yorker includes pianist Nellie Sandahl. She transferred into Local 47 in September 1931. See *The Overture* (September 1931): 14.

[234] B.B.B.'s club was called The Cellar, with a floor show, "Boys Will Be Girls." *Variety* (October 4, 1932): 53.

[235] Advertisement, *Los Angeles Times* (March 19, 1936).

[236] "Fete Marks Milestone," *Los Angeles Times* (March 19, 1936).

[237] "Sheetz, Candy and Restaurant Chain Owner, Taken by Death," *Los Angeles Times* (September 16, 1941).

[238] Conversation with author (August 6, 2006).

[239] Beginning operations in March 1922, KFI was one of the earliest of the clear channel radio stations in the country.

[240] Peggy Gilbert, saxophone and leader; Helen Ireland, saxophone; Jerrie Stanley, saxophone; Katy Cruise, saxophone; Helen Kay, trumpet; Mabel Hicks, trumpet and mellophone; Janet Spaulding, trumpet; Naomi Preble, trombone; Evelyn Savery, trombone; Helen Boyd, bass; Kathleen McArtor, drums; Della Anderson, guitar; Lona Bowman, piano.

[241] Vol. IV, no. 12 (September 11, 1937).

[242] Oral history interview (1985).

[243] Ussher, 133.

[244] See Pool, "The Story of the All-Women's Orchestras in California."

[245] Audrey Hall (Petroff) was born in Roubaix, South Dakota, in 1907; both of her parents were musicians. She attended Illinois College Conservatory of Music and Chicago Musical College. As alto saxophonist, clarinetist, flutist, violinist, and vocalist, she played with Bobbie Grice and The Fourteen Bricktops, 1930–32; Babe Egan and Her Hollywood Redheads, 1933; and Ina Ray Hutton and Her Melodears, 1934–36, 1950–56; Jean Wald Orchestra, 1937; Peggy's big band, beginning in 1938; KMPC Radio with Peggy; sang in trio with Danny Thomas; Ina Ray Hutton's Band on TV. In 1931, she transferred into Local 47 (see *The Overture* (September 1931): 18). In the 1940s, she performed in the classical group The Golden Strings, as well as with various small combos in Los Angeles. She told the story of her own experience as a female musician: "That year [when I was 18 years old] the Chicago Musical College was offering scholarships to students of strings, piano, and voice. I went to Chicago to try out for a violin scholarship. The three judges, one of whom was the great Leopold Auer, were seated behind a screen. This way the evaluation of each contestant was based solely on what the judges were hearing. (Yes, I won the scholarship). . . . A few years later I found myself playing lead alto sax with the Ina Ray Hutton Band. Our second musical short for Paramount Pictures was being shown in N.Y. City so several of us went to see it. The opening scene took place in the office of the Mills Booking Agency and shows Mr. Mills talking to a prospective buyer. Finally, via an intercom system Mr. Mills tunes into what is supposedly a rehearsal hall so that the buyer can hear the band. He is very favorably impressed with what he hears, but still doesn't know that it's coming from an all girl group. Then Mr. Mills takes him to the rehearsal hall so he can see us. It is at this point that the band is flashed on the screen for the first time. So, all right . . . here we are in the theater and setting directly behind us is a row of male musicians. Some of the remarks overheard by us were: 'Wonder what band that is? . . . Don't know, but it sure has a good sound. . . . Yea, they're great! . . . Sounds a little bit like the Lunceford Band, etc.' All praises. Then when the band appeared on the screen—the remarks were like this, 'A girl band *(followed by snickers)* . . . Yea, they sure sound corny don't they? . . . Well, what do you expect from girls? . . . Wonder who writes their choruses for them?' . . . and on and on.'" See Gilbert, "Tuning in on Femme Musicians," *The Overture* (August 1980). She died in 1995. See Placksin, 78–82, for her discussion of Audrey Hall's career.

[246] Born in Los Angeles, Bee Turpin (Butler) studied piano with Madame Flora Ferraro; she started her professional career in 1931, while she was still in junior high school. In the local press, she was called "tiny Bee Turpin, the personality pianist" (*The California Broadcaster*, November 21, 1936). She played with Peggy's big band, 1937–43; Rita Rio's Orchestra, 1940; Victory Belles; Zenda Ballroom; and toured with Jane Wyman, Janet Blair, and Nan Wynn, and other USO groups, during World War II. She also had her own group, in places like the Club Circle on La Cienega, G.G.'s and the Riviera Country Club; and was a soloist at the Knickerbocker Hotel. In addition to playing with La Virginia Massey Trio at Keith Jones

Restaurant (with Virginia Massey and Betty Reilly), she also performed regularly on radio stations KAFJ and KFAC. Bee was the staff pianist for Chauncey Haines's KFAC radio show, "Artists' Parade." As official pianist for the Los Angeles Fire Department, she played on a Fire Prevention Radio Program on KNX and KHJ. She also appeared in films, including *The Great Waltz* (1938). From 1944 to 1955, she worked as a pianist and musical advisor-supervisor at Universal Studios, where she played piano for Jane Wyman and Deanna Durbin. As rehearsal pianist for auditions and screen tests, she researched music to be used in films. She left the music business from 1955 to 1962, due to marriage, and in the 1960s moved to Bakersfield, California. In 1972, she moved to Indianapolis, where she continued to perform until her death. This information is from a letter to the author (1986).

[247] Marie Ford O'Sullivan was born in 1914 in Bridgeport, Connecticut, and died in 1991. She played violin, viola, and "Mexican rhythm" (hand percussion instruments). She appeared in the film *The Great Waltz*; and performed with Peggy's (later McArtor's) band, called the Four Grace Notes, at The Rice Bowl. She also was a member of the Pasadena Symphony, 1932–36; concertmistress for Pasadena Junior College Orchestra; Dr. Stallcup's All-Girl Orchestra, 1937–38; and had her own trio, in the early 1940s. Marie left the music business in the 1940s. Peggy recalls that, "Marie's history in our business goes back almost as far as mine, but not quite. . . . Many years ago, I met Marie at a rehearsal for Dr. Stallcup, who had an all-girl orchestra. I saw this beautiful young girl walk in, swinging her violin case. She played and I heard a big, gorgeous tone with technique to match. She continued her professional career from then on, featured in combos and orchestras, motion pictures, presentations, etc., and was concertmistress for the Burbank Symphony Orchestra. Then she gave it all up to become a housewife and mother." See Gilbert, "Tuning in on Femme Musicians," *The Overture* (March 1980).

[248] The price for licensing a clip from the film for the Peggy Gilbert documentary was prohibitive; the production company would not approve use of a freeze-frame "still" from the scene. However, Bee Turpin provided photocopies of pictures of the women in costume, taken on the MGM lot. Peggy did not recognize herself in the film clip, and thought that perhaps, as contractor, she might not have been allowed to appear on screen. However, Bee Turpin's photograph includes Peggy in costume; given her unique hairstyle it is easy to identify her in the scene. None of the women received on-screen credit for the appearance.

[249] Fern Buckner (1910–1981) was a violinist and composer. She played with Peggy's band on KMTR radio; Fred Waring's Pennsylvanians, along with Rosemary and Priscilla Lane, Patsy Garrett, Les Paul, Kay Thompson, Leo Arnaud, Robert Shaw, and Frank Perkins, among others. Her father was the Rev. Henry W. Buckner of Pasadena. Fern's parents had a business making jams and jellies from fresh fruit, which they sold from their shop, Buckner's, at the Farmers' Market near Fairfax in Los Angeles. She was a schoolmate of later-to-be-famous arrangers Ken Darby and Roy Ringwald, who together learned sight-singing from Mae Nightingale at Lincoln Junior High in Santa Monica and had five semesters of harmony. At Santa Monica High School, they performed in the school orchestra, formed a string quartet, and along with the entire school put over a drive to buy the school a pipe organ. She graduated in 1928, and was later inducted into the high school's Alumni Hall of Fame. At age 17, Fern won a scholarship from the Santa Monica Bay Cities Music Association for her work as a composer and violinist. At the Curtis Institute in Philadelphia, she studied violin with Efrem Zimbalist, Sr., and composition with Rosario Scalerio. She retired to Santa Fe, New Mexico, opening a shop to sell blankets made by Native American women. See Roy Ringwald, "Tribute to Fern Buckner," *The Overture* (July 1981).

[250] Ibid. At Fern's request, Peggy sold her violin and used the funds to set up the Fern Buckner Scholarship, which Peggy administered for many years through Local 47.

[251] Gilbert, "Tuning in on Femme Musicians," *The Overture* (October 1979).

[252] Chicago-born Gene Krupa (1909–1973) was a Swing Era drummer and bandleader.

[253] These are references to bandleader Louis Prima, trumpeter Roy Eldridge, and saxophonists Vido Musso and Frankie Trumbauer.

[254] *The Overture* (August 1939): 18.

[255] June 9, 1939, 3.

[256] This undated clipping was provided by Bee Turpin, who played in Peggy's band in those years.

[257] The broadcasts for 1939 and 1940 can be confirmed with the daily listings, "Your Radio Today," in the *Los Angeles Times*, calling the band "The Early Girls." However, the band may have been playing earlier on KMPC, under a different name.

[258] Grace Pappalardo (Dunn) (1918–1992).

[259] Della F. Anderson (1907–1990) performed with Fanchon and Marco; she married William F. Smith.

[260] Oral history interview (1985). From the newspaper's daily radio listings, it appears that the time of the program varied over the years.

[261] An excerpt from one of Peggy's KMPC air-checks can be heard on *Peggy Gilbert and The Dixie Belles* (Cambria Master Recordings, CD 1024, 2006).

[262] At the Pacific Pioneer Broadcasters in 1982, they indicated that the KMPC show was in 1942, at which time Peggy was musical director of the station. Peggy remembers, however, that the KMPC gig took place at the same time her band appeared in *The Great Waltz*, which was 1938.

CHAPTER VI: God Bless the Girl who's Got Her Own [Band]

[263] George T. Simon, *The Big Bands* (Toronto: The Macmillan Company, 1967), 260.

[264] Ibid., 261.

[265] Some sources incorrectly spell Ina's second name as "Rae." There has been much rumor and speculation about Ina Ray Hutton being of mixed race. Some black musicians, claiming to be her first cousins, said they resented her, because she could have integrated her band in the 1940s, but did not. In fact, they said, she was known for not wanting black musicians around her, professionally or socially. Who knows the truth? Chicago jazz musician and composer Ed Bland said, as a young jazz musician in Chicago, he heard the rumor that she was "passing." The Ina Ray Hutton story would make a great film or book, if someone would research this rumor and tackle the complicated matter of race in American music in the 1930s and '40s.

[266] Some sources report her birthday as early as 1910; others as late as 1916.

[267] Sister June followed suit.

[268] Frank Driggs, "Women in Jazz, A Survey," published in 1977 as part of the Stash Recordings, Inc., double album, "Jazz Women, A Feminist Retrospective," 16.

[269] The cue sheet for *Accent on Girls*, dated January 14, 1936, includes the following tunes: "Devil's Kitchen," "Truckin,'" "Topic of the Tropics," and "Hobo of Park Avenue." It was filmed at the Paramount News Lab on West 43rd Street in New York City.

[270] Ruth Lowe later wrote two great Frank Sinatra hits, "Put Our Dreams Away" and "I'll Never Smile Again."

[271] The Grammy Foundation restored historical footage of Ina Ray Hutton and Her Melodears, as part of their archiving and preservation initiatives. Several clips are available for viewing on Youtube.com: Ina Ray Hutton and The Melodears playing "Truckin'" (2:33); "Hutton Club Shake" (1:40); "I'm a Hundred Percent With You" from *Star Reporter*; and "Doing the Suzy Q" (2:17).

[272] Marnie Wells later played with Peggy Gilbert in Los Angeles.

[273] Others in the band included: Jack Purcell, guitar; Randy Brooks (1917–1967), trumpet (who married Ina Ray in 1949); Stuart Foster, vocals; Lou Parris, saxophone; Hal Schaefer, pianist. In 1943, the band added the Kim Loo vocal trio. Paxton left in 1944 to start his own band.

[274] Jackie C. "Zackie" Walters (Cooper) [a.k.a. Zackie Cooper Florio, Zackie Cooper Alexander, due to her several marriages] played alto saxophone, clarinet, and keyboards, and was an ASCAP songwriter. She was born in Lee's Summit, Missouri, a suburb of Kansas City, in 1912 and started performing at age twelve, playing in the band and orchestra in her high school from 1926 until 1930. In addition to appearances in local Kansas City clubs with the Gladys Beatty Girl Band, which also toured the Midwest and South, she also played in several men's groups, including at the Amos and Andy Club, Mary's Chicken Dinner House, and Wiggle Inn. In 1939, she joined Ina Ray Hutton's Band, with whom she played for five months until the women's group was disbanded to use men. She settled in New York City, joined Local 802, had her own group, and played with Count Berni Vici. In 1941, she got married and did not play for a few years, except at Hotel Amityville on the weekends. She moved to Los Angeles in 1947. She was working on a book on the all-girl bands when she died in 1987; the manuscript has not been located. This information is from a letter from Jackie Walters to the author (1986).

[275] Deedee Ball (Glee), also known as "Glee" or Mrs. Roland A. Ball, was born in 1917 in South Dakota. A pianist, organist, accordionist, and bandleader, she played with Ina Ray Hutton's band; toured with the Hormel Show; performed with Lawrence Welk, 1936–37; Kay Starr Radio Show with Buzz Alarm Orchestra, 1948–49; was a "sub" for Ada Leonard. Deedee led the Union Oil Company band for six or seven years, as leader and arranger for industrial shows. In the 1980s, she performed with Big Band Commotion in Newport Beach, a mostly male band.

[276] Some sources give her first name as Harriet, instead of Helen.

[277] Trombonist and vibraharpist Lois Cronen Magee was born in Mapleton, Minnesota, in 1928. She performed with the Hormel Girls Band, 1949–51; Ada Leonard's band, 1951–53; Ina Ray Hutton's band 1952–57; with Frankie Carle, 1954–55; with Alvino Rey, 1955–57, and had her own jazz group, 1951–67. She left the music business to raise her children and complete her college education. "I played with some female groups, some male. No difference—some musicians very good, some not, in both male and female groups. Treated well in both groups by fellow musicians and leader." From Lois Cronen Magee, letter to author (1986).

[278] Evelyn "Evie" Howeth Campbell was born in 1920 in Globe, Arizona. On saxophone, clarinet, violin, and vocals, she performed with Jean Tighe, Rube Wolf, Singing Strings, and Dinney Fisher (bass, who had her own band at The Strand in Long Beach). She was managed by Dr. Leonard Stallcup (who also produced the Miss California Pageant for many years), doing stage shows, trade shows, radio program, film shorts, and films, 1939–42. She also played with Ada Leonard's band, 1951–53, and with Ina Ray Hutton, 1955–57. During World War II, Evie served in the military, following her husband, Jerry Campbell, into the Air Force. Later in her career, she taught in the Los Angeles Unified School District and became a school psychologist. She told Peggy, "It is a far cry from being a musician, but the pay is steady!" Peggy responded, "It all goes to prove that musicians must be psychologists, public

relationships experts and keep a happy, smilin' face in order to prepare for a profession in other lucrative fields—right?" See Gilbert, "Tuning in on Femme Musicians," *The Overture* (September 1979). Evie Campbell died in 1994.

[279] Van Euer is today an accomplished painter in Los Angeles. She also played with *The Spade Cooley Show* on KTTV.

[280] Russian-American violist–Hollywood studio contractor, Phil Kahgan, asked Peggy to do the contracting for the Ina Ray Hutton television show, when it was starting up. Peggy had to decline, as it was considered a conflict of interest, because she worked at the union. Interview with author (July 19, 2006).

[281] Guitarist and producer Audrey Barnett (1918–2005) performed with Peggy's band at The Rice Bowl; with Ada Leonard's band; and with accordion player Dorothy Ray. She had her own production company and did shows with Liberace, Bob Hope, and Angela Lansbury, among others. Audrey's longtime partner, Dorothy Ray, wrote Audrey's obituary for *The Overture* (November 2005).

[282] Born in Crestline, Ohio, in 1912, Genevieve B. Howell began classical piano training at the age of five. Two years later, she contracted polio, which crippled her left leg. She played piano and improvised for silent movies in the pit at the Ohio Theater in Mansfield. She also played with the Paul Lowry Orchestra, 1937–39; Femminaires Vocal Trio, for which she made vocal arrangements, 1938; Peggy's band, 1939–42; Ina Ray Hutton band on KTLA TV, 1950s; Zepher Room at the Chapman Park Hotel and at the Peppermill Restaurant in Pasadena, 1960s. From a letter to the author (August 10, 1986). She died in 1995.

[283] Lucille B. Silverstone was born in Madisonville, Kentucky in 1912. She played piano, flute, violin, and trumpet, performing with Sam Damen in Phoenix, 1934–35; as a sideliner with Ada Leonard's band, 1940s; in a piano team with Judy Winsor, 1941–43, 1951; with her own trio and duo, 1944–45; and at the Brown Derby Restaurant.

[284] Trumpeter Doris E. Pressler was born in Janesville, Wisconsin, on January 17, 1911 (sharing a birthday with Peggy Gilbert). She joined Local 47 in 1940. During her long career, she performed at the Roseland Ballroom in New York City; toured with the Sally Rand Show; played with Annette Dieman's Orchestra at the Chez Parée, the Hollywood Debs at the Top Hat Club, and The Biltmore Hotel and Coral Gables Country Club in Miami in 1939. She also played with Bobby Grice and The Bricktops, with Sally Banning's Orchestra, and with Peggy Gilbert's band. After the war, she earned an engineering degree at the University of Southern California, and worked for the Los Angeles County Road Department until 1974, when she retired. She then moved to Las Vegas and resumed performing with a professional Senior Citizens Orchestra. She died in 1999. See Peggy Gilbert, Doris Pressler obituary, *The Overture* (January 2000).

[285] *The Overture* (September 1940): 8.

[286] Oral history interview (1985). For more information on the black music scene in Los Angeles in the 1930s, '40s, and '50s, see Bette Yarbrough Cox, *Central Avenue—Its Rise and Fall (1890–c.1955) Including the Musical Renaissance of Black Los Angeles* (Los Angeles: BEEM Publications, 1996); and Clora Bryant, Buddy Collette, William Green, Steven Isoardi, Jack Kelson, Horace Tapscott, Gerald Wilson, and Marl Young, *Central Avenue Sounds: Jazz in Los Angeles* (Berkeley: University of California Press, 1998).

[287] Elvira "Vi" Redd was born in 1928 in Los Angeles, the daughter of drummer Alton Redd. She was known as a bebop player, performing on alto saxophone and vocals with Earl Hines, Dizzy Gillespie, Count Basie, and Max Roach in the 1950s and '60s. She married drummer Richie Goldberg.

[288] Jazz trumpeter Clora Bryant was born in Denison, Texas, in 1927. Her mother died when she was three; she and two older brothers were raised by their father, who took them to see Count Basie, Duke Ellington, Lionel Hampton, T-Bone Walker, Jay McShann, and Jimmy Lunceford. She started playing her brother's trumpet while he was in the service, during World War II. While a student at Prairie View Agricultural and Mechanical University, she joined an all-girl band, the Prairie View Coeds, playing throughout Texas, including at military bases. In 1945, the family moved to Los Angeles, where she attended University of California, Los Angeles, and joined Local 767. She moved to New York in 1954. In addition to the Sweethearts of Rhythm, where she performed at the Million Dollar Theater in 1945, she was a member of Queens of Swing in the late 1940s–50s, appearing in 1951 as the "Hollywood Sepia Tones" on Los Angeles Channel 5, KTLA, the first all-female jazz group on television, according to Clora. See Cox, Chapter 17, in which Clora Bryant describes how the Central Avenue club scene influenced her playing and launched her professional career.

[289] Melba Liston (1926–1999) was born in Kansas City, Missouri. She started playing the trombone at age seven, and came to Los Angeles in 1937, joining Local 767 at age sixteen. Her music teacher Alma Hightower organized a band that included Melba, Alice Young, Minnie Moore (Alma's daughter), and Vi Redd. Melba played with Bardu Ali's band at Lincoln Theater at age seventeen, for which she wrote music and made arrangements. She toured with Gerald Wilson's band, as the ensemble's only woman; she (and Gerald) joined Dizzy Gillespie's band in 1950, for whom she wrote several charts. See Cox, Chapter 12, in which Melba Liston tells her story.

[290] The Sweethearts of Rhythm began in 1939. See D. Antoinette Handy, *The International Sweethearts of Rhythm* rev. ed. (Lanham, Maryland: The Scarecrow Press, Inc., 1998).

[291] Peggy went to New Orleans in the late 1940s and '50s with her partner Kay Boley to visit Kay's family. Both recall that they often went to black jazz clubs to hear the musicians and Peggy would take her horn and "sit in." Kay says that, if her family had known, they would have tried to stop them from going, because the black neighborhoods were rough and most whites avoided those areas at night.

[292] Oral history interview (1985). For a fascinating account of the events that led up to the merger, see Bryant.

[293] Ernestine "Tiny" Davis also led Tiny Davis' Hell Drivers.

[294] Like all bands, members varied. Others who played with The Sweethearts include: Nova Lee McGee, trumpet; Helen Jones, trombone; Ellarize Thompson, alto saxophone; Alma Cortez, tenor saxophone; Roz Cron, saxophone; Roby Butler; and Roxanna Lucas.

[295] *The Overture* (November 1940): 8–10.

[296] Anyone researching music in Los Angeles in this period needs to look over these listings. There are details about which bands appeared where, including Local 767 black jazz clubs and radio bands. Orval's band was at The Stock Club in 1941.

[297] Some have been identified.

[298] Doris L. "Dody" Jeshke was born in 1918 in Santa Paula, California, and attended school in Boyle Heights in East Los Angeles, joining Local 47 in 1937. She played drums, marimba, vibes, harp, chimes, xylophone, tympani, and was also a copyist. Born in Santa Paula, California, she attended school in Boyle Heights, East Los Angeles, joining Local 47 in 1937. She played with the Victory Belles and appeared in the film *The Second Time Around* (1961). She died in 1995.

[299] *The Overture* (July 1941): 8, Los Angeles Band Directory.

[300] Born in 1904 in Milwaukee, Evelyn M. Pennak played baritone saxophone and clarinet in Peggy's big band, appeared with Ada Leonard on her TV show, and toured Europe with the American Legion Band. With her partner Lillian Anderson, she owned a music store in Los Angeles at 330A Western Avenue. She died in 1994.

[301] *The Overture* (September 1941): 10, Los Angeles Band Directory.

[302] "Girl Loses Life Hiking in Park: Tragedy Ends Vacation Outing as Young Woman Falls on Rugged Slope," *Los Angeles Times* (March 20, 1940).

[303] Bee Rock, a popular climbing site, got its name from the millions of bees storing their honey in the tiny caves that honeycomb the rock.

[304] His biography, *Trumpet on the Wing*, was published by Doubleday in 1948. In 1954, he moved to Las Vegas.

[305] Pianist Annis Cannie "Annie" Elliott (a.k.a. Annsaelio A.) was born in Stephenville, Texas, in 1910. She played in Peggy's band at The Rice Bowl in the 1940s; and joined Local 47 in 1942. She married photographer Dick Elliott, Jr., whose father was Richard Damon "Dick" Elliott (1886–1966), an actor in television and film, beginning in the 1930s, best known as Mayor Pike of Mayberry on *The Andy Griffith Show*. She died in 1993.

[306] Lois Robbins Isaacs (b. 1924) is the sister of Natalie Robin. In addition to Count Berni Vici, she played trombone, bass, and cello with Rita Rio (1938–39), Peter Miremblum (1938), and Ann Wallace (1938–39). In 1946, she married and had a family.

[307] Gilbert, "Tuning in on Femme Musicians," *The Overture* (April 1980).

[308] Videotaped interview with author (August 18, 2005).

[309] "Serena Kay Williams Receives Prestigious Grande Dame Award," *The Overture* (October, 2005): 1, 6.

[310] Ada Leonard, letter to author (1986).

[311] Danny Ray Johnson, "Another Response," *The Overture* (June 1980).

[312] Also known as Russell's Hacienda Club.

[313] By the March 1943 issue of *The Overture*, only the club names are listed, along with names of a few bands. Judy Winsor is also known as June Winsor.

[314] *Pacific Coast Musician* (November 1, 1941): 1.

[315] Ruth Haroldson, "Unbalanced Symphony," *Music and Dance in California* (Los Angeles: Bureau of Musical Research, Inc., 1948), 41, 142. See also Carol Neuls-Bates on Frédérique Petrides.

[316] Radie Britain's personal papers are at the Cook Music Library of Indiana University. For information on Elinor Remick Warren, see the recordings of her orchestral works on the Cambria Master Recordings label and www.elinorremickwarren.com. A biography of Mary Carr Moore, *Mary Carr Moore, American Composer*, written by Catherine Parson Smith and Cynthia S. Richardson, was published in 1987 by University of Michigan Press.

CHAPTER VII: The Victory Belles and USO in Alaska

[317] World War II began September 1, 1939, when Germany invaded Poland. In January 1940, FDR called for increased production of planes. Germany invaded the USSR on June 22, 1941.

[318] Oral history interview (1985).

[319] *The Overture* (July 1942): 5.

[320] Grandma Hazzard died in 1943, at the age of 89.

[321] Spike Wallace, "Musicians Open Hollywood Canteen, 'The House That Labor Built,'" *The Overture* (October 1942): 18–19.

[322] The movie *Hollywood Canteen* starred, among others, Jack Benny, The Andrews Sisters, Joe E. Brown, Eddie Cantor, Joan Crawford, and Bette Davis. For more information about the Hollywood Canteen, visit www.hollywoodcanteen.net.

[323] See Emily Yellin, *Our Mothers' War: American Women at Home and at the Front During World War II* (New York: The Free Press, 2004), based on her mother's papers found after her death, including letters sent to her parents in Oklahoma. During the war, she worked at *Reader's Digest* in New York City; in 1945, she joined the Red Cross and was sent to Saipan.

[324] Oral history interview (1985).

[325] "Jean Hay, 87, Host During War of 'Reveille with Beverly' Show Dies," *New York Times* (October 3, 2004). A web site (www.reveillewithbeverly.com), which no longer exists, included radio transcriptions of *Reveille with Beverly*, along with some rare photographs, and a description of the KNX Victory Belles.

[326] This was Sinatra's first credited appearance in a movie. He sang "Night and Day."

[327] The soundtrack from the film is available on the Howard's International label.

[328] An original Broadway play called *Victory Belles,* written by Alice Gerstenberg (1885–1972), ran for thirty-two performances between October 26, 1943, and January 22, 1944, at the Mansfield Theater in New York. Directed by Henry Adrian, the comedic plot had nothing to do with an all-girl band, but rather with women trying to find husbands during the war years. An actress, playwright, and activist in the Little Theater Movement, Gerstenberg is remembered as founder, producer, and president of The Playwrights' Theater of Chicago.

[329] See Axel Madsen, *The Sewing Circle: Hollywood's Greatest Secret: Female Stars Who Loved Other Women* (New York: Birch Lane Press, 1995).

[330] These words may have been written by Beverly Beyette of the *Los Angeles Times*. It was not clear on the web site, although on the front page of the site's music section was a headline, "A Jumpin', Jivin' Weapon . . . During World War II," with the byline Beverly Beyette, *Los Angeles Times*. Attempts to locate the owner of the site have been unsuccessful.

[331] Oral history interview (1985).

[332] Peggy's surviving cassette copies confirm the versatility of The Victory Belles.

[333] One source is Bill Sparks Old Time Radio, www.billsparks.com.

[334] Martha Mears (1908–1986) was the singing voice for many 1940s on-screen actresses, including Rita Hayworth, Veronica Lake, Lucille Ball, Marjorie Reynolds, and Hedy Lamar.

[335] Bee Turpin, who played in Peggy's band during the 1930s, was a lifelong friend to Peggy. It is not clear why Bee is listed as bandleader for this broadcast; perhaps it is because Peggy was working at Local 47 at the time.

[336] It could have been Allie Wrubel (1905–1973) or Bobbie Worth (1912–2002), both well-known big band arrangers working in Hollywood at that time. Arranger Van Alexander suggested that it might have been Al Woodbury.

[337] See Thelma White and Harry Preston, *Thelma Who? Almost 100 Years of Showbiz* (Lanham, MD: The Scarecrow Press, 2002), 226.

[338] Oral history interview (1985).

[339] Frances Shelly [or Shelley] also performed on radio, in motion pictures, including *Rain or Shine* (Columbia, 1930), and in Broadway musicals, including *Mystery Moon*, *Nine-Fifteen Revue*, and *Wake Up and Dream*, where she introduced the song "What Is This Thing Called Love?" June Derry (Weston) [a.k.a. June Safford, June Weston, Julie King] was born in Chicago in 1915. On piano and accordion, she was a sideliner and studio musician at Paramount, Columbia, and Universal Studios in the early 1940s, before making USO tours to Alaska, Japan, Korea, Thailand, and the Philippines in World War II, as well as to Vietnam in the 1960s. In a letter to the author (1986), she says, "Some of my side men included Mel Torme (before he became the star that he is), Barney Kessel, etc. Have played with many of the greats including Jack Teagarden, Charlie Teagarden, Tony Rizzi, etc. Played at the Hangover Club with groups, Radio Room with Mike Riley; Bob Surke used to come hear me play and offered to give me additional lessons 'for free.' While in Orange County played a lot of the places there, Newporter Inn, Jolly Roger, Disneyland, etc. Worked summer resorts in Northern Wisconsin during the summer months and also the Holiday Inns and Ramada Inns in Michigan, and many clubs in Washington and Oregon. . . . Played with black musicians before it was the 'in' thing to do (while I was still in high school, not in California), and knew Charlie Christian and played with him when he first left Oklahoma and long before he joined Benny Goodman and became famous. Phil Moore was one of my biggest boosters when I was playing jazz in LA during the 40s." In the 1970s, she played on such cruise ships as Sitmar, Princess, Cunard, and Prudential lines. Now in her nineties, she continues to perform in and around Thousand Palms, California, where she lives.

[340] See White, 226.

[341] Thelma mentions in her memoirs (226) that, although Peggy Russell was missing a lung, she was nevertheless determined by the Army doctor to be fit for the tour.

[342] This would have been offensive to some. Many blacks and liberals rejected the show-business antics of Louis Armstrong, Fats Waller, and Cab Calloway, as perpetuating degrading racist stereotypes.

[343] Thelma White's autobiography discusses her own and Liz's drug use in this period, but does not say what happened to Liz in the 1950s.

[344] Videotaped interview (August 6, 2006).

[345] *Reefer Madness* was rediscovered in 1972 by Keith Stroup, founder of the National Organization for Reform of Marijuana Laws. After he screened a copy from the Library of Congress as a benefit for his advocacy work, it became a cult favorite.

[346] One version of this story was that she ate some contaminated fish in Alaska and contracted a rare disease. Peggy doubts this story, because all of the women ate the same food on tour and no one else became sick.

[347] A Quonset hut is a lightweight prefabricated corrugated steel structure, modeled after a Nissen hut developed by the British during World War I, and manufactured in large numbers for the United States Navy, beginning in 1941. They could be shipped anywhere and assembled without skilled labor. More than 150,000 were manufactured by the George A. Fuller Company for the war effort. They were sold to the public after the war and are found today throughout the United States.

[348] Nellie Neal Lawing, *Alaska Nellie* (Lawing, Alaska: Alaska Nellie's Inn, Inc., 1990).

[349] In 1936, MGM made a nine-minute documentary called *Land of Alaska Nellie*, narrated and produced by James A. Fitzpatrick (1894–1980), with cinematography by Bob Carney, and original music by C. Bakaleinkoff and Nat W. Finston. Today one can visit Alaska Nellie's

Inn, Mile 23, Seward Highway, Moose Pass, AK. Alaska Nellie's homestead is on the list of Registered Historic Places in Alaska.

[350] Videotaped interview (August 6, 2006).

[351] This information agrees with the data provided in Thelma White's autobiography. They were USO Troupe No. 406.

[352] Many things in Thelma's memoir did not ring true to Peggy Gilbert or to pianist June Derry, both of whom had different—and less pleasant—memories of the USO tour. Despite Thelma White's claims, according to a letter from June Derry Weston (October 15, 2006), she was never "Miss California."

[353] This has appeared recently on YouTube.com, but ownership of "Soundies" is questionable. UCLA Film and Television Archives have some in their collection, including *Zoot*, also recorded by Thelma White's band.

[354] Wilma Wescott also played tuba.

[355] Videotaped interview (August 6, 2005).

[356] The pianist may have been Lona Bowman and not Annis.

[357] After retiring as an entertainer, Kay Boley worked at the beauty salon at Sportsman's Lodge for fourteen years. In her later years, she volunteered at Providence Saint Joseph Medical Center in Burbank.

CHAPTER VIII: BACK TO WORK AT LOCAL 47

[358] Oral history interview (1985).

[359] Ibid.

[360] Penny Colman's *Rosie the Riveter: Women Working on the Home Front in World War II* (New York: Crown Publishers, Inc., 1995) contains many photographs from the period. Books and articles about "Rosie the Riveter" often fail to mention women musicians.

[361] Ruth Haroldson, "Unbalanced Symphony," *Music and Dance in California* (Los Angeles: Bureau of Musical Research, Inc., 1948), 41, 142.

[362] *Moments of Charm*, a short from Paramount Pictures, featuring Phil Spitalny & Orchestra, was filmed on August 11, 1939, and included "My Isle of Golden Dreams," "The Pretty Girls," "Bugle Call Rag," "I Love You Truly," and "William Tell Overture." Another short, *Moments of Charm of 1940*, was filmed November 16, 1939, and included "My Isle of Golden Dreams," "Toy Trumpet," "Ave Maria," and "Begin the Beguine."

[363] This photograph could be from The Rice Bowl.

[364] When Peggy was honored by the Pacific Pioneer Broadcasters with their Diamond Circle Award, they mentioned the Danny Thomas radio show, but did not specify dates.

[365] Phone interview (July 15, 2005).

[366] There is a copy from January 30 through February 6, [probably 1946], also stating that the Peggy Gilbert's Jacks and Jills were playing nightly at the Garden of Allah.

[367] A photograph of Peggy when she worked in the Recording Secretary's Office as the Trial Board Secretary is found in *The Overture* (1953): 21.

[368] See *The Overture* (January 1949): 18, for a list of committee members and their photographs. Peggy Gilbert is listed first.

[369] Videotaped interview (August 6, 2005).

[370] Ibid.

[371] Lenore [Lenora] Holcomb Leblanc was born in 1914 in Dallas, Texas, and died in 1957 in Inglewood, California. She played cello and trombone and transferred her membership to Local 47 in 1936. Her obituary appeared in *The Overture* (July 1957).

[372] The entire program is available online at Local 47's web site, www:promusic47.org/program.

CHAPTER IX: The Fifties and Sixties

[373] Phyllis Chesler, *Women and Madness* (New York: Doubleday, 1972). The whole tragedy of women being forced out of the job market and back to prewar roles and positions was a dramatic boost to the entire American psychiatric profession, due to the preponderance of women in need of treatment and counseling.

[374] Gilbert, untitled manuscript (1998).

[375] Oral history interview (1985). Ted Knight hosted Channel 11's *KTTV 35th Anniversary Show* in 1984, and *KTTV's A 47-Year Legacy* in 1996; Ada's band appears in both. DVD copies of these specials are available for through Kinevideo@aol.com.

[376] Ada Leonard, letter to author (1986).

[377] Kay Boley performed on the same show with Ada in Chicago.

[378] Jane Sager's extensive account of those USO tours with Ada's band is found in Sherrie Tucker's book, *Swing Shift: "All-Girl" Bands in the 1940s* (Durham, NC: Duke University Press, 2000), Chapter 8.

[379] International Movie Data Base, www.IMDB.com.

[380] Maxine Bleming (1914–1993) transferred to Local 47 in 1942 from Chicago; she worked at the Warner Bros. music library.

[381] Trumpeter Jane Sager was born in Milwaukee in 1914, and played violin and piano as a child. She supported herself while attending Stephens College by playing trumpet. After college, she moved to Chicago to study with Edward Lewellyn of Chicago Symphony Orchestra. She performed with the Chicago Women's Symphony; with the Platinum Blondes of America, touring Cuba; with Rita Rio's all-girl band; and with Ada Leonard on USO tours. She also played with Peggy Gilbert, and with Ina Ray Hutton on TV in the 1950s. In addition, she played in Johnny Richards' (1911–1968), a.k.a. Johnny Cascales, orchestra during World War II, as well as a CBS Studio band in Hollywood; with the house band for the Casino Gardens; and with Charlie Barnet and His Orchestra. Jane started her own all-girl band and comedy show called "The Frivolous Five," with other veteran women musicians. Jane Sager describes her role in the creation of Ada Leonard's All American Girls Band in Tucker, *Swing Shift*, 262–66.

[382] Mary Demond (b. 1921) was a trumpeter and bandleader. She played with Frances Carroll and The Coquettes (appearing in a 1940 Warner Bros. short directed by Roy Mack), 1939–40. In addition, she performed with singer Edith Dahl, 1940–41; Ada Leonard, 1941; Count Berni Vici, 1942; radio, TV, and film actor Alan Reed (1907–1977), 1943; Virgil Whyte, 1945; Betty McGuire Orchestra, 1945; Thelma White, 1946; and The Hormel Girls, 1951. When not playing with a big band, she had her own group. Mary left the music business in the early 1950s, because: "Reason #1 'Rock & Roll' poison came in and I decided to 'go-out!'; #2 I wanted to buy a home and stay in one place and get a job with a steady paycheck." About playing with all-girl bands, she said, "Men were more reliable and less petty, at least they were during my experience. I had a wonderful time in the music business and I shall always

treasure the memories and the friendships." This information is from Mary Demond's letter to the author (1986).

[383] Francis Rossiter (1918–2000) was born in DeWitt, Nebraska.

[384] Rosalind "Roz" Cron (b. 1925).

[385] Betty "Roz" Rosner was born in 1925 and died in 2005. She also played clarinet. She joined Local 47 in 1957.

[386] Trumpeter Bernice Lobdell was born in 1906 in Huntington, Indiana. She joined the AFM in Chicago. Among the groups with whom she performed are The Harmony Girls, 1924–25; Babe Egan's Hollywood Redheads, Bobbie Grice and Her Fourteen Bricktops; Helen Compton's band; Ada Leonard's band; Ina Ray Hutton's band; Count Berni Vici; and Rita Rio. In 1944, she became a film technician for motion pictures and television productions. She retired in 1971 after twenty-nine years, with a lifetime membership in Local 683. This information is from Bernice Lobdell's letter to the author (1986).

[387] Norma Teagarden (Friedlander) was a pianist and bandleader, who was born in 1911 in Vernon, Texas. Her mother, Helen, was a ragtime pianist; her father played trumpet; and her siblings were also musicians: Cub, drums; Charlie, trumpet; Jack, trombone. She played in her brother Jack's band, at Army and Navy bases during World War II; as well as with Pete Daly, Wild Bill Damian, Matty Matlock, Ben Pollack. As a soloist and with her own groups, she played clubs in Long Beach, including the Bomb Shelter, N.C.O. Club, Wilto Hotel, and Hangover Club in Hollywood. She was a member of Local 47 in Los Angeles and Local 6 in San Francisco. Norma taught piano and performed little from 1955 until 1965. In the 1970s and '80s, she played in Washington Square Bar and Grill in San Francisco and at numerous jazz festivals. She died in 1996. From a letter to the author (1986). For a longer profile, see Placksin, 73–78.

[388] Videos and DVDs of Ada Leonard's band from the television show are available. *Back Home in Indiana* shows Peggy (on the far right, first row). It is mislabeled on YouTube.com as being from 1943; actually, it dates from 1952 or 1953. Ownership of the clip is unclear. Bootleg copies of this footage exist, including on YouTube.com.

[389] Peggy Gilbert, "Ada Leonard Honored at Reunion," *The Overture* (April 1992): 15.

[390] A Duke Ellington/Irving Mills/Mitchell Parrish tune, often sung by Ella Fitzgerald.

[391] Kay remarked (June 2005) on the irony that, after entertaining all those years, few invitations were returned. But most of their friends were not in a position to reciprocate. In retrospect, Kay felt it was good that she and Peg "had been able to take them in," because they needed a place to go where they felt at home.

[392] "Phony Bunny," *Los Angeles Times* (June 15, 1958).

[393] At some point in the 1970s, Peggy destroyed her paintings.

[394] *The Overture* (1961).

[395] A peck horn is a tenor horn.

[396] Pages 6–8. The problems began in 1952 and continued throughout the decade.

[397] *The Overture* (November 1957): 1.

[398] The papers of Dave E. Dexter (1915–1990) are at Miller Nichols Library at the University of Missouri, Kansas City. This information is from Nellie Lutcher's letter to the author (1986).

[399] In the last years of her life, Nellie lived in a retirement home in Los Angeles. Marl Young's article, "The Amalgamation of Locals 47 and 767," is available at www.promusic47.org/benefits/amalgam.asp.

[400] Peggy had hoped that they would appear in the television show, but they did not. The documentary, *Peggy Gilbert & Her All-Girl Band*, shows them in the Alaska sequence.

[401] Oral history interview (1985). Ellington was born April 29, 1899. His sixtieth birthday would have been in 1959. He wrote the score for *Anatomy of a Murder*, a Hollywood film (Columbia) directed by Otto Preminger, that same year, so he may have been in Los Angeles at that time. She may instead be recalling his fortieth birthday, in 1939.

[402] Videotaped interview (August 6, 2005).

[403] In discussing the fifty-two-week contracts in Europe of Babe Egan's band, members told me that they did have lesbian relationships ("love affairs") among band members; they were safer than the girls picking up "customers" for one night stands. In fact, Babe encouraged this pairing off among band members, to ensure their personal safety and emotional well-being, and to ward off homesickness. She viewed herself as chaperone of the teenage (under-aged) girls in the group and forbid them from dating men in the audience. But when the band returned to the United States, several of these girls married and had families and never gave it another thought. This was told to me in confidence by several of the band members, because they did not want their families to know.

[404] Tony Horowitz, letter to author (August 14, 2005).

[405] Billie Cutler, "Surprise Tribute to Peggy Gilbert," *The Overture* (August 1967).

[406] Ibid.

[407] She was buried at Inglewood Memorial Park.

CHAPTER X: The Dixie Belles: "And Away We Go!"

[408] *The Overture* (February 1970): 9. Peggy would have been successful in that field, because of her extensive experience in the music business. Instead, she used those talents to promote The Dixie Belles.

[409] According to Local 47 Archivist Gordon Carmadelle.

[410] Videotaped interview with Serena Williams (August 18, 2005).

[411] Naomi had a stroke in the early 1980s and died in 1986. Peggy could never find a replacement for her, so The Dixie Belles continued without a trombonist.

[412] Bassist Karen Donley was born Brunelda Hawkins in 1919. She performed with Ina Ray Hutton's band on KTLA-TV, with USO overseas, and in Las Vegas; also with Manny Harmon and with Jerry Rosen. During the early 1980s, she was a member of The Dixie Belles. With a B.A. in English and an M.A. in music education, Karen could play anything from jazz to symphonic music. She taught elementary and secondary school for sixteen years in the Los Angeles Unified School District, and had Lifetime California teaching credentials. Besides raising a family, teaching, and performing, she also worked as a secretary in the administrative offices of the Los Angeles Community College District. See Gilbert, "Tuning in on Femme Musicians," *The Overture* (June 1980). Now living in Oceanside, California, she continues to play bass with drummer Dusti Druer in "The Groovin' Grannies." Dusti Druer appeared in numerous MGM films, and worked with The Andrews Sisters, Jimmy Durante, Ricky Nelson, Johnny Mathis, and Frankie Carle. She also performed with the USO.

[413] Oral history interview (1985).

[414] "Hot Jazz and Cool Sounds," *Los Angeles Times* (December 18, 1974), Part IV, 21.

[415] Leo Walker wrote *The Wonderful Era of the Great Dance Bands* (Cambridge, MA: Da Capo Press, 1990), and *The Big Band Almanac* (Cambridge, MA: Da Capo Press, 1989), and founded the Big Dance Band Academy of America.

[416] Gilbert, "Tuning in on Femme Musicians," *The Overture* (February 1979).

[417] Gilbert, "Tuning in on Femme Musicians," *The Overture* (July 1980).

[418] See Appendix A for descriptions of these columns.

[419] These three gentlemen had tremendous influence and dominated the published literature on big band and jazz history, during their lifetimes and today. Their omission of women instrumentalists needs to be rectified.

[420] Gilbert, "Tuning in on Femme Musicians," *The Overture* (June 1979).

[421] Ibid.

[422] Letter from Tony Horowitz (August 14, 2005).

[423] Reprinted with permission of Irreptuous Music Co. (ASCAP), 1983. Music and lyrics by Peggy Gilbert and Anthony Horowitz.

[424] Gilbert, "Tuning in on Femme Musicians," *The Overture* (July 1982).

[425] Leonard Feather (1914–1994) was a writer, producer, educator, and an important jazz critic and journalist. He wrote a jazz encyclopedia and several books, and although he empathized with female vocalists, most women jazz musicians feel that he did not give women instrumentalists their due.

[426] Gilbert, "Tuning in on Femme Musicians," *The Overture* (March 1980).

[427] *The Overture* 68, no. 8 (December 1988): 1.

[428] Gilbert, "A Very Special Thanks," *The Overture* (December 1980).

[429] Videotapes of the Pacific Pioneer Broadcasters' luncheons make up one of the largest quality collections of transcriptions and tapes of early radio programs. They have scripts, publications, music scores, premiums, and other memorabilia. The collection is housed at the Thousand Oaks Public Library. See www.pacificpioneerbroadcasters.org/

[430] An article in *Local 37 News* (January 1, 1980) mentions that The Dixie Belles were appearing on an upcoming Bob Hope Special on NBC. This was not accurate; they played on a show in Las Vegas with Bob Hope, but as far as Peggy knows, it was not broadcast on television.

[431] "We Salute Our Own Peggy Gilbert," *The Overture* (August 1981).

[432] Actor Robert Blake was also a guest on *This Is Your Life*, when Peggy appeared on that show in 1957. Blake was one of the young actors represented by Thelma White's talent agency. In 2005, he would face charges of murdering his wife, Bonnie Lee Bakley, for which he was acquitted of criminal charges but held responsible in a civil case brought by her family.

[433] Marylouise Oates, "Rams, Dodgers Big Hit at MS Benefit," *Los Angeles Times* (November 19, 1981), Part V, 2.

[434] "Phil Harris Gets Festival Off to a Rousing Start," *San Diego Union* (December 18, 1981), A-58.

[435] Baldinger.

[436] Gilbert, untitled manuscript.

[437] Marian "Marnie" M. Elzea Wells, letter to author (1986).

[438] In her letter to the author (1986), Marnie said that The Dixie Belles actually started in 1971, and not 1974, as reported by others.

[439] In a letter to the author (1986), she said she was born in 1921; but her Local 47 card gives her birth date as 1919.

[440] Natalie Robin, letter to author (1986).

[441] Many thanks to Pearl's daughter, Michael Strange (also a bass player), for providing this information. See Michael Strange, "Pearl Powers," *The Overture* (February 2006): 14.

[442] Karen Young, "Jerrie Thill Still Keeps the Beat: 88-year old drummer celebrates seventy years of performing," *Studio City News* (September 2–15, 2005): 1, 16.

[443] This information may be incorrect. By the time she reached 18, in 1935, vaudeville was over.

[444] See www.jerriethill.com.

[445] The complete interview is found in the documentary *Peggy Gilbert & Her All-Girl Band.*

[446] Marie Wilson (1916–1972) was an American actress on radio, film, and television, who gained national prominence for her role in *My Friend Irma* (Paramount, 1949). The quintessential blonde bimbo, she appeared in more than forty films and was also a volunteer performer at The Hollywood Canteen. She played "Camille Casey" in *Melody for Two*, a film in which Peggy's band appeared. Toby Wing (born Martha Virginia Wing, 1915–2001) was the archetypal Hollywood chorus girl.

[447] On the cue sheet, the composer is listed as Hughie Cannon. The show number is 007-40011-004.

[448] Throughout the eighties The Dixie Belles were represented by Aimée Entertainment Association, Joyce Aimée and Helen Barkan of Van Nuys, California.

[449] *The Overture* (September 1982): 3.

[450] Serena Williams, "Women's Committee," *The Overture* (December 1983).

[451] Saxophonist, clarinetist, and bandleader Ann Patterson was born in 1946.

[452] Page 5.

[453] It was added to the Cambria compact disc. At one point, producer Lance Bowling decided to issue "When You're Smiling" as a single CD, for Jerrie Thill to sell at her weekly gig at El Cid's in Hollywood.

[454] Although Peggy often did arrangements for her band as early as the 1920s, she did not consider herself a professional arranger. In those days, few women were. Peggy did not publish or copyright her arrangements.

[455] Television broadcasting pioneer Ruth Ashton Taylor is a fifty-year veteran broadcaster and longtime friend of Peggy's. She did several reports on The Dixie Belles over the years, before she retired in 1989.

[456] Fred Hyatt hosted KPFK's Sunday opera show for several decades; "Uncle Ruthie" Buell hosted a family program, "Up the Down Staircase," that featured her performances as a vocalist and guitarist and her readings of children's stories.

[457] Betty O'Hara (1926–2000) played all the brass instruments from piccolo trumpet to euphonium. In addition, she was a composer, arranger, and jazz vocalist. Born in Earl Park,

Idaho, she began to play trumpet at age nine. She performed with bands including Freddie Schaeffer's Band, a band led by Joan Lee, with Abe Luboff and Dick Cary, among others. She also played second trumpet for five years with the Hartford Symphony and was a studio musician in Hollywood. She married bass trombonist Barrett O'Hara in 1960. Betty was featured at the Sacramento and Monterey Jazz Festivals and, from the late 1970s, she performed with Ann Patterson's band, Maiden Voyage. With trumpeter/flugelhornist Stacy Rowles, she formed the Jazzbirds in the early 1980s. She can be heard as soloist on the soundtracks for many prime-time TV shows, such as *Hill Street Blues* and *Magnum P.I.* Her original tune, "Pretty Good for a Girl," was played by Maiden Voyage on *The Tonight Show Starring Johnny Carson*. Her solo albums include: *Horns Aplenty* (1995) and *Woman's Intuition* (Sea Breeze Records, 1999). She also played a variety of instruments on other recordings, including John Allred's *In the Beginning*, Dick Cary's *All His Tuesday Night Friends* and *Catching Up*, and Rick Fay's *Endangered Species*. Peggy mentioned Betty in her *Overture* column (September 1980).

[458] Peggy and Jeannie heard from many of the family members of those honored that day that, for many of the honorees, the event was a highlight, if not of their lives, then certainly of their senior years. They finally received the recognition they deserved as "Pioneer Women Musicians." Many of them were interviewed at the event, the videotapes of which stand as important documentation of their careers.

[459] "Struttin' Their Stuff, The Dixie Belles Are Having A Ball," *People Weekly* (July 3, 1989): 98–99.

[460] From the film *Hatari* (Paramount, 1962).

[461] For a while, the driver was Linda Crane, now of the Schutrum-Piteo Foundation.

[462] *Who's What/What's Where* (February 1998): 1. This text, written on a steno pad in 1998, was found after Peggy died.

[463] Videotaped interview (August 6, 2005), when Peggy was one hundred.

[464] Gilbert, untitled manuscript.

CHAPTER XI: Celebrating the Nineties and Beyond

[465] This letter was framed and presented to Peggy; it hung on Peggy's wall for many years. Because Peggy Fredericks was a large, tall woman—probably twice Peggy Gilbert's size—she referred to herself as "Peg (the big one that is)." They were the two Pegs who ran Local 47 for many years.

[466] Interview with Judy Chilnick (August 18, 2005).

[467] Interview (August 18, 2005).

[468] It was organized by a committee consisting of Serena Williams, Judy Chilnick, Ann Patterson, and Jeannie Pool, with the help of Local 47 staff members.

[469] Videotaped interview (August 18, 2005).

[470] George Liberace died in the fall of 1983. Peggy often mentioned that he hired many Local 47 women musicians throughout his career and was very supportive of women instrumentalists.

[471] Because the certificate has no date, it is not known whether it was presented in the 1940s or more recently. Bette Davis died in 1989.

[472] A photograph that appeared in *The Overture*, October 1983, has the caption, "Three well-known Local 47 members recently were given the Bronze Award of the Southern California Motion Picture Council 'for special merit in the field of music.' (L to R) George

Liberace, Peggy Gilbert and Nellie Lutcher. (That's actress Alice Ghostley . . . sitting between Peggy and Nellie.)"

[473] Bassist Marilyn Mayland (1923–2006) was born in Corona, California, and studied with Herman Reinshagen; she graduated from Occidental College. She performed with the California Women's Philharmonic, under Ruth Haroldson, as well as the Los Angeles Women's Philharmonic. She also formed her own group and did five USO tours. Beginning in 1953, she was director of Sigma Alpha Iota Radio/TV Committee, where she wrote, announced, and directed more than seven hundred live music shows for the fraternity over radio station KPCC in Pasadena. See Marcia Williams, "Marilyn Mayland, International Strings Founder, Dies," *Pan Pipes* (Winter 2007): 7.

[474] Announced on the front page of *The Overture*, 68, no. 8 (December 1988).

[475] "Peggy Gilbert and Jane Sager Receive Awards," *The Overture* (February 2002): 24.

EPILOGUE

[476] The Peggy Gilbert Collection is in the Special Collections, Oviatt Library, California State University, Northridge.

[477] Dennis McLellan, "Peggy Gilbert, 102; blazed a trail for women in jazz," *Los Angeles Times*, February 18, 2007, B10.

[478] "Brief Lives," heard on BBC Radio, March 3, 2007.

APPENDIX A: "Tuning in on Femme Musicians"

[479] E. Ginger Smock Shipp (b. 1920) was heard regularly by the age of sixteen, playing violin on the radio with the Gold Classical Trio. She also performed with the Sepia Tones, 1943–45, including Nina Russell, piano, organ; Mata Roy; and occasionally with Camille Howard, playing at Last Word and Shep's Playhouse on San Pedro Street. She was a soloist on several television shows, including *Chicks & the Fiddle* (1951), *Dixie Showboat,* (1951–53), *Rhythm Revue* (1959–60), and *The Spade Cooley Show.* She toured with the Red Caps; and organized Shipmates and Ginger, playing in Las Vegas from 1959 to 1961. In 1971, she moved to Las Vegas to perform in the hotel orchestras at Caesar's, Sands, Tropicana, Hilton, Flamingo, Desert Inn, and Riviera hotels. When asked if she experienced any discrimination as a female, she answered, "[I] lost several gigs because I would not date the bosses and was told that I wouldn't 'play ball.' Told them 'where to go,' walked out and kept my dignity. Praise God! Being of Irish, black, and Indian descent, [I] threatened to 'punch' a few of them in the nose. Luckily I didn't have to." This information is from E. Ginger Smock Shipp's letter to author (1986).

[480] Philip Kahgan was a music contractor at Paramount Pictures for forty-eight years; he died in 1986 at the age of ninety-three.

APPENDIX B: Filmography

[481] This list is incomplete, because Peggy did not keep accurate records about her film and TV appearances. Included here are only those appearances which could be confirmed.

[482] She recalls that Debbie Reynolds hung out with the band and often jammed with them. For a photograph of the musicians with Debbie Reynolds which appeared in *The Overture*, the caption indicates that Debbie Reynolds played a "peck horn."

APPENDIX C: TELEVISION APPEARANCES

[483] Cohosts were Morgan Fairchild, Sarah Purcell, Lynn Redgrave, and Betty White. Advertisements in the newspapers said, "Women Throw Men a Hot New Curve! Resident Cast of Comics and The Chippendale Exotic Male Dancers!" According to Howard Rosenberg, writing in the *Los Angeles Times* (April 7, 1982), "'Shape of Things' is not satire and it is not irreverent. It is an insult that trivializes everything and everyone it touches."

APPENDIX D: PIONEER WOMEN MUSICIANS OF LOS ANGELES

[484] As printed in the program booklet, March 8, 1986.

[485] Barbara Ann MacNair (1934–2002) was originally from Dallas, Texas.

[486] Drummer Bridget O'Flynn (b. 1923) played in Los Angeles with Sally Banning, Clifton Rawnsley, Dale Reed, Fanchon Alexander, William Collins, Dell Everette and Jack Rossi; in New York, she played with June Rotenberg, Jack Dinnerman, Mary Lou Williams, Ann Winburn, Margie Hyams, and Joe Springer. She also appeared on radio and television.

[487] Eunice Wennermark Price was under contract to MGM and NBC.

APPENDIX E: DOCUMENTARY

[488] For more information, visit www.peggygilbert.org.

Bibliography

"The AFM Congress of Strings." *The Overture* (February 1983).

"ASMA Annual Christmas Brunch." *The Overture* (January 1984): 7.

Balboni, Alan. *Beyond the Mafia: Italian Americans and the Development of Las Vegas.* Las Vegas: University of Nevada Press, 1996.

Baldinger, Jo Ann, "The Dixie Belles—Peggy Gilbert's Not-Ready-For-Retirement Band." *Los Angeles Times*, November 8, 1981. Calendar Section, 4.

"B.B.B. Makes New Find in Peg Gilbert and her 'Femmes.'" *Hollywood Filmograph* [1935].

Bryant, Clora and Buddy Collette, William Green, Steven Isoardi, Jack Kelson, Horace Tapscott, Gerald Wilson, and Marl Young. *Central Avenue Sounds: Jazz in Los Angeles.* Berkeley: University of California Press, 1998.

"Can You Find Our April 11th 'Guess' Star?" *Hot Notes/Monterey Bay Hot Jazz Society*, April 1981.

Chesler, Phyllis. *Women and Madness.* New York: Doubleday, 1972.

Cohen, Aaron. "Film Highlights Gilbert's Youthful Spirit." *Downbeat* (January 2007): 20.

Colman, Penny. *Rosie the Riveter: Women Working on the Home Front in World War II.* New York: Crown Publishers, Inc., 1995.

"Congress of Strings." *The Overture* (January 1984).

"Congress of Strings 1984." *The Overture* (May 1984).

Cox, Bette Yarbrough. *Central Avenue—Its Rise and Fall (1890–c.1955) Including the Musical Renaissance of Black Los Angeles.* Los Angeles: BEEM Publications, 1996.

Cruise, Katherine "Katy." "Rebuttal to Walker." *The Overture* (June 1980).

"Dance Tonight." *This Week in Los Angeles.* August 8, 1937.

Davidson, Harriet. "Rebuttal to Walker." *The Overture* (June 1980).

Dressler, Marie. *The Life Story of an Ugly Duckling: An Autobiographical Fragment in Seven Parts.* New York: Robert MacBride & Co., 1924.

Dreyfus, Kay. *Sweethearts of Rhythm: The Story of Australia's All-Girl Bands and Orchestras, To the End of the Second World War.* Sydney, Australia: Currency Press, 1999.

Driggs, Frank. "Women in Jazz, A Survey." *Jazz Women, A Feminist Retrospective.* New York: Stash Recordings, Inc., 1977.

Faderman, Lillian and Stuart Timmons. *Gay L.A.: A History of Sexual Outlaws, Power Politics, and Lipstick Lesbians.* New York: Basic Books, 2006.

"From Margaret Teegarden." *The Overture* (1982).

Fry, Stephen M. *The Story of the All-Women's Orchestras in California, 1893–1955: A Bibliography.* Compiled with the assistance of Jeannie Pool. Northridge, CA: CSUN Music Department, 1985.

Gilbert, Douglas. *American Vaudeville: Its Life and Times.* New York: Dover Publications, 1962.

Gilbert, Peggy. Untitled manuscript, 1998.

———. "Ada Leonard Honored at Reunion." *The Overture* (April 1992): 15.

———. "Albert Steinberg Becomes Director-Conductor of Life Members Orchestra." *The Overture* (October 1979).

———. "Billie Cutler by her Friends." *The Overture* (May 1984).

———. "The Blonde Bombshell: Ina Ray Hutton." *The Overture* (April 1984).

———. "Celebration-Women." *The Overture* (November 1975).

———. "Drummer Boy." Manuscript, c.1988.

———. "How Can you Play a Horn with a Brassiere? 'Sissy!' Pens Skirt Swinger to Writer Who Said Women Are Inferior." *Downbeat* (April 1938): 3, 17.

———. "In Memoriam: Ada Leonard." *The Overture* (February 1998).

———. "A Living Legend: Fern (Spaulding) Jaros (Trombone-French Horn)." *The Overture* (July 1995): 12.

———. "Members' Headquarters Throughout the Federation." *International Musician* (February 1962).

———. "A Special Message from Peggy Gilbert." *The Overture* (February 1983).

———. "Tuning in on Femme Musicians." *The Overture* (February 1979–January 1984).

———. "A Very Special Thanks." *The Overture* (December 1980).

"The Great Life." *The Hollywood Reporter*, July 21, 1982.

"Guests at Press Club Luncheon." *The Overture* (November 1979).

Handy, D. Antoinette. *The International Sweethearts of Rhythm,* rev. ed. Lanham, Maryland: The Scarecrow Press, Inc., 1998.

Haroldson, Ruth. "Unbalanced Symphony." In *Music and Dance in California.* Los Angeles: Bureau of Musical Research, Inc., 1948.

Harrington, Bob and Rex Downing. "Tales of Coon-Sanders." *The Mississippi Rag* (April 1991): 10–14.

Hensley, Harold. "Country, Western Scene . . . ." *The Overture* (January 1980).

———. "Country, Western Scene . . . ." *The Overture* (May 1984).

Herman, Max. "From the desk of . . . The Best Congress of All." *The Overture* (February 1980).

Hicks, Mabel, arranger. *You Just Drive Me Screwy* (sheet music). Camp Publishing Co., Hollywood, 1936.

"Hot Dogs, Live Music, Old Friends Are Features of Local 47's Picnic." *The Overture* (September 1960).

"It was potables with Peg at the ASMA Xmas Party." *The Overture* (January 1984).

Johnson, Danny R. "Another Response." *The Overture* (June 1980).

Kernfeld, Barry. *The Story of Fake Books: Bootlegging Songs to Musicians.* Lanham, MD: The Scarecrow Press, Inc., 2006.

Kraditor, Aileen S. *The Ideas of the Woman Suffrage Movement, 1980–1920.* New York: W. W. Norton & Company, 1981.

Lauder, Harry. *Roamin' in the Gloamin'.* Philadelphia & London: J. B. Lippincott Company, 1928.

Lawing, Nellie Neal. *Alaska Nellie.* Lawing, Alaska: Alaska Nellie's Inn, Inc., 1990.

"Let's Talk Legit." *The Overture* (1982).

"Live Music Award to Teagarden." *The Overture* (September 1982).

"Local 47 at the Rose Parade." *The Overture* (January 1980).

"Local 47 Brings Dixie to Los Angeles." *The Overture* (October 1977).

"The Local 47 Dixieland Jamboree." *The Overture* (August 1975).

Madsen, Axel. *The Sewing Circle: Hollywood's Greatest Secret: Female Stars Who Loved Other Women*. New York: Birch Lane Press, 1995.

"Manners, Di Bari and Palmer Win Top Offices." *The Overture* (December 1982).

"Manny and Peggy at Happy Tribute." *The Overture* (August 1979).

McBride, Renee, "Women in Music Roundtable." *Music Library Association Newsletter*, February 2002, 25; www.musiclibraryassoc.org/pdf/news128.pdf.p.25.

Michele, Jimmie de, ed. and pub. *Musicians Advertising Graphic*, Issue A, Volume I (1940).

"Musicians Union AFL-CIO, On Strike Against Motion Picture and TV Film Producers." *The Overture* (September 1980): 15.

Neuls-Bates, Carol, ed. *Women in Music: An Anthology of Source Readings,* 2nd rev. ed. Vancouver: University of British Columbia Press, 1995.

"The New Local 47 Trial Board." *The Overture* (February 1983).

"Peggy Gilbert Popular." *Dancing Topics*, c.1937.

"Peggy Gilbert Submits Some Fascinating Musical History." *The Overture* (August 1980).

"Peggy Gilbert's one hundredth birthday Celebration," *The Overture* (March 2005): 13.

Placksin, Sally. *American Women in Jazz: 1900 to the Present, Their Words, Lives, and Music.* [n.p.]: Wideview Books, 1982.

Pool, Jeannie. "Peggy Gilbert." *The Overture* (April 2007): 12.

———. "Peggy Gilbert Celebrated one hundredth birthday," *IAWM Journal*, vol. 11, no. 1 (Spring 2005): 10–12.

———. "Peggy Gilbert, Saxophonist and Bandleader, Turns 90!" *ILWC Journal*, February 1995.

———. "Researching Women in Music in California." In *California's Musical Wealth: Sources for the Study of Music in California*, compiled and edited by Stephen M. Fry. Los Angeles: Southern California Chapter of the Music Library Association, 1988.

———. "The Story of the All-Women's Orchestras in California." Northridge, CA: CSUN International Institute for the Study of Women in Music, 1985.

———, producer. *All Women's Orchestras*. Documentary film, 1985.

———, producer. *Peggy Gilbert & Her All-Girl Band*. Documentary film, 2006.

Rasmussen, Cecilia. "At 101, 'All-Girl' Bandleader Can Toot Own Horn." *Los Angeles Times*, August 27, 2006, California Section: 1–2.

Ringwald, Roy. "Tribute to Fern Buckner." *The Overture* (July 1981).

"The Rogue Song" with Jazz Temple. *Fox-Poli Newslette*, April 1930.

Shotwell, Walt. "Why no women in big bands?" *Des Moines Register*, June 11, 1984.

Simon, George T. *The Big Bands*. Toronto: The Macmillan Company, 1967.

Slide, Anthony. *The Encyclopedia of Vaudeville*. Westport, CT: Greenwood Press, 1994.

Smith, Ronald L. *Who's Who in Comedy*. New York: Facts on File, 1992.

Snyder, Libbie Jo, "Peggy Gilbert: L.A. Ladies of Jazz." *The Overture* (May 1988): 14.

Stevens, Joe. *Hoover Dam: An American Adventure*. Norman: University of Oklahoma Press, 1988.

Stewart, D. Travis. *No Applause—Just Throw Money: The Book that Made Vaudeville Famous.* New York: Faber & Faber, 2005.

Strange, Michael. "Pearl Powers." *The Overture* (February 2006).

"Struttin' Their Stuff, The Dixie Belles Are Having A Ball." *People Weekly* (July 3, 1989): 98–99.

"Surprise Tribute to Peggy Gilbert." *The Overture* (August 1967).

"Three well-known Local 47 members." *The Overture* (September 1983). Southern California Motion Picture Council Bronze Award.

"3rd International Congress on Women in Music." *International Congress on Women in Music Newsletter*, December 1983.

Tucker, Sherrie. Interview with Peggy Gilbert. Jazz Oral History Program, Smithsonian Institution, National Museum of American History, September 22–23, 1998.

———. *Swing Shift: "All-Girl" Bands of the 1940s.* Durham, NC: Duke University Press, 2000.

———. "Telling Performances: Jazz History Remembered and Remade by the Women in the Band." *Women and Music: A Journal of Gender and Culture,* volume 1 (1997).

Ungar, Arthur. "Loew's State ("Jazz Temple"-Unit)." *Variety* (October 30, 1929).

———. "A Five Year Achievement." *Variety* XCVII:3 (January 29, 1930).

Ussher, Bruno David, ed. *Who's Who in Music and Dance in Southern California.* Hollywood: Bureau of Musical Research, 1933.

Walker, Leo. *The Big Band Almanac*. Cambridge, MA: Da Capo Press, 1989.

———. *The Wonderful Era of the Great Dance Bands*. Cambridge, MA: Da Capo Press, 1990.

Wallace, Spike. "Musicians Open Hollywood Canteen, 'The House That Labor Built.'" *The Overture* (October 1942): 18–19.

Wertheim, Arthur Frank. *Vaudeville Wars: How the Keith-Albee and Orpheum Circuits Controlled The Big-Time and Its Performers.* New York: Palgrave MacMillan, 2006.

"We Salute Our Own Peggy Gilbert." *The Overture* (August 1981).

Wheeler, Marjorie Spruill. *One Woman One Vote: Rediscovering the Woman Suffrage Movement.* Troutdale, OR: New Sage Press, 1995.

White, Thelma and Harry Preston. *Thelma Who? Almost 100 Years of Showbiz.* Lanham, Maryland: The Scarecrow Press, 2002.

"Women in Music." *The Overture* (February 1947).

"Women's Committee." *The Overture* (October 1983).

"Women's Committee." *The Overture* (December 1983).

"Working." *The Overture* (July 1983).

Yellin, Emily. *Our Mothers' War: American Women at Home and at the Front During World War II.* New York: The Free Press, 2004.

Newspapers

Arizona Republic (Phoenix)

Bakersfield Californian

Burbank Daily News

Burbank Leader

Daily Sundial (California State University, Northridge)

Dealer News

Des Moines Register

Desert Sun (Palm Desert, CA)

Diablo Beacon (Concord, CA)

Downtown News (Los Angeles)

Hollywood Citizen-News

Independent

The Kansas City Star Magazine

The Legion Liar

Local 37 News

Los Angeles Daily News

Los Angeles Herald Examiner

Los Angeles Times

Marina Mail (Santa Monica, CA)

Morning Oregonian

News Chronicle (Thousand-Oaks, CA)

Newsette (Fresno, CA)

Oakland Poet-Enquirer

Oregon Daily Journal

Pacific Pioneer Broadcasters

Pasadena Star News

Phoenix Gazette

Plaza Pulse

Reader (San Diego, CA)

Riverside Enterprise

San Diego Union

Santa Monica/Venice Independent

Seattle Star

Sioux City Journal

The Sportlight (San Diego, CA)

Sunday Courier Express (Buffalo, NY)

Toluca Lake Review

TV Times

Valley Daily News

Weekend

Web Sites

Early Television Foundation. Hilliard, OH. www.earlytelevision.org/museum_information.html.

Haddix, Chuck. "The Coon-Sanders Original Nighthawk Orchestra: Radio Aces." Club Kaycee: Kansas City Jazz History. www.umkc.edu/orgs/kcjazz/

Internet Movie Data Base. www.IMDB.com.

KSJC. www.ksjc.com.

Markstein, Don. "Boots and Her Buddies." www.toonopedia.com/boots.htm.

Millar Family web site.

Orpheum Theater. Sioux City, Iowa. www.orpheumlive.com.

Pacific Pioneer Broadcasters. www.pacificpioneerbroadcasters.org

Peggy Gilbert & Her All-Girl Band. www.peggygilbert.org

Sioux City, Iowa. www.siouxcityhistory.org

Swing Music. www.toodeadtoswing.com/swing.html

Thill, Jerrie. www.jerriethill.com

U.S. Television History. http://members.aol.com/jeff99500/tv9.html.

Women Marines Association. www.womenmarines.org

Young, Marl. "The Amalgamation of Locals 47 and 767." www.promusic47.org/benefits.amalgam.asp.

YouTube.com

Index

About the Author

Jeannie Gayle Pool.
Photo by Beverly Simmons.

Jeannie Gayle Pool is a composer, filmmaker, musicologist, film music consultant, producer, and college instructor. She lectures and writes frequently on film music history and preservation, contemporary music, and on women in music.

Dr. Pool has taught music history and appreciation, theory, and solfège at various California universities. She has served as an independent music consultant for Paramount Pictures since 1995. An award-winning radio producer, specializing in contemporary music of the Americas, she was heard weekly on KPFK-FM, Pacifica Radio in Los Angeles between 1981 and 1996. As a music historian and producer, she was executive director of the Film Music Society from 1990 to 2002. As a composer, her works have been heard in California, Washington, D.C., Florida, Ohio, Canada, China, and Europe.

Since 1980, Jeannie Pool has organized many conferences and concerts, including the International Congresses on Women in Music in New York, Los Angeles, and Mexico City. She has produced recordings for Cambria Master Recordings, an independent label in California which specializes in contemporary American music. She serves as an advisor to the Board of the International Alliance for Women in Music, which she helped to establish.

In 1995, she was honored by the National Association of Composers, USA for her work to promote American composers and music, and served on its National Board of Directors. She is currently on the Board of the American Society of Music Arrangers and Composers.

Born in Paris, Illinois, Jeannie Pool grew up in Ohio and studied music in New York City at Hunter College of the City University of New York, where she earned a B.A. in music. She also studied musicology at Columbia University, and holds a Master's degree from California State University, Northridge, where she did a thesis on music in Los Angeles in the nineteenth century. She received a Ph.D. in music at the Claremont Graduate University in May 2002, with a dissertation on the black Creek Indian composer Zenobia Powell Perry (1908–2004).

For more information: www.jeanniepool.org.